TEACHERS

STRAIGHT TALK FROM THE TRENCHES

Other books by Susan Dichter:
The Disposable Parent
Major European Art Movements

TEACHERS

STRAIGHT TALK FROM THE TRENCHES

Susan Dichter

LOWELL HOUSE
Los Angeles
CONTEMPORARY BOOKS
Chicago

To Tom Dichter and the memory of
Belle Kushner Beges

Library of Congress Cataloging-in-Publication Data
Dichter, Susan.
    Teachers, straight talk from the trenches/Susan Dichter.
    p. cm.
    ISBN 0-929923-07-3
    ISBN 0-929923-22-7 ppbk.
    1. Teachers—United States—Interviews.   2. Teachers—
United States—Biography.   3. Teaching satisfaction.
4. Education—United States—Evaluation.   I. Title.
II. Title: Straight from the trenches.
LA2311.D53   1989
370 ' .973-dc20   89-37284
                                                                   CIP

Lowell House
1875 Century Park East
Los Angeles, CA 90067

Publisher: Jack Artenstein
Vice-President/Editor-in-Chief: Janice Gallagher
Marketing Manager: Elizabeth Wood
Design: MIKE YAZZOLINO
Manufactured in the United States of America
10   9   8   7   6   5   4   3   2

Contents

Your Move, America

When I began this book, I knew that our schools were in trouble. At least I knew what you know: the three-minute spots on television, stories heard from parents, the evidence in front of my eyes–the checkout boy at the supermarket who didn't know how to divide the price of a dozen eggs in half–and the official reports.

The reports, and school authorities, have a formal kind of language that by now I think we are beginning to distrust. We don't connect with them, but we do want answers. That is one reason we elected as our chief executive someone who wants to be known as the "education president." It's also why our major corporations have begun to act like big brothers, singling out certain schools and "adopting" them.

But what will it take to improve our schools, and what has gone wrong?

What do the people in the trenches have to say? I wanted to know and interviewed dozens of teachers to find out.

Their voices are heard in this book. They, too, are disturbed about our schools–far more disturbed than even the official reports–but not for the reasons you might suppose. The standard lines, the horror stories, are a big ho-hum for them. They regard students who lack even fundamental skills, the new crop of ill-prepared teachers, and schools without real standards or adequate resources as the givens, the tip of the iceberg.

What really worries them is us—you and me—and the world we have made.

That covers a lot of ground, more than I can explain in this introduction. But the issue should be clear from the outset: virtually every teacher I interviewed said that changes in our world have invaded our classrooms and are too much for schools to handle alone.

They talked about our troubled social climate and showed me how that climate—not the school in a vacuum—is our problem. They charted not just the test scores, but changes in attitudes and values. And who teaches those? they asked. They described the garbage-strewn streets around city schools and the suburban school yards filled with late model cars owned by kids. What does garbage teach? they wanted to know. Or unearned automobiles?

They gave eyewitness accounts of how our schools reflect the divisions in American life and reveal our segregation by income, color, and social class—all the things we as a nation do not usually like to face.

They questioned our priorities. We say we value our schools, but some of them have no heat in winter, no windows, and walls that are near collapse. Makeshift classrooms, often with two or more classes going on at once, are found in gyms, boiler rooms, and basements—making it clear we care more about our shopping malls than our schools.

They all came up with the same acid test: we say we value teachers, but we don't want our own children to become teachers.

They also responded to changes on the domestic front. They asked who is "home" to make sure kids do homework and they had a laundry list of complaints about parents who don't have time to pack a peanut butter sandwich or see that their children are warmly dressed in winter. They talked about young kids who find it hard to concentrate and older ones who come to school high.

Should teachers feed the kids who don't bring a lunch? And how can they help the ones who work an eight-hour shift after school and fall asleep at their desks? Should they give the class some busywork so they can talk to the child who hasn't seen his father in six months or the one who doesn't understand why her parents are always mad at each other?

You get the idea. Of course, all the finger pointing can get tiresome and, yes, teachers were defensive. Some even struck me as being played out, only going through the motions and picking up a paycheck.

But most of the time, I was moved by how much our teachers care about other people's children. And most of the time, the teachers I met were far more dedicated than we have a right to expect.

Their stories, uncannily alike from New York to Los Angeles, had a cumulative effect on me and made me realize what should have been very obvious: we can tinker with this or that program, but our schools will not seriously improve until we recognize and acknowledge that they are part of a larger social context.

For instance, when we abandon our inner-city schools to those too poor to escape them and equip our suburban schools with all that money (and perhaps only money) can buy, we send out a message. Some teachers may try to soften its impact. I think that's why many teachers in our inner cities worry about their students' "self-esteem" and why in suburban schools the subject of "character" comes up a lot.

But the larger social context is a powerful teacher and can sometimes defeat the teacher in the classroom.

Teachers know that. For while we look at teachers, they look at *us* through our schools. For them our schools are social mirrors. Schools reflect our values, and they reflect certain problems we have as a nation, problems that did not start, but often end up, in the classroom.

I do not want to sound dramatic. The truth is dramatic enough. But it is difficult to summarize what teachers say and not sound like some Jeremiah in the wilderness.

Teachers are fed up, and they have their own three Rs—all negative: no recognition, no respect, and not enough remuneration. These have been well publicized, but perhaps readers do not realize (I certainly didn't) how deep they run. It's bad enough that they earn far less than their neighbors, but the lack of respect and recognition seem to teachers to be the unkindest cuts of all.

They are also skeptical about what we want to do about our schools. Yet they still care. It amazed me how much they care.

When I began these interviews, I was stunned by the floodgate I had unleashed. I felt as if I had stumbled on a lost people who had not seen anyone from earth in a long while. Teachers all wanted to talk about their work, but no one had ever asked them before!

There was no stopping them—*after* I cut through a thicket of suspicion. Why, they asked, did I want to know? Was this an academic study? An exposé? Many assumed I had prejudged them and knew what I would find.

They were wrong. I was shocked by what I heard and unprepared for it. But the fact that teachers are suspicious and very wary of any visitor to their classrooms, tells you what mine fields our schools have become. Teachers feel attacked from all sides. "What's it to you?" has become their motto, a defensive question posed by an angry and demoralized profession.

Everyone blames everyone else and everyone (I think) plays politics–whether it is the far right who think if we eliminate welfare, kids will have more incentive to learn or the left who argue that schools teach the poor how to fail and the rich how to rule.

I, too, have a politics, but I don't believe I can spell it out. Will it do if I say I still believe in cornball things like the life of the mind and all that rhetoric about a democracy being only as good as its schools?

It is true, of course. But somehow the stake we all have in the future of our schools has become a cliché–the kind of thing we expect to hear from a candidate for public office.

Closer to home, I've watched my stepchildren muddle through a variety of schools, public and private, and my own son–now six– has just started the great adventure.

And I used to teach college English. Some of those I passed on are now out there (oh Lord) pretending that they know more about the English language than their pupils–a case of my own low standards and flagrant grade inflation.

I am also intrigued by the classroom because it is where our young spend their time. I was curious about what happens to them in schools today, and I wanted to know how teachers see not only their own profession, but their charges.

There's an old Jewish joke: "Don't ask."

Teachers *are* negative. They have a lot to lament and little comfort to give–no comfort, but a much needed perspective on the issues. For example, we hear a great deal about how our schools have fallen behind those of Japan and other advanced nations in preparing our kids for a technological age. Teachers would agree.

They would point out, however, that the problem isn't merely that the math curriculum has been watered down or that our children think the simple math they are being given is tough enough, thank you. Teachers say our kids believe it is enough if they have "tried." They don't quite understand what more can be asked of them. "Trying," not "succeeding," defines their shrinking horizons.

Similarly, teachers are concerned because they do not believe their students make a connection between effort and rewards. "They don't have their foot on the gas, but they expect to go far" was an observation made by teachers in affluent districts as well as the ghetto. They say everyone expects to be a brain surgeon TV-style: a few late nights with the books and *presto*, a white jacket and a BMW.

There seems to be no way of getting around it: for a nation built out of the wilderness by men and women with no capital but their energy and will, this is a major cultural shift. It is never reported the way drugs in the school yard or weapons in the classroom are reported, but it seems to be taking its toll.

Parental attitudes have also changed. Judging from what I heard, parent-teacher relations are at an all-time low. In the suburbs some teachers complain that parents send out mixed signals: they want their kids to go to Harvard but not to feel any school "pressure"; or they want to pull their kids out of school for a trip but still tell them education comes first. In the inner cities they say most parents are not around.

Either way, there is the widespread perception that people only pay lip service to education and educators. They do not value or understand the teacher's job well enough to supply the help and support that are desperately needed.

Where once parents and teachers were natural allies, they are now at an impasse or even antagonists. Mutual blame and recriminations are common. For teachers, many parents are at best victims; at worst, cop-outs and enemies.

As teachers see it, they have lost the support of the home, and in many cases there is no home and no support they can lose. Everyone is working, and no one has time for the kids, no one except the teacher. Teachers are picking up the pieces that parents haven't the time, energy, or interest to handle themselves. Not only that, but they are also taking on roles that used to be left to the church, the family doctor, Grandma, and even the neighbors.

Our teachers see more and more children in trouble, and there are no adequate services—academic, social, psychological—to help them. Nor is this only a problem for the poor. School after school in the suburbs seems to be taking on a social worker because, I was told, the youngsters need help.

Somehow we expect our schools to handle it all: if the inner-city teacher fights a situation in which kids are exposed to drugs, violence, and despair at a very early age, then the suburban teacher wants to know how to compete with tennis lessons, Bloomingdale's, trips to Bermuda, and so on.

One suburban teacher said, "This is what is driving me crazy. We are not the center of kids' lives anymore. We are just one more acquisition." And from an inner-city teacher: "I can bring them up to grade level and in the third grade even motivate them. But they'll regress, I know it. The streets will consume them."

The problems these teachers describe will not be solved by a new curriculum, merit pay, or higher salaries. They see that, and they want us to see it too.

Meanwhile they do what they can and they seem to me a strong conservative force. They do not usually want to undermine the American dream, only to see it work.

But it cannot work if we ask more of schools than they can deliver *alone* (an old problem: we were sold on public education in the nineteenth century partly because we were told that schools would keep our poor from joining the criminal classes) and if we ask more and more of our teachers. Teachers now serve as low-level cops so that our children will not attack one another on school time (this is called lunchroom duty, hall duty, attendance duty). And they are involved in a fantastic amount of red tape—some of it worthwhile (like getting a child a pair of glasses) and much of it nonsense. All of it takes time away from the classroom, and all of it suggests the more-than-academic roles our teachers are being asked to handle alone.

When you add it up—the lack of support from within and outside the system, the social ills that schools are asked to somehow overcome, and the way none of us brings an apple for the teacher anymore—it's a miracle anybody is still in the classroom.

How much longer will they be there? And who will be there? Judging from these interviews, for every dedicated and talented teacher who stays, two more are on the way out—too demoralized, too frustrated, and too angry to continue.

Your move, America.

About the Interviews

There are 35 interviews in this book. Many were held in and around New York and Los Angeles, our nation's two largest school systems. A few come from the Midwest and others from elsewhere on the East coast.

They do not pretend to cover the nation, and this is not a scientific study. But for those who are comforted by statistics, the 35 voices in this book were echoed by 22,000 teachers in a recent survey undertaken by the Carnegie Foundation for the Advancement of Teaching (and published in December 1988, after most of my own interviews had been completed).

Summing up the survey, Carnegie Foundation President Ernest L. Boyer said that teachers feel a sense of frustration in the classroom, both "over the lack of support they receive from parents" and over a "feeling of powerlessness in teaching." He also said that teachers are deeply disturbed by what they see as America's "emotionally needy" children and that "they really did feel that something has changed dramatically in America and that far more children are at risk."

Precisely what I heard. Apparently, teachers in American

schools share the same problems and hold many of the same views no matter where they live.

Their impassioned views—not mine—are my subject. But I am not a Martian. As I listened, of course I reacted; and the more I heard, the more some patterns, as well as further questions, seemed to emerge.

I have identified these patterns and brought up some of my unanswered questions in small asides to the readers. These "postscripts," as I call them, along with the introductions to each interview, are my chance to talk back.

They are sometimes critical of teachers and just about everyone else in the education business. But I hope they avoid throwing stones or making educational reform sound like a simple matter. The solution to our problem is not simple, and if I have learned anything, it's how difficult the contemporary world of the classroom has become.

In the Cities

_____

In the Cities

With the 1983 report of the National Commission on Educational Excellence, *A Nation at Risk: The Imperative of Educational Reform*, our troubled school systems made front-page news. We heard about how all our schools were threatened by a "rising tide of mediocrity" and how, for the first time in our history, the educational skills of a new generation would not surpass, let alone approach, those of its parents.

Recommendations were made—including a call for a tougher "new basics" curriculum, higher standards, and an improvement in the status and income of teachers—and we were cautioned not to make scapegoats of the "victims...our beleaguered teachers."

Of teachers and other groups the report said that "their frustration threatens to overwhelm their hope."

That is still true six years later, and it applies especially to those who teach in our cities. But surprisingly, the report did not make much of a point about the disparities between our urban and suburban schools. It did mention that our schools are meant to provide "an equitable treatment of our diverse population," but it left out how our urban schools are increasingly dominated by one segment of that diverse population–disadvantaged and minority youth.

This is the population schools also find hardest to reach and the reason why programs like Head Start were begun. Unless, it was argued, children can be reached early enough, it becomes increasingly difficult to put them on track.

Teachers all agree, but they know there are not enough Head Starts and that once kindergarten has begun, there are few outside supports for the children of poverty. As they grow older and forces in their larger world begin to impinge on them, it becomes harder and harder for teachers to keep students motivated and interested in school.

For elementary school teachers this translates into the feeling that they are sitting on a powder keg. As many said, they look at young, eager faces and are almost sure that they will be angry, blank ciphers in a few years' time. For high school teachers, many of whom confront the violence head on, "excellence in education" isn't much of an issue right now. If kids show up and do some work, that looks like an achievement.

Also, in the 1960s and 1970s teachers lived what the report only wrote about. They saw a breakdown in the authority of the school. It became, many said, not very different from the streets; truancy and assaults on staff and other students were common, and the need for police patrols to protect them and to keep weapons and drugs out were also common.

Perhaps some of that violence has abated, but it is hard to know if it has just shifted locations. For example, street gangs are on the rise in Los Angeles, but they have diminished in New York; both cities, however, report the confiscation of many more weapons than ever before in their schools.

And less dramatic problems–the bureaucratic tangle that is most urban school systems, the way many administrators seem more caught up in public relations than in serious support of their teachers, and the dilapidated state of our underfunded city school systems–all remain.

For urban teachers, perhaps the most serious problem of all has to do with their students' attitudes. Kids are not motivated, they report, and sometimes it seems as if kids have given up on the system. They don't think it works for them and therefore have no incentive to do well at school. They know McDonald's will hire them without a diploma, so why study? Education is not much valued in their culture, and perhaps most critically, there are few role models in the classroom for them (a point all teachers made, but one that minority teachers seem to feel more intensely).

A bleak picture, and one that makes it look as if our educational system has become almost two-tiered—divided into suburb and city, middle class and (that new phenomenon) underclass. And should there be any doubt which classroom is easier to handle, I can only add that I rarely heard any military metaphors in the suburbs. But in our cities teachers speak about "the front line," "combat pay," and "the trenches" all the time.

"In the L.A. Unified School District status is centered around *leaving* the classroom. For teachers who look at the classroom as the trenches and think the sooner they can get out the better, it doesn't matter.

But some of the best teachers I have known leave to become specialists, resource people, advisers, administrators. They take these routes for better pay and higher status.

The kids I'm around—they need all the good teachers they can get. We need a career ladder you can climb *within* the classroom. That's where teachers belong."

DAVID WILLIAMS
high school English teacher
and football coach
Los Angeles, California

Where Teachers Belong

David Williams was the first teacher to point out the ironic way the educational system works: it rewards those who get out. So far his parents have not (both teach), and he is still in the classroom after nine years.

Dedication is a cliché, but this teacher seemed to me to be the real thing. He described his students with candor and concern, and he also knows their world. Like the majority of them, David Williams is black and he lives two miles away from the school.

He teaches English—everything from A Midsummer Night's Dream to 1984. But he also spends time helping his students learn how to think things through and how to make decisions.

He says most of his students "raise themselves" and need a surrogate parent. It sounded to me (although he did not say so) that David Williams often fills that role.

He teaches minority students who are anywhere from poor to middle class. I started out (and returned a number of times) by asking what they were like.

Nine years ago Dorsey High had perhaps 50 white students. There are none now; our ethnic mix is about 70 percent black, 20 percent Hispanic, and the rest Asian.

My own childhood was spent here. I know the area well, and I know what kids face. I think that helps.

What are they like? They're very, very seasoned—much more so than the students in places like Temple City, a white suburb where I have also taught. They are quick to size you up. They know who cares and who doesn't, and they behave accordingly.

It isn't cut and dried, but for the most part I teach kids who have a lot of ability but are used to neglect. They are not poverty stricken, but they also do not know affluence. It's unlikely that anyone in their family has been to college, and rarely does anyone at home talk to them about the future.

How are they neglected?

I'm not talking about material neglect. Most of the young people I know are very well fed and clothed. But their parents are at work a lot of the time, and the kids can do what they want. They can come and go as they please. They get away with an abnormal amount.

I normally have about one hundred and fifty students, not counting the football team. On open house night I get five or six parents—usually the parents of the better students. Most parents are either at work or they are very apathetic.

I don't understand the parents. You live in the area. Nobody can claim you would alienate or intimidate them.

We call, we send notes. They are not at all intimidated. I think they just do not make it a priority. They have their own lives, two or three jobs, divorce, other problems. It's hectic.

Many of my students raise themselves and their kid brothers and sisters. They often make scary decisions based on whim, and that leads them down some poor paths.

There are the girls who get pregnant, and, sad to say, a number of my students are in jail. Last year I was a character witness in a murder trial. It broke my heart. This student of mine was easily led. He didn't choose his friends but went along with anybody. He was in a car when a couple of these people robbed and shot someone. He had nothing at all to do with it, but he was with them and they sent him up Sometimes you wonder, did you do enough?

What can you do?

Whatever I do, I didn't learn it in any training manual. We're trained to teach the curriculum, but all these other realities—child abuse, divorce, drugs—are never mentioned.

It's tough. I've been told several times by young ladies that they were pregnant—before the boyfriend knew, before the parents knew. And what do you do?

It would be wrong to state what I think. I am supposed to be objective. I do not say "keep the baby" or "have an abortion," but I walk the girl through and try to help her use some critical thinking on the issue.

These girls—their self-esteem is very low. They hook up with much older men. They need the support, not just from me. There ought to be more support services.

What do you mean?

It's nothing like it was, even 10 years ago. It's worse, much worse. You've heard that in some parts of L.A. there is increasing violence and gang activity? Are you familiar with that? I'm not physically threatened on a day-to-day basis, but it exists. We take strong measures on gang clothing, gang signs, gang hair. We don't allow it on campus, but it is in the neighborhood.

It's a neat neighborhood and does not look like some areas in Detroit or Philadelphia, but the violence is there.

I lost one student who had been in my advanced-placement English class, a girl who had graduated. She got off the bus after work and was shot. She was in the wrong place at the wrong time. I've had that happen twice, and that is a real thing.

In a given school year you'll lose at least one student to violence. It's devastating, it really is.

Are other teachers afraid?

Some are, but I wonder: some teachers exaggerate, and when they do not know how to behave, they almost invite trouble.

It's hard to describe. They've been away at college, and where we work may be a shock—not visually, but we are dealing with some pretty rough characters. Not all are in gangs, but lots are.

Once you get to know the kids though, you realize that the violence is not directed at you, not at all. In fact, this girl—who is 15 and has lived the life of a 35-year-old—isn't going to do anything to you. She will probably be nice to you.

It's hard, very hard. They have seen so much violence and have often been its victim. A lot of times the adolescent discovery, the joking, is missing from their lives.

They're cynical, and they are very seasoned. Their view of the world is bleak. If you saw many of my students, you would not believe that they are in high school. They look 29, but they are still 15 and very young inside.

Many have been in the courts or are runaways. I had one 10th grader who had been out of the house for a year. She was a runaway, but still she came to school. Academically she could compete with anybody. Her father had died, her mother was never sober, and she was on the streets. I could go on and on.

Do you feel you have a mission?

I am successful sometimes and not others. But I do take pride. I have many students who now attend UCLA [the University of California, Los Angeles]—a former student is the school's newspaper editor. Others are at [U.C.] Berkeley, and some go on to junior colleges. I ride them pretty hard if I can see a spark of willingness. In fact, a few of my A.P. [advanced-placement] kids are now teachers themselves, and some now own their own businesses. Every year I get on the phone and have 30 grads come talk to the seniors.

What kind of education are the kids getting?

It depends on what schools they come from (there is broad busing in the L.A. area); on what teacher they have in the high school; and of course on whether their parents are going to be cautious about tracking them properly.

Is discipline a problem?

That, too, depends on the teacher. I think if you set rules and are fair and if you allow for some humor and let them be 17, then there will be very little trouble.

Does being the football coach help you as the English teacher?

Maybe. I am not the typical football coach who cracks a whip and curses [laughs]. But I know how to manage large groups and how to keep my explanations brief.

What helps even more is that in a school with a high turnover rate I've been around for nine years. I have the cousins and younger brothers and sisters of my old students now. Since their relatives know me and think well of me–I hope!–the new students will usually behave.

Why is there such a high turnover of teachers?

And administrators. I've observed a lot of teachers, counselors, and other personnel who use the school as a stepping-stone. They work here, but their ambition is someplace else. They initiate programs for self-aggrandizement and not for the benefit of the kids.

Are there many white teachers?

It's about 50-50. There are only four Hispanic and Asian teachers, which doesn't represent the student population. The district is trying to ethnically match staff and student body.

That's important?

To a degree, but I would not stress it. I think what matters is the quality of the person.

Of course, some teachers are racist. I've seen that. There are also several white teachers who are among the most popular in the school.

You have to think before you speak and get to know the kids first. Some teachers do not do that. One teacher I know is condescending. He used to publicly reprimand Hispanic kids, and that is not the best approach. Hispanic kids are very macho, quick tempered, and easily embarrassed in public. To put them down in front of others does not work.

Some white teachers have also told me that the kids are prejudiced.

Very much so. It is something I am always battling. The kids are also prejudiced against one another–the upper-middle-class blacks against the lower, blacks against Hispanics, kids on the west side against those on the east side. (Conditions on the east side are much more severe than what I am describing to you. There is a high school called Jordan in Watts. It is an attractive school in the middle of miles of blight. There is far less control there. It is much worse.)

How would you feel about being reassigned to Watts?

I could make it there now that I have some experience, but I would not choose willingly to go there. Believe me, there are enough challenges where I am. Students tell me there are few enough of the kind of people that they need where I am. They want someone they cannot run all over but who is not a mean autocrat. They really need a surrogate parent.

Money isn't always the problem. I have some fairly affluent kids. Their homes have everything that the Cosby kids have, but there are no Cosby parents, no magazine subscriptions, and very few books. They barely read a newspaper. It's a video age.

They will not do it on their own, but they have the ability. I make magazines, paperbacks, and newspapers available. Sometimes I teach a class from sections of the newspaper or a segment of "Donahue" or "Oprah Winfrey" when a meaningful adolescent issue is discussed. They are good writing props.

How is the students' writing?

I had three or four kids last year who wrote very well. But many of my students speak very well and write like three-year-olds. None of them, not even my brightest kids, read enough.

The bottom line is that they haven't been asked to write enough.

Are you able to change the writing in a year?

A little. I help them with structure and organization but could do more about their grammar and punctuation. I think most of them need more individual help. There are no resources for this, and our classes are too large.

My number-one negative complaint is the paper load–both the administrative papers and the papers I correct. Compositions take a lot of time. I have spent weekends on the papers. I am not in a good mood after I do that too many times. That is a common complaint, especially among English teachers. And I am sorry to say that we sometimes lower our standards to compensate.

Is there grade inflation?

Yes. I've been guilty of it myself at times–mostly when it's the difference between failing and a D. One of my kids got in with a bad crowd and stole a girl's bus pass. Charges were pressed in juvenile hall, and he was out of the class from February to April. He did satisfactory work in my class from April to June, but I didn't have his grades from juvenile hall. In instances like that, or when girls leave to have babies, I'll slide them through.

Are you considered a "softie"?

No. I am always sensitive to that. If I heard that I was, I would correct it immediately. I'm sensitive to the other extreme too. There are some teachers who have some sort of pride in never giving an A.

What kind of books are being taught in high school English in Los Angeles 1988?

I teach different books in regular and A.P. English. I'm very proud of my A.P. kids. Four years ago the school did not offer advanced English, and so we have made some strides. What do I teach them? *Death of a Salesman, The Great Gatsby, Hamlet, A Midsummer Night's Dream, 1984, Brave New World*.

Do the kids ever question the relevance of these books?

Sometimes. But the teacher's approach means all the world to them. You have to make it come alive.

I mean do they ask, "What does *A Midsummer Night's Dream* have to do with my life?"

Their world is narrow. I teach Shakespeare after I have gained their trust, not at the start of a semester.

We also have very frank discussions about drugs, sex, crime—you name it—and we talk about values.

I don't know if this is true elsewhere, but our kids are very tied up with material things. They have a real need to display what they have—gold chains, cars—to gaudy excess. They judge other people based on what they have. If you don't have this, you are nothing; if you do have this, you are everything. In fact, a lot of them dress far better than their family's income would allow.

I have more than a few who work very late at night and then are sleepy during the day. Attendance is a problem, and it's more of a problem the older they get. Mondays are the worst days. No one is there. You often teach a four-day week because of attendance. The day before a holiday no one is there.

What do teachers do to unwind after a week when one kid goes to jail and a lot more don't show up?

[Laughs] I've had days when I'm really frustrated, but that is not the norm. I have lots of success stories, and I think I have a young frame of mind. When there's time, I love the movies and athletics.

I'm busier than most though. I'm the football coach, the senior class sponsor, and up to this semester a mentor teacher.

A mentor teacher?

I helped guide a new inexperienced teacher, but a new ruling doesn't allow me to both coach and be a mentor teacher. I think that's a mistake.

You lose extra income?

Yes. Most of my friends make far more money that I do; they have more. I have the same old car that I had in college. But I think they understand.

I think teachers don't get paid enough. Consider this: When I go to a football game, I may be the only adult supervising 70 to 80 kids, and that includes getting them there and back. The bus driver who drives us makes more money than I do. The janitor makes a comparable salary. That's a reality, a fact.

Do you work summers?

I work in a Volkswagen plant in Pomona. I do very menial labor and make more there than I do teaching.

If you could change anything about education, if you had the power and the money, what would you do?

First of all there ought to be creative scheduling. I've heard of some schools where you do not have the same six periods every day. I'd be in favor of creating blocks of time where students could read and blocks of time in which teachers could plan lessons or correct papers—not this burnout. Also I've noticed a lot of schools in the L.A. area where the counseling could be better. A bright mind is not discovered until very late, and the average kid will take the *bare* minimum but will never say a word. They have to be pushed, they will not do it on their own.

Grouping is also a problem. It is tough to be effective when one-third of the class is barely literate and another kid is almost genius level. I had a class like that fifth period last year, and it was just exasperating. Perhaps classes have to be segregated by skills—it has to affect a teacher's style when the range is that vast. That's what many people say.

The counselors are to blame in part for this. They change so frequently. All but one left my school this year, which means new ones coming in. Frequently they come from the junior high level and don't know about the sports program, the work program, class sequence. They don't know about the kids, the families either. They don't know who is likely to be bright and who needs extra help; they just shove the kids anywhere, and it is trouble for the teachers.

I get a kid in 11th grade, and he is really bright; I'd like to get him in advanced placement, but he has not had the sequence and hasn't been tracked from the beginning. Those are my biggest gripes, and I make them known very regularly. But it doesn't help, because the staff changes so much.

What else would you change?

There needs to be a larger concerted effort for teacher recognition and a career ladder you can climb *within* the classroom.

I turned down two offers from the board of education. Knowing what I would be leaving behind, I could not justify a move. But I wouldn't always have that luxury. I'm married now and have a child. Money will have to influence my decisions more and more.

The bottom line is that this is an education system. The kids I'm around—they need all the help they can get. Shouldn't the best be with the kids? The board of education building in L.A. is a huge place, like a big hospital; there are thousands of people—I wonder what they all do.

Put you on hold when you phone them?

[Laughs] It's second only to New York in size. All I know is, we can use some of those people in the classroom. We have some teachers who teach because they don't make enough money in the real-estate business. Because teaching does not pay as well as it should, you don't always get good teachers. And the kids know it, they know it right away.

I work with a few who are suspect. They have trouble spelling and things like that. Competency testing might help here. But merit pay? I don't know. Who would decide? I'm not antiadministration, but I don't think they can decide.

Do you think your education courses were useful?

A friend of mine who left Dorsey to pursue a Ph.D. in education is in classes with people, none of whom has spent a day in the classroom. Only two or three of his professors have ever been in a public high school. Many of the things he hears them say, he has to start laughing. I've had valuable instruction in how to prepare a lesson plan, handle machinery, but as far as people skills–zero. A lot of the science and math teachers are that way; they are geniuses in their subject, but when it comes to teaching a class of 17-year-old kids, forget it.

"I had kids in 1970 who were already mothers when I left in '81. When a 13-year-old has a baby, she thinks it is a doll. But when the baby makes demands on her and isn't cute any more, the mother turns off. I can't always handle the demands my own children make. How can a child raise a child?"

JILL MARVINOWSKI
elementary school teacher
Yonkers, New York

How Can a Child Raise a Child?

Jill Marvinowski collects crystal. On days when kicking the broken toilets in the teachers' room or making half-serious plans to open a cleaning service with fellow teachers did not make her feel a whole lot better, she went to a good china shop.

Twelve years in an inner-city school add up to a lot of crystal—delicate glass bells, candy dishes, bud vases. They are her own purple hearts, the rewards that she gave herself.

Now she teaches at a magnet school for the gifted. (A magnet school is one in which the student body is determined by interest in a special subject or by special skills, not by where the students live. There are more than 1,000 magnet schools in the nation at present, and most are successes: a way to educate and to maintain an integrated student population.)

In Marvinowski's new school, life is much better: parents tend to be older and more supportive. Just getting a thank-you card from a parent makes a difference. "There is something about working hard and getting recognition," she said. "It makes you want to go back the next year. Who wants to go back when the students are ready to beat you up?"

Being where parents are appreciative rather than hostile has done more than improve Jill Marvinowski's morale. She is sure it also affects the education her students receive. She is convinced that neither the school (regular or magnet) nor the teacher can make a big enough difference alone: it is the life children lead outside the nine-to-three classroom that determines how they will fare in school.

Her schools are in Yonkers—a city just north of New York that has a large minority population. When she first started out, back in the seventies, there was money available for minorities and for school programs. But the money has long since been cut back or has disappeared. Budget cuts, bureaucratic red tape, and the hornet's nest of school integration have taken their toll.

Yonkers—which is now fighting integration in housing—was then integrating its schools. The school-integration process was not as violent as that of Boston, but it was still very difficult. Though some people saw busing as "the thing to do," it was still not a popular solution to the problem of second-class classrooms. White flight—and also, said Jill, teacher flight—was almost immediate:

We were always being compared to the east side and shown their higher test scores. But when integration came and the school population on the east side changed, a lot of teachers on the east side bailed out. Or they gave it one year and then they retired. They could not handle the inner-city child.

All of a sudden it wasn't the teachers who were to blame for failures in education. But we knew that. For years those of us who had been on the avenue [on Yonkers's west side] had been telling people that we were not the problem. The teachers that I worked with in the inner city were some of the best I've known. They were great. You just don't last if you are not that good.

When I started out in 1970, they were putting a lot of money into the inner-city schools. We had money for guidance counselors, social workers, a full-time psychologist, and full-time art and music teachers. We also had what was called "double-teaching." I had a "cluster" teacher in my room a couple of hours a day and a full-time aide as well.

Sounds great.

It was good, and it helped to some extent. But then came the budget crisis, and our programs were the first to go. Even when money and energy were being expended though, we could not keep up with the east side. The kids who came from sound homes—whether professional or blue-collar families—had an advantage. Our kids didn't cut it. We never made it.

Why?

The school cannot become the life of the child, because the child goes home. Whatever I did from eight to three, he still had to go home and deal with his problems. The problems were bad then and are even worse now...the drugs, the lack of a structure, the lack of a parent figure, or the parent who is herself a child.

So many kids went home to terrible places, and nobody took care of them. There were kids who were ironing their clothes in the kindergarten. Can you imagine? Mine didn't even plug in the iron at that age.

It's a totally different life from the one you and I know, and it is just very frustrating. The more you put in, the less you get back, the less you see someone grow. If you have twenty-five kids and only four of them show any progress, it is depressing. You know, I read in the paper about kids I had in class. They are murderers.

Parental involvement?

Mostly negative. Once I wanted to retain a kid, and his mother absolutely refused. The kid should have been in special ed. [Special education, a program for children with special academic, emotional, or psychological needs—including the learning disabled and gifted.] I was trying to have him repeat the grade, get some help, and then go on. But she refused; she threatened my life. She'd call me and threaten to beat my white f—— rear end. I'd lock my door so that if she was in the building, she could not get to me.

This mother wasn't alone. It happened repeatedly, and each time I'd think, This parent will be different.

All year long I'd try to reach parents to say, "Your kid has some problems; so let's talk about what we can do." I'd tell them to do the things a typical mom would do—get involved, see that the child has his books and does his homework. But they didn't listen. At the end of the year, when report cards went home and I'd put "retain" on some of them, parents suddenly woke up. Then they carried on like lunatics.

[She shrugs, as if reliving the times she threw up her hands.]

After a while I began to feel pretty defensive. I'd think, Okay, if you do not want my opinion of your kid... I learned to keep a low profile. I set classroom rules but did not ask for help very often because I did not want to be attacked anymore.

[Remembers something] Look! I couldn't even get much help within the school—not after funds were cut.

In every class there were kids I couldn't reach, not in a class of 25. They were kids who did not retain information. Perhaps some were dyslexic. I don't know—I can't spot dyslexics or even tell you why some kids can't retain information. All I know is, you stand on your head and spit wooden nickels, and the next day they look at you and you do it again. Those were the kids that I believed would benefit from a class of eight.

To place them in small so-called special-education classes, you go through reams of paperwork. You write them up, get them interviewed, see the parents, get their permission, and then—and this takes some time too—the kids are placed.

The special-ed. program was wonderful—eight kids and a teacher.

But after a while we were told that too many minority kids were being referred, and it didn't look good. These kids were not "learning disabled" or "emotionally disturbed," we were told. They were "socially deprived," [and so they were rejected from the program].

So what were we going to do? All of these kids were socially deprived. Do you think I was going to spend hours and hours writing up papers to get them into the small classes only to be turned down?

In the end I felt the same way I had about the mother who did not want me to retain her kid. She's the mother—no retention. It's your city—no special ed.

Did you choose this school?

When I graduated, I didn't have a planned direction. I had minored in education, and at that time women were not doing what they are now.

My mother thought becoming a teacher was great. It was a step up for my mother and dad, who were immigrants.

We lived in Yonkers, and I knew the assistant superintendent. She had once been my teacher. She told me to go over to the avenue, and I went. I was there for 12 years.

You had minored in education?

And student-taught in a well-to-do Long Island school. But my ed classes—except for the practice teaching—were a waste of time. I didn't know what it was like to be a teacher until I appeared in the classroom that first morning, and then I was scared to death. I had 26 kids that I was totally responsible for from eight to three. If you stop to think about it—you as a mother send your child off on the bus, and he comes back at three—and there is this one poor woman who is responsible for everything during that time.

I'd take them to the zoo. Then all night long I'd be worrying. Did I have everybody? You count them, all the time you count them. But then you think, Wait a minute—did I actually see Valerie's mother come for her?

It's a major responsibility, and in the inner-city schools—where parents are not involved scholastically but may come after you physically—it can be a nightmare.

How did you last as long as you did?

My friends. In fact, I still see them. We laughed, we joked, we kicked the toilets—out of frustration. You'd come up for lunch after a day of frustration, and you'd go to the bathroom and the toilet wouldn't work. You'd kick the toilet—grown women lashing out at a toilet!

When I got to my magnet school, I thought, Who died and went to heaven? Parents send me cards: "Thank you for taking care of my son. You were wonderful." They must know I am giving 100 percent.

We are what is called a magnet school for gifted kids, and we now are integrated. But even our magnet school has its problems. There are many bright nonminority kids who do not make the program. Why? It's the quotas: the law states that we must have at least a 40 percent minority population, and the low IQ cutoff is 120. Minorities are actively recruited—at churches, nursery schools, everywhere. All the minority kids who pass the IQ test are admitted. But white kids with 160 IQs may not get in.

That's not fair. All who qualify should be taken. The way it is, we are driving even more people out of Yonkers.

In fact, as more people do leave Yonkers, I'm sure that even at the magnet school we will start to see the parents who are not interested. To be honest, I am planning to look for a job up county because, as I get older, my patience is wearing thinner.

It is white people who are leaving Yonkers? Are you saying that they tend to be the more interested parents?

Not at all. But white people have a better chance of getting out, and if most do leave—along with the more-affluent minority parents—then the school will be left with a less-involved group of parents.

The parents are the key to everything. It's the parents who care, the hardworking PTA moms, who make teachers' lives livable. It's *their* kids who learn.

You see it right away. When I taught kindergarten, it was the kids from Head Start who did very well. They had parents who cared enough to get them there on a daily basis and to pick them up. They didn't just shoo them out the door.

Is teaching a gifted child different from teaching any kid?

No. It is very difficult to say that the school has 700 truly gifted children from age 3½ to age 8. They are potentially gifted when tested at age 3, and some of them are truly gifted. But they are a puzzle. Their motor coordination is poor; they can think, but they cannot write. They can tell you wonderful stories, but they can't put them on paper.

There's a new push now to discover ways to deal with the gifted minority student who is very bright but not academic. It's very difficult to get remedial math or remedial reading services for our school because the administration doesn't want to admit that there are some problems, and we need those services. I had one child who was a scientist and into experiments. He was very bright but could not read at all. I couldn't give him the help he needed. His mom took him to be tested. Again, she cared enough to go that extra mile and pay for the tutoring. But most minorities are not financially able to pay for that kind of help. The city should provide the remedial instruction. We ask for it, but it isn't there.

Are you measured by your students' scores?

I guess so. But as long as I feel I am doing everything I can, I am not especially threatened if their scores don't measure up.

It is outrageous to be held responsible for student progress *if* you are doing your job. If you are sitting back and relaxing, then it is up to the administration to see that you get to work or get out. The administration should not wait until the scores come back and then point out that Mrs. So-and-So's class had higher scores. If you measure by scores, then measure how far you brought *your* students up from their previous year's scores.

And do the kids measure you? How do they see you?

I don't know. I think they like me. I once got a note from a kid in the ghetto. He wrote, "Mrs. M is a very nice teacher. She has brown and yellow hair and roars like a lion." [Marvinowski shows me a book her students assembled for her when she was on sick leave for an operation; clearly she is very proud of it, and not for the first time I realize that it is recognition–not merely money–that teachers want.]

Is your administration supportive?

I've worked with administrators who were very supportive and aware that it is teachers who really run a school. I've also worked with some who have swollen egos, like kings. It's hard to support their projects because they are the people who ask, "How will it look for me?" rather than "What will it do for the kids?"

In truth, I had only two really terrible principals. One was fired, and the other one came on like gang busters and then found out that it's not that easy to change the world. She has a desk job now–director in charge of something or other.

How do you feel about the issue of not living in the community where you teach?

I feel good about it [laughs]. That woman who came after me was not atypical. On open-house night we all came at the same time, and we never left alone.

Was race a problem?

Kids don't see color, but they do reflect their parents' attitudes. There are white kids with a poor attitude toward integration, and there are some black kids who say, "You don't like me because I'm black." I say, "You could be purple. If you are a nice person, I'm going to like you."

I tell them all that I care. "But," I say, "you have to care, your mom has to care, your people have to care."

Do you think integration was a good thing?

I think it hasn't worked. I had a friend who taught in the best school in Yonkers. When integration came, they really sold that school–tremendous fanfare and tours. They bused the children in. Now it is a minority school and again does not meet integration guidelines! They have to try and get the white kids in there.

Also, it became so difficult there that the good teachers left.

You know how the children are assigned to schools now? Now each year we have a fair in Yonkers. Interested parents come to the fair and choose which school their child will attend.

But when September 7 comes around, hundreds of kids haven't even been registered for kindergarten. Despite all the efforts to reach parents—through churches and newspapers and on the radio —the kids are not there on the first day of school. On September 7, I had eight kids in my last kindergarten. By January, there were twenty-seven. They come in slowly.

Many times it's the grandmother who finally brings the kids to school and registers them—and the grandmother might be 35. Her daughter—the 15-year-old mother—might have been one of my former students.

Would you become a teacher if you were starting out now?

I think so. Teaching affords me time with my children. If I didn't come home until seven at night, I could not function as a mother. Also, I like the vacations.

But I am not compensated for the amount of work I have to do. I don't want to brag, but I think I give it my all, and I should be paid more.

This may seem very superficial, but in all those years on the avenue, I never got a thank-you card. Once I received a card and it said, "Happy Birthday, Grandfather." It touched me because the kid actually thought of me.

Now at Christmas time the parents at the magnet school give me a check for $100, pearl earrings, that Lenox crystal [points to a vase on her wall]. That's nice, to feel recognized.

Where do you think teaching is going?

Fewer people are going into it because those who might become teachers see bigger opportunities in business. My feeling is that it is very important to continue to recruit people who care.

But as the country goes, so go the schools. If our cities decay and the minorities fall apart even more, then the schools will suffer. Schools cannot meet the needs of what amounts to homeless children.

"Clean house—from the administration all the way down. We need to get rid of the principals who have been there for 25 years and get in people who are going to turn things around. We need to put teachers in there who enforce the same standards: we do need pencils and papers, we do need books, we will do homework, we will come to school on time, and we will not leave in the middle of a class without a permission slip just because we have to go to work at Wendy's at one o'clock even though school ends at three."

MARY KLEIN
high school English teacher
Kansas City, Missouri

Clean House

Mary Klein has taught English for 15 years and is now about to start her own business. She's getting out because, she said, "I just couldn't handle it all."

She has been involved with children all her life. Before her 15 years in the public schools she taught in a Hebrew school and also worked in camps and with preschool children. But "teaching became too stressful" and too great a battle. If the schools are to change, they will have to "clean house"—a top-to-bottom sweep that will put everyone on the same side.

In the meantime, Klein has started a "creative storytelling" business. "I go to play groups, churches, hospitals, nursing homes—everywhere— and I'm using my literature when I enact stories and ask my audience to re-create them. I'm still in the field but on my own time. I just can't do it anymore. I know it was wrong of me to get out. It was wrong because they need me."

Mary Klein has a strong desire to serve. So why did she leave her inner-city school?

I will tell you. You get to be a certain age, and I think you get tired of fighting the glassy eyes, of having a student tell you to just f——off.

(Excuse me.) I really no longer wish to fight the drug scene and the discipline scene. I left it to somebody else if you want to know the truth.

Students told you to f—— off?

Oh, sure. We are talking all the schools—inner city and suburb. Neither group is motivated, both talk back, and they both use drugs. But the suburbs are a lot easier to handle.

This past year I was in an all-black inner-city school. It's in the same neighborhood where my husband's business is located, and he was not happy I was there. I didn't need to be in a place like that. I didn't need it in order to survive.

What was it like?

I will tell you that I never took a pocketbook in with me at all. I carried 50 cents in change to buy a soda for my lunch. My coat was locked up in a teacher's closet. There was no classroom for me; the school was overcrowded. I taught three hours a day in a cafeteria, one hour a day in an ROTC room with no windows, and only one hour a day I was able to go into a classroom.

Six teachers started the day I did. We were all in the same boat and had to teach without classrooms.

How many in a class?

Fifteen in a class. Usually I had eight or nine there, and it was very difficult. Many of these kids will not go on to college, and they are in high school because they must be. They are not interested.

You could not reach them with nine in a class?

I reached some, not all. There was no homework given, because they did not do it anyway. There were no pencils, no paper, no books. Many of them could not read. Literature books were of low interest, and so I dug out my own old sixth- and seventh-grade-level reading material. I copied stories that I felt they would like. But we still had to look at the stories in class and read them aloud—they couldn't take them home to read, because many of them could not read.

I was not secure there. The security was not what I wanted it to be, and I am being a lady when I say that to you. I had a sense of fear, and many other teachers did too. Only one of the six I started with returned this year.

Was race an issue?

Wasn't relevant.

I asked a teacher about whether our cars were safe, and she said that sometimes on the last day of school the kids will slash the teachers' tires; another time they threw India ink out the window and literally ruined the top of a teacher's car. Vandalism was high.

I didn't need to be in a place like that. I am fortunate because I could leave.

What teachers remain?

There were a lot of black teachers who had been there since before the school had turned black. They are locked in because if you choose to leave and change districts, you lose a lot of money.

Why didn't you just change schools?

After this experience I felt it was time to move on. But I've stayed in the field so that I can continue to work with children. With creative storytelling, I can still reach out to kids, but it is on my own time. I feel very badly about having to leave.

It's terrible because these kids need somebody who is going to teach them about Edgar Allen Poe and Mark Twain—even though it wasn't on a high level, I felt they got something out of it. The kids did not know how to write a paragraph when I walked in there. They did not know what a topic sentence was.

How could they be in high school and—

[Interrupts] Easy. Their teachers passed them on.

What accounts for a system in which white kids at least learn the rudiments, and black kids are passed on?

The fact that so many of the faculty members in the black schools have been locked in for a long time—since the time when their schools were white—and they are stuck there because of the money factor. They have lost their vim and vigor, but they can't leave. And the young people, the new teachers, don't go to the black schools;

they go into the suburban Kansas schools. (Salaries may be a wee bit higher in the ghetto, but there isn't that much difference.)

Are there changes that could be made to the schools that would cause you to return?

I don't know. Things are very different now. Here in Kansas City, Missouri, we have magnet schools.

I'd welcome a definition.

[Pauses a long time, then sighs] Let's say this. They have schools dedicated to science, to computers, to drama; if, as a student, your interest is computers, you will be bussed in to the computer magnet school, and along with the basics your program will zero in on computers. After high school, if you are unable to go on to college, you may possibly be able to get somewhat of a decent job after the magnet specialization you've had. That is the theory.

Not the practice?

To get a decent job and to fulfill an obligation to yourself, I feel you have to go on to college. The magnets don't make that clear.

Also, they recently announced that it will take 1,000 students from suburbia in order for the magnet schools to work. I'm not sure how many white families who live in suburbia are going to send their children to an inner-city school. They need this mix in order to get the money from the government and so on. It's quite a problem here. It's a real problem.

Why don't white kids go to these schools?

The schools are not located in the good parts of town, and parents are physically afraid. Kids would have to be bussed in.

Are the schools inferior?

Parents may think so, but that may not be true of the academic program. There is racial distrust and the risk of physical danger: there are security guards on every floor, and very often students are caught with weapons.

What can be done?

Clean house. Change the administration and make it clear to kids that they are responsible for some things. We need rules and regulations, and the students have to abide by them. They will if somebody puts it to them.

Somebody?

Everybody has to work in unison. It can't be one teacher. It needs to be the English teacher, the math teacher, the history teacher, the gym teacher. It needs to be everybody doing the same thing at the same time so that these kids know that this is the way it's going to be. Now it is too permissive.

Why are there few demands being made now?

It's easy. It is easy to just pass them on; the key is the administration—teachers can't change it alone, and a lot are very insecure. They are afraid for their jobs. They need their jobs.

In Kansas and Missouri there isn't a great deal of tenure anymore. Teachers can be shifted from one school to another and can also be asked to leave. They are sitting on a keg of dynamite.

You don't make teaching sound very attractive.

I love teaching! I love working with children and adults. I feel there is a very strong need for good people to share their knowledge with the public, whether it be young or old. There is a lack of this sharing in communities. Nobody has time.

Yet you cannot continue.

I am a highly motivated person, and I expect people around me to work as hard as I do and to produce. That wasn't coming through for me. I felt it was time for me to take a break.

In 1974, when you began, were kids more motivated?

Definitely—no question about it. I realize I was probably more patient then, but 15 years ago kids were more apt to do and to listen.

In suburbs and cities?

There's less motivation in both populations today, but when I taught in the Kansas schools, I found the students to be interested in learning and parent interest was high. These students went on to college.

In the inner city there was a lack of parent interest, and many of the students don't even have a father or don't know who he is. They have a mother, but she works, and there is no interest there.

That must be rough for the kids.

Yes, I'm sure it is rough. The kids are not stupid, just not motivated —the complete opposite of the kids I taught at the Hebrew Day School some time ago.

The Hebrew Day School was like a cult—the students are in school from eight to five, they take ten subjects a day, and they're too busy to do anything but go to school. These kids work their little tails off; and Friday night, Saturday, they go to synagogue. They don't work outside of school.

In the ghetto—I saw it this past year—the kids have to work to survive. Schools may have to change their structure to accommodate kids who work. A lot of kids are working today to survive. It's hard.

"What is it like to teach, to *try* to teach, to a group of kids who are looking at you with glassy eyes, who are dozing. What is it like to ask a kid to go the blackboard or to answer, and have the kid say, 'I don't feel like it'?"

MANUEL MONTALVO
ex-high school Spanish teacher
Bronx, New York

What Is It Like to Teach?

Manuel Montalvo did not ask these questions when he first began teaching back in the early sixties. At the start he was excited by his work and wanted to learn all that he possibly could about teaching. He worked in a number of schools, all quite different—rich, poor, traditional, innovative, racially mixed, and racially segregated. He tried to learn about them all.

When he'd been teaching for about 10 years, a new school opened in his own neighborhood. Truman High began amidst great fanfare, and its teachers were all enthusiastic, none more so than Montalvo himself. For Manuel Montalvo, who is Puerto Rican, the racially mixed school was a chance to give something back to his own neighborhood. He regarded the school with great hope and eagerly joined its staff.

At Truman he helped create a new language program. "As it had been," he said, "kids moved from the present to the subjunctive in three years. But after all those classes, when somebody said, 'Hello, how are you?' in Spanish, they would pause and have this terrible discomfort. They could not speak the language."

But, Montalvo said, the new program failed. The pressures from without—drug pushers who walked into the school to conduct business, violence that led Montalvo to carry a bat and patrol the basement, racial strife and community power struggles—were part of the reason.

Another reason was that few people within the system backed Montalvo up. His school life was a bizarre rerun of an old fairy tale, "The Emperor's New Clothes." Though there was no thread on the loom, his school bragged of its new clothes—its better scores, lower truancy rates, and new programs.

None was real. Better scores meant lower standards, and the truant rate only appeared to go down: attendance at homeroom was made a condition of graduation and that is when the school counted heads.

Montalvo called it "passing off paper plates as Lenox china." He fought it as long as he could, and last fall, after 26 years as a teacher, he decided he could not continue the charade any longer and he left the classroom.

When we talked, the experience was still very raw. Tales of 26 years in the classroom poured out of him—a nonstop torrent of ironies, insights, memories.

Reliving the decision to quit, and visibly shaken, he said, "I had to get out because the experience had destroyed me and a profession that I loved. It has been very difficult—the way teaching could not continue to be the thing that it was."

Many teachers I spoke with said that schools have changed and the profession has changed. But few made the impression on me that this teacher, for whom teaching was more of a calling than a job, made. We talked for a long time, and this interview abbreviates what was said. His decision to leave was traumatic. It colored all that Montalvo said.

His first subject was the language program that he helped start at Truman:

We had a language program that might have taught kids to speak Spanish. But at Truman a good idea became a ploy. What became important was not the value of the program, but how many people it passed.

We were told that we failed too many students and that grades would have to improve. But simultaneously, when this "grade" issue came up, we had grave drug and absentee problems. The schools were not facing these problems, and when we studied our language-program rolls, we found that the academic failures were very small. It was the absentees who were failing.

You were asked to pass kids who were not there?

The name of the game was survival, not education. This wasn't a mistake or a difference of opinion. It was survival of an individual's job, of a department, of the school.

It bothered me—the idea that if it sells, it's okay. When you have a good product—say you have Lenox china—you can sell it. But when you try to sell paper goods as Lenox china, that is something I cannot philosophically accept.

Did schools pass off paper goods as fine china in the sixties?

I think the attitude has changed. You once walked into a school, whether you were a teacher or a pupil, and you knew you had a job to do there.

Slowly the street has crept into the school. It may have started with the struggle for community control; it may have started when the pupils began seeing their teachers strike, seeing them as people rather than gods. But the atmosphere in the school kept changing, changing to the point where there were confrontations: if you put your hand on a black kid or a Latin kid, you might hear him say, [mutters] "Get your hands off me, man." Simple gestures were misunderstood, and any encounter could turn into a racial thing.

I remember teachers being challenged or ignored but still thinking that they could say, "If you don't do this, you will fail, *madam.*" I remember them walking down the halls and telling students, "Take off your hat." Take off your hat! As if that had been the major problem. It was culture shock.

Culture shock?

The school population was changing, and we had to undergo a whole relearning. With all the changes many schools were living in the past...in dreams. I remember going into Taft High School in a changing ghetto area, and having the principal tell me that we were teaching in a silk-stocking district. It was hard for people to face, or understand, all the change.

You mean the school is in some Dick-and-Jane world with one set of rules and—

[Interrupts] Yes, yes. So much was going on and teachers were still telling kids, "Take off your hat!" To a certain degree you find that today, in 1988.

When I was a dean (I was called a dean, but it was more like being a cop. Not that I went to school to be a cop, but if I can't teach and you need a cop in order to provide education, then let me at least make it possible for somebody else), I met with the principal about a kid who the principal thought had a weapon. The weapon was a bracelet with studs on it. I think it might have been pink. The principal said, "What about the points on it?" "Please," I said, "that is a fashion thing he is going through. Sometimes the kids who dress the most offbeat are the ones who are most afraid."

But the principal said that it was a weapon, and the kid was suspended.

Somewhere along the line the father came in—infuriated. And he was wearing two of these things, the bracelets. The kid had tried to adopt something of the father. The father walked in with the bracelets, tatoos, the whole number [laughs]. The principal could not see; he had not been dealing with street life and could not tell the difference between a weapon and this pink bracelet.

At Truman they were concerned, and still are, when a student came in wearing a hat—never mind the boom box blaring in the halls. The hat…you know, you are supposed to take it off when you come into a building and to tip your hat when you see a lady. These were old values and particularly white values.

It's astounding when you watch Jamaicans, even in the heat of summer, wearing a tam—you wonder how they do it. But the school could not let go of the hat, ordering them to take it off even though it is like saying, "Take off your *yarmulke* [a skullcap worn by Orthodox and Conservative Jews]."

When the teachers address children, they don't see.

Cultural misinformation is a major problem?

Even today blacks and whites do not speak the same language. Once, I remember, a white girl was giving a report and using some music with it. A black kid objected to the music because he thought she was dodging the report. She rebuked him, and he said, "If you were nicer, you would 'get it over.'" She told him that the kind of people she knew did not have to "get it over." Obviously the black kid meant—in white talk—you'd be able to "get your point across without throwing in all this music as if we were jerks." But the girl misunderstood and responded with a racial slur, and a terrible situation developed. The language of communication wasn't there, and you see that very clearly in the school.

In fact, the tragedy of the school is that it is not a change agent. Rather, it seems that the school reflects society. It reflects it so painfully that your hands are tied. I mean, what is it like to teach, to *try* to teach, to a group of kids who are barely awake?

What is it like?

Like having to be the dentist. I think they liked me personally, and it was all right to be with them. But to teach them? They did not want me to give them "work" or "homework." If I was doing my job, then I was a source of constant torment to them.

Yet the reality is how do you help kids grow and how do you grow? The roles of teacher and pupil are confused. I don't want to "relate," but to be engaged in a cooperative effort. We are partners. They must study, and I must teach.

That does not happen anymore.

Historically the administration blames teachers for their students' lack of achievement. But I can give you all the books and all the papers and all the notes in the world, and if you don't study them, you go no place. Part of my problem, personally, in teaching was that I realized that the amount of effort I was putting into planning, thinking, testing did not matter. No matter how good my classroom effort was, if you don't study it, you will not learn. After a kid failed, he'd say, "Oh, yes...I remember that." But that does not make you a success.

In desperation, education–certainly at Truman–has had an "I tried" attitude. Rather than feeling that education is measured by success, it has come down to that level. The word *try* is used so often that kids now feel they should pass because they tried.

That attitude has hit affluent school districts also.

Yes, I know. But when people are struggling for understanding, they somehow get on the wrong boat. Rather than speak out, the teachers bend back liberally. But the good intentions of a liberal person can kill you–whether it's done through neglect or good intentions, the end result is the same.

What do you mean by "rather than speak out"?

No one tells kids their behavior is inappropriate. When minority students–for whom the interchange is everything–block the steps or joyously shout to one another across a long hallway, they know exactly what they are doing. But no one says to them, "This is a school. There is learning going on here."

Why not?

The street has crept into the school; the language of the street is the language of the school, and the actions of the street are the actions of the school. There is no separate thing.

Is this misplaced liberalism?

It's certainly a breakdown in public mores. You see it in theaters and in libraries as well. For myself, I think being a member of a minority is an advantage here. I can go to another person and say to him, "That is not appropriate. That is low class." Period. And that person will know, *they will know.* There is nothing they can say to me about it. The case is closed.

They accept your reprimand because they see you as one of them?

Yes, if you like. You see, just because minorities are misunderstood does not mean they should not be held accountable.

I remember one school in which I taught that had a lot of problems. It had opened too soon, and at one point I shared a room with a French teacher. Half the period she taught in French; the other half, I taught in Spanish. We were all seated there with coats—October, November, it was cold and there were no windows.

There was a special locked-room class for difficult kids. That's where I saw a little boy squirt a can on a girl's hand and then light a match. He set her hand on fire.

This was the atmosphere. Could we make it?

We watched over the kids, and we were always counting them. One day I count, and there's a kid missing. I look outside, and I see him coming in from the street, a little kid *in the street.* I went berserk. I was responsible. What happens if a truck runs over him? What do I tell his parent? I was livid. I grabbed that kid as if he were my own—how dare he!

The principal's response? He felt minority kids did not eat enough, so when something like this happened—like this kid running into the street—he took the kid to lunch and the two of them talked it over. He did not hold that kid, or any kid, responsible. Here we were, all the teachers, in desperate need of help, and that was his contribution to the situation.

It sounds as if he tried to start with the kid. In any case, if schools are not agents of change, then what can be done?

I think the problem is not what we can do. That idea may represent a problem we cannot solve: a teacher should not come into the classroom with the idea that he is going to change society. But he should be given some foundation, or basis, for what he is going to be doing in the classroom.

Even classroom preparation is a problem we have not solved. Take behavioral objectives: what I will teach and how I will evaluate whether it has been taught. They always sound good, but time does not usually permit them to be carried out.

There is no time for workable, let alone creative, programs. There are too many restrictions; so there's no time for students to learn to speak in a foreign language!

This thing about going along at the student's own rate is a dream. In language study you must complete the curriculum and get them through the Regents in three years. [Regents exams are end-of-course achievement exams in grades 10 through 12, based on New York State courses of study. All students who want a Regents, as opposed to a regular, diploma are required to take them.]

We'd work very hard to prepare them for the Regents, and then I'd see the exam and want to die. The test assumes that the kids' English is good enough to recognize cognates. So if they see "inundar," they'll say, "Oh, yes, inundate."

They can't do that. They don't know how to think either. Teachers should encourage students to think, and yet many do not.

Worse, there are many excellent things in education that are tried and quickly discarded. We "innovate" every year and do not learn from our past experience.

How about the kids' experience? One teacher in Cambridge, Massachusetts, said that children don't see any connection between school and the jobs that are out there. They don't see education as leading anywhere.

Stereotypes can be dangerous, but ever notice how a Spanish mother dandles her child and dances and sings to it, "See the boy, see the girl," while a Jewish mother introduces her infant as "Doctor Joe"? At a beach club in Brooklyn I saw this once—Doctor Joe!

My thing is not that the kid makes no connection between school and goals, but that there is no reinforcement at home. You know, my parents spoke a lot about education, but when they gave a party, I was aware that I was the one who was going to have to lock myself up in a room and close the door because the party was there, the people were there.

Parents may pay lip service to education but very often they, too, are lost. At Truman there was so much guilt—the parent was already the victim of what he had done or not done. By this point [when the child reaches high school] the parent is not an ally. The parent is a person who dies when parent-teacher night comes, and he knows that if he comes in, it will be to hear the bad news. Will he come in? He knows what is going on and does not know how to deal with it.

Did you spend time following up with parents?

No, you can't do that. It requires more than just talking. It requires your getting very much involved in their lives and being almost intrusive. Has the kid got an area he can call his own? Has he got an appropriate place to study? That kind of thing goes beyond what a teacher can do. You would have to ask such personal questions to try and help.

Yet you wanted to work in your own community, and now you say you cannot reach the parents.

I wanted to give them the best education I could—not to be involved in social work. Nowadays they talk a good deal about the need to "educate the whole child." But they do not have the people or the resources to do it. If I refer a kid to one of the agencies that are supposed to help, it takes at least a year before anything happens. The kid is worried because his mother is sick and she is his only parent. Do I intercede? It is better to stay away than make a promise I cannot keep.

Inner-city teachers all say that the home is a problem, and yet you are telling me that little, if anything, can be done about it.

The true impact of family—you know, you can talk about all these things, but unless you are there, unless you experience these things.... I asked a kid once, "How you doing? I didn't see you yesterday, what happened?" And he said, "I slept on the subway."

He then proceeded to tell me a gruesome story about how his mother was in an insane asylum and how he had been brought up by his aunt and her uncle. Now, at 17, when he was going to graduate, he had asked the uncle's permission to use his name. But the uncle said to him, "No. In case you go wrong, I do not want you to have my name." The impact of this is beyond talking about "problems of the family." When to get involved, when to withdraw, where to go—you end up with a terrible frustration. You want to help but don't know how. If you send him to a counselor, he becomes lost in the mass machine.

The school implies that there is a referral system that works. It does not.

Every teacher has said that. It takes forever or you have to exaggerate what is wrong in order to get any help. Another kind of grade inflation!

Look, even the honors system doesn't work. In the honors class at Truman I caught kids cheating. I was horrified, which shows you how simple I am. I could not believe that the kid would cheat. So you are not 99, who cares? What is your evaluation of yourself as a person that you must cheat? You are wonderful the way you are. God gave everybody a gift.

I spoke to my chairman about this, and he said, "What did you expect?"

I cannot tell you the impact this had on me: "What did you expect?" So I took it further, and I saw the parents. And I swear to you, I am not making this up, it is like a record playing in my head. For the parents, the cheating was acceptable. "What did you expect?"

[Montalvo paces up and down. He picks up a bundle of papers.] Look, I wrote this out before you arrived. Question: What do you think will happen if educational standards rise and students don't rise to the level expected and teachers are on the line in terms of accountability? a) Will teachers cheat? b) Will students cheat? c) Will standards be lowered? d) All of the above. Answer: All of the above.

This is what is happening, and like a good teacher I have offered it to you as a multiple choice. The public is being lulled into a complacency with these pronouncements that everything is going to be all right—you know, don't worry, it's *mandated*.

I'm still unclear. The villain in the piece is the administration? If they had been different, you would still be there?

No, no. The administration is a reflection of our educational system, of the way the ball bounces. They personally destroyed me, but they are not the ultimate villains.

In our educational system it means nothing if kids fail. Here is an example: A kid cuts my classes first and second marking period. He shows up third marking period because someone told him this is the one that counts. I don't think teachers told students that each period is 33 percent of the grade, and the administrators, well, they've said, "Don't tell him he will fail—he's there. Tell him we will see." I am not into that kind of hypocrisy crap. I think kids should be made aware that what you put into something is what you get, and for you to expect otherwise is naive. The world does not carry you—okay?

But is it the educational system or your particular school? If it is this school, why not change schools and keep teaching?

Moving to another school, there might be similar problems or different problems, but basically the problem is that education is not going on. Whatever is the reason, it doesn't seem to work. Education is not going on, and that is why I'm out.

Education is not going on anywhere?

I can't say that. But look, it's like working on a sculpture. You mold it this way and that [gestures], trying to make it look good. But after eight *years* or ten *years* it's a horror story. Do you want to start another one and go to another place and start with a new piece of clay?

Well?

We started out at Truman with so much hope. It was a brand-new school and was designed with entrances on three levels. That was one of the first mistakes. Drug dealing was at an all-time high, and here were these three entrances; dealers used to walk through them and push drugs in the school.

Did you say you started with hope?

Despite the drugs, it was a new chance. We had all the latest equipment and had attracted remarkably talented people who started out full of hope and ambition. With all these resources we were a better school and, yes, we had fewer problems than other schools.

But?

But were we teaching? Were they learning?

They came to school—but that was because we took attendance, homeroom attendance, in the third period. The school gets paid for the students who show up, and that is why they made a rule that you fail if you don't come to homeroom. The school took this stance not because it is right, but for gain.

It is public relations: the appearance is what matters. In this respect, the administration is just an extension of the educational system.

Would you teach again if—

[Interrupts] I don't think I can. I struggled to make heads or tails of the diversity of goals and the problems that we faced. But I had to get out. I didn't know what I was doing or why I was there.

After a while I began to feel like an incompetent teacher, and I think I was because I kept lowering standards—wanting them to fly, wanting them to run, wanting them to walk, hoping that they would crawl and maybe that they would come in.

I realized that I was still teaching based on the idea that we were in a cooperative arrangement. But we were not.

Can I show you something?

Sure. [We are looking at a certificate of appreciation from the New York City Board of Education, a citation of merit from the president of the Borough of the Bronx, and an exit questionnaire from the board of education, which, I might add, is multiple choice.]

Also, here's an award from the school in which I could not function and an invitation to a retirement party. They all contributed to the unreality of teaching. The board of education questionnaire asks questions that even Dear Abby can answer.

[He hands me a "Dear Abby" column that reads in part, "Teachers are leaving the profession because of low pay, lack of cooperation from parents, and a tendency to blame the schools for all the ills of society."]

Dear Abby knows more than the board of ed.! Or this thing from the borough president—his name is at the top in Gothic print with gold lettering, and mine is somewhere at the bottom in very small print. These sum up not only why I left, but they're also an appropriate close to the lack of reality in educational experience.

They do not mention any of the things that have happened in the years I taught. I think it would have been more appropriate had they sent me a Purple Heart. I really do. Because then I could say, "Well they understand that it was combat conditions."

And the flourish of the borough president's citation—when you end up leaving like a beaten dog.

**I see at the end of the questionnaire that they ask a few questions that
are not multiple choice: "Under what conditions would you return to
teach in the NYC public schools?" You write, "None. My love for a
beautiful profession was destroyed by racial strife, community power
struggles, the rise of drugs, problems of safety, and finally economic
game playing, which changes teachers from professionals to
frightened bunnies who fear for their jobs in a bureaucratic hell."
I think you've explained that statement here. I will be curious
to see how they respond to it.**

I'm never going to send the questionnaire back though. Again, this
is just like my efforts to create a conversational dimension to the
language program. It is expedient. It is important in the realm of,
"Did you run a test to see what are the problems and solutions?"
And they did that: they sent me the form.

If I didn't get out, I was going to be sick. You have to realize that
the very same kids who were involved in the community conflict
and in the destruction of education—and in the education that did
not go on—are now my colleagues. The products of those years of
massive turmoil have now become teachers.

What kind of teacher ends up being a teacher when every six
months is being excessed [what schools call laying teachers off]
out of the school system? What kind of teacher sticks it out? What
happens to this teacher?

What help does he get? What is in today is out tomorrow. Today
they mandate this, and tomorrow they mandate that. Russia did it;
so we'll do it. Russia stopped; so we'll stop. The system lacks all
reason. Yet we are taught there is a philosophy of education. Whom
are they kidding?

Cultural Barriers

Manuel Montalvo knew his students. But he, too, said that the language of communication isn't there. When a boy is suspended because the school principal thinks his bracelet is a weapon—and then the boy's father comes on the scene, and he is wearing that same bracelet—the distance between school and home is absurd enough to be funny.

But most of the time the distance is cause for alarm. It is so extreme that it resembles a kind of colonialism: for some teachers, their students are the "natives"; the teachers will do what they can, but, after all, these are natives.

(I lived in Yemen once, and I remember how some of the staff from the U.S. Embassy played the same game. They agreed to try to do whatever the task at hand might be, but they reminded one that they were working with "the Yemenis"—sufficient explanation for all the things that were sure to go wrong.)

It worried me when teachers began sentences with such phrases as "Asian kids feel..." and "With Hispanic kids you have to remember..." It's true that they knew these were stereotypes and that we all do use them, but it is still not quite the best way to figure out who your pupils are.

Worse, it is usually a way to remain comfortably blind. Many times, for example, teachers told me what their students did not have: no manners, no morals, and even no experience. But what they often meant was no white middle class _____ (you fill in the blank).

This is not news. The blind spots some teachers reveal when they look at minority students have been described before. (Good examples are Jonathan Kozol's *Death at an Early Age* and James Herndon's *The Way it Spoozed to Be*.) But it seems to me that this is the kind of issue writers recognize and prominent reports on education ignore.

In this respect the cultural misunderstanding of teachers is like the social climate of the inner city. Both seriously impede education, and both are very difficult to change unless we, as a nation, decide change must come.

At present one hears of workshops or courses in sociology and the like that are meant to open teachers' eyes to their students' cultural lives. Perhaps they are of some use. But for myself, the only start (I don't say solution) to the problem that I see is to first recognize it: make the breakdown of cultural barriers between teachers and students an issue, and make everyone aware that a problem does exist. Then encourage teachers to learn more about their students by spending time with them and with their parents —time that can be credited just the way the dumb courses teachers must now take in order to qualify for salary hikes and the like are credited.

I can't work if I see no hope. We would not
have a Writing Center if I and others had not
believed it could work. There would not
have been a Pilot School—there were many
reasons to believe it could not work—if we
had not believed in it. In my experience,
then, attitude has a lot to do with reality.

ROB RIORDAN
high school English teacher
Cambridge, Massachusetts

Making Things Happen

*The Pilot School is a public alternative school in Cambridge, Massachu-
setts. It was started 20 years ago with 60 9th graders and now has 220
students in the 9th through 12th grades. Rob Riordan taught English
there for 14 years.*

*Now he has moved into the regular program at the high school, Cam-
bridge Rindge and Latin School [CRLS]. It has a mixed population of
some 2,200 kids and all are welcome at the Writing Center, which Riordan
directs.*

*The Writing Center is a fairly informal place that uses student, or
peer, tutors and encourages teachers, as well as students, to come together to talk about their writing. The emphasis is not on correct grammar
per se, but on work that is meaningful to the writer. The idea is that the
grammar will then follow.*

*When he describes the center and his ideas about how writing can
best be taught, Riordan's attitude toward education also comes across. He
describes the center as a place where "teachers don't see kids as the enemy or as empty vessels to be filled. Rather, kids can be pro-active in their
own learning."*

Involving kids in their own education is part of his philosophy and of that of the sixties-inspired Pilot School. At the Pilot School the students influence what is taught, who is hired, and so on. The Pilot School is critical of traditional classroom life, and so is Rob Riordan.

In itself, that is not unusual. I met many teachers who are critical of how their schools work. But few have been able to do much about it. More often I listened to teachers who felt isolated and who felt they worked in a vacuum—without confirmation, recognition, or power.

(It made me wonder if relatively content, or at least positive, teachers were going to become an endangered species. Certainly, they are not all that easy to find.)

Rob Riordan is one of the exceptions. He worked for change in the school system and for self-renewal, and he has found them both. But what he has not found is wealth: with a doctorate in education from Harvard, he is at the top of his school's pay scale, roughly, $41,000.

While he is articulate about some of the larger issues his own school as well as the nation's schools face, it is the particular that engages him. We started by talking about "making things happen" in his own back-yard—the Writing Center:

The city of Cambridge wanted to do a remedial lab on basic skills. I was interested, but instead of a remedial lab, I wanted a place where any writer could come at any time or stage of composition and get some help. I had worked with heterogeneous groups throughout my years at the Pilot School and knew it could work. But I felt that if it were called a "remedial lab" or "skills lab," students would not come.

For tutors, I recruited kids whom I had taught, and I approached the seniors—who had to write college essays—first. They started coming in to see us, and slowly the word spread. Kids would tell each other to "go to the Writing Center."

We were in a tiny room with six word processors, and soon we had to turn kids away. Now we have twenty word processors and a big room where bilingual ESL [English as a secondary language] kids and mainstream kids work side by side.

One complaint you hear all the time from teachers is, "My class isn't working, because I have these three kids who don't belong." I think those three kids do belong, and there are strategies—like peer coaching—to bring these kids into the class. The kids learn from one another, and I coach, rather than instruct.

Of course, the center wasn't going to work unless teachers knew how to use it. There were English teachers who assigned very little writing. That is changing now. I was trying to help teachers see that writing is a way to learn. It doesn't have to be a performance every time—or graded. And I was trying to get kids to see that writing is a process of multiple drafting, of revisions.

There was an element of risk about the center because we didn't know if it was going to work. I could walk into the Pilot School with my eyes closed and do a creditable job of teaching, and people would say that I did a good job; but I could feel it wasn't the same. The risk wasn't there. So the Writing Center brought a whole new excitement to my professional life. It was starting from scratch.

Bluntly, if English teachers were doing their job, why would you need a Writing Center?

Partly because of the way the teacher's work is structured: the number of classes, the class load, and the isolation all make it difficult for teachers to find time to meet and talk with each other. The Writing Center brings them together and gives them a chance to talk about writing; and it brings teachers and kids together in a relatively collegial setting.

Also, our notions of how to teach writing have been so screwed up. To exaggerate, the assumption has been that if you teach grammar, you are teaching writing. That's just not true. At the center we are trying to turn it around and say, "Let's teach writing by writing." I mean, there are 50 years of research that indicate there is no connection between grammar instruction and the quality of kids' writing. It doesn't carry over.

You're not advocating that they make up their own grammar?

No, the notion is that writing is self-expression, articulation, and communication. If there is no audience and all we are doing is drills for the teacher, that is not writing. It's doing puzzles.

First, we work on getting across what the student wants to say—structure, clarity, and so on. We work on grammar when it interferes with meaning and when we can see typical, or consistent, errors. Then we will proofread before publication. But we are not going to put kids down for their poor grammar or make them "do" grammar—apart from their own writing.

We try to convince teachers that they don't have to put a red mark on every error they see. Some teachers say they cannot let the student leave with an uncorrected error. But the kid isn't going to look at the paper anyway when there is so much red all over it.

As teachers we're very good at telling where they're wrong. But we need to help them see where their writing is strong. Often we assume that if they have done something right, they know it. That's not always so.

I still don't see why kids would go to the Writing Center unless they are in some sense forced to go.

The issue is, what are you asking kids to write, and why are you asking them to write? If you are asking them to write in order simply to demonstrate competence in the written language, then they are going to turn off. They have been told for years that they are incompetent, and they don't want to hear it again. They think they can't write. But if you can convince kids that writing is something else—that they can really say something—and if they can see themselves as writers, it turns around. Even though it's not always easy and not always fun, writing is something that can be rewarding. We publish a lot of student writing, and kids are proud when they see themselves in print.

And you are assuming that conventional competence will follow? Because people reading this will say, "Fine. So the kids can 'express themselves,' but they can't write an English sentence."

I know competence follows, because I have seen it. Very often in schools we have taken writing out and tried to separate it in an artificial way from other language-arts skills. You write and are graded on what you write, but the writing has not been connected to reading, to listening. When I work with the tutors, we devote a lot of time to listening, to finding out how people use the language.

Don't you need more than 40 minutes a day for this?

Learning to write is a lifetime process, and that's what we have to recognize. The way it's done is just crazy. There should be writing and response to the writing. That is how development occurs. You write, you show it to somebody, you get some kind of response, and you go back and write it again. As you write more and more, and show more and more, you learn; and you begin to define both a personal style and a public style. It happens *if* you do a lot of writing and you get response to it.

What is the general level of skills?

It varies. We have a very mixed population. We are over 50 percent minority: Afro-American, Asian, Hispanic. About 10 percent of our kids are in the bilingual program, and many more have made the transition from bilingual program to mainstream. While there are kids whose parents are academics and professionals, many others come from much less affluent backgrounds. When you eliminate the university overlay, Cambridge is the third poorest city in Massachusetts (behind Boston and Chelsea).

There is placement by skills level at my school, and in the middle range there is a great deal of diversity. We need to face the reality of what we have.

[The high school shares a small campus with the main Cambridge library. It is about a mile from Harvard in an area of single family homes and more and more condominium conversions. We talk about school discipline ("pretty mellow"), a murder that took place seven years ago, the school weapons policy, parent involvement ("pretty good").]

Do you take the view that kids today are different from the kids of 15 years ago?

Yes and no [laughs]. I'm struck by how many live in single-parent households or live alternatively with mother and father in two different households. That's a lot different from the time I was growing up. But I don't know that the kids are really less motivated. They watch a lot more television, and I know that when the high school kids we hire as baby-sitters leave here, it's after 11, and their night has just started. It's a faster life, a higher burn. Kids today seem more sophisticated but perhaps less academically skilled than in the past.

More experience and less ability to express it.

More experience and sophistication. Lots of kids can watch the debates and pick out what Quayle is all about and make some pretty savvy comments about the packaging of candidates. But when they sit down to write that stuff, they have trouble doing it.

What about the way they see each other? It's not a very macho thing to write poetry.

Yes, that kind of pressure is still there, and I think it's especially there for some minority students. It is not strictly an issue of being academic, but also that things like poetry are seen as the white world.

At our school, except for Asians, there are very few minority students—Afro-Americans, Haitians, Hispanics, Portuguese—in our advanced courses. We're trying to do things to make that academic image more attractive. In the Writing Center I try to get as many minority kids as I can to be tutors and role models. I think we can make some headway with that.

But another big problem is that there are not many black teachers at our school. I can't speak for other urban schools, but my guess is that in many places you have a basically white staff and a minority-student population.

It's a serious problem. We are seeing larger and larger minority populations in our schools, and we're not providing programs or adults to help these kids.

Some teachers say their minority students have totally unreal expectations. They don't work at school and are barely literate; yet, they expect to drive a Mercedes and live in a fancy house.

I think both tendencies are there—the McDonald's reality and a whole fantasy world. "I'm going to be a rock musician or make it in the movies, 'get discovered'"—those kinds of things. You do see black and white kids whose expectations are out of whack with their skills, and it's a judgment call as to what to do about that—tell them they will never be a brain surgeon?

But aren't schools in complicity with those false expectations? Kids are moved along, cheered on, but not given the skills. Is there a pushing-them-along grade inflation in your school?

I think there is, yes, but by and large there is a genuine effort to impart skills in our school. There's a lot of attention now to passing the Massachusetts Basic Skills Test. There is intensive work being done with kids who are not passing it, and there's an attempt to get 100 percent of the kids to pass. So there is a lot of effort going into basic skills. But the other thing is, you cannot keep a 17-year-old in 9th grade—you just can't do it. So the kid moves up.

Up to what?

That raises larger questions. We lack a sense of national purpose, and kids know it; they don't feel, when at school, that they are buying into something the country is really behind. All they are told is that school is a place to get some skills in order to get a job. But many students know that the only job out there for them is at McDonald's. And you don't need to go to school to get that job.

The middle-class kids know there is something in education for them. But the students who qualify for free or reduced lunches in Cambridge or who work 25 to 40 hours a week don't necessarily see that. They don't look 5 years down the road. They see that they can make $5 an hour at McDonald's and buy some things with the $200 a week they earn.

So this lack of national purpose refers to the poor kids?

No, the plight of poor kids is a reflection on the whole society. If we are talking about the biggest problems facing education, one is that we are not meeting the needs of the poor or even the needs of those populations that have been lower-middle class but upwardly mobile—we are not meeting those needs. The mobility isn't there. Kids lack the sense that when you go to school, you buy into something that is important for you and for your society, something that is available to all.

[As parenthetic aside about how the textbook industry provides a lunatic, but lucrative, solution to our disintegrating national purpose, Riordan points out that educational publishers have taken E. D. Hirsch's cultural literacy (from his book, *Cultural Literacy*)—the sense that the transmission of our culture is falling apart—and packaged it: "The problem is that for education, Hirsch's work leads to more of the same model of cultural transmission. You see textbook publishers saying, 'Don't worry—buy our textbook, because every one of those 100 items on Hirsch's list is in it.' The problem isn't that those items haven't been in the textbooks: it's that we have those textbooks in the first place—textbooks that are dumbed down, watered down, appealing to the least common denominator, with no values in them."]
What are the other big problems you see facing education?

I've mentioned the lack of programs—or adult role models—to help minority kids.

A third, big problem is the teaching profession itself. It is a dead-end profession. There's low pay, low incentives, and no power. The only way is out.

I'm an anomaly really. Teachers at the Pilot School have always had a lot of power, and our principal at CRLS tries to run a very consultative organization.

In general, though, I agree with all that stuff in the reports—especially Ted Sizer's work and the kinds of things Albert Shanker has been saying. [Author of many books on American education,

Theodore Sizer is the chairman of the Education Department at Brown University. Albert Shanker is president of the American Federation of Teachers. Both men are highly critical of what they see as the routinized, assembly-line structure of our schools.] I think schools are structured all wrong. The whole business of where power lies is all wrong. Teachers don't *have* any power, and everywhere, I think, many teachers feel stymied.

It's my impression that many teachers want to get out but don't know how.

Many teachers do feel stuck. They are teaching 5 classes a day, and they deal with 100 to 120 kids or more. They are teaching the same stuff they have been doing for years and years. They are teaching out of a book, and they don't have time to read a book themselves. There is no stimulation in that job.

In many cases, because of that whole structure and the way teachers are responding to it, they are not getting very much from the kids. They are trying to feed in some stuff to kids, and the kids aren't absorbing it by any method the teachers can devise. The teachers are not feeling appreciated. They are not appreciated.

Do you feel appreciated?

A couple of years ago I would have told you I was pretty tired; but I've been lucky to carve out a nice little niche for myself, and I do have a pretty free hand. I get respect and support from the administration, perhaps because the Writing Center has been successful and people trust me with it.

How about student power? Students at the Pilot School have some power over hiring and curriculum. How do you feel about that?

It works; it still works at the Pilot School. It has to be done carefully, and you have to know how to do it. It is not the kind of thing where you just walk in and say, "Okay, kids, we are going to choose our teachers today."

I think the education kids are getting at the Pilot School is super. And yes, I would like my kids to go there. Though with Proposition 2½ [tax-cap legislation in Massachusetts], the program is being chipped away. Classes are larger, and the teachers are overextended.

Who do you see going into teaching today?

I'm worried about that because all the statistics tell us that the folks going into teaching now tend to come from the bottom sections of their classes and that their motivation is not so much their wanting to have an impact on kids or to do meaningful work but, rather, that they go into teaching because it can be a relatively secure job—albeit low paying—and because they feel there is not much else they can do.

Sounds like the old joke: "Those who can, do; those who can't, teach."

Yes, I'm worried about it. There are so many things a bright college graduate can do—and especially the way the world is opening up to women....

What about you, personally? To be a male, over 40, and still in the classroom. Isn't that unusual?

If I were not happy, I would not be a teacher anymore. I really need to feel that I am involved in meaningful work, and I would find something else if I couldn't create a meaning for myself in teaching.

Feeling positive about your work and seeing it as meaningful seem to be very difficult to accomplish in the inner city. Teachers feel overwhelmed by problems larger than the classroom.

I sympathize with that point of view because sometimes the situation can seem pretty hopeless. But I think it is a self-defeating attitude. You have to assume that there is something you can do. And at CRLS we are finding that there are things you can do for kids to make their lives a little easier and to give them a better chance—whether it be creating teacher-advisor programs, mediation and advocacy programs, writing centers, or teen health centers.

Some people have said that the inner-city school should be open 24 hours a day because the minute kids get back on the street, it is all over.

Our school has lots of things that go beyond the school day, and there could be more. If you're going to talk about schools having an impact on kids' lives, then yes, more availability and services and longer hours make sense. But so do ways of accommodating kids who work long hours. The only time many youngsters have for school is when they are in school.

I know that you will teach a seminar at Harvard's Graduate School of Education in the spring. What are the educators there doing about this issue of how to reach minority kids?

I think Harvard has an interest in the subject but not a lot of access as to how to accomplish it. They are not doing a lot in terms of programs right now, and they're having trouble recruiting minority candidates for their newly reestablished teacher education program. Harvard got out of teacher training for about 12 years, after they decided that their mission was not to train teachers, but to train people in public policy and administration.

So Harvard embodied the whole status shift. But didn't the academics have it wrong? Shouldn't the emphasis be on the teacher in the classroom?

Yes, and now with a teacher shortage on the horizon, everyone has rediscovered teachers. In fact, Massachusetts has passed legislation to try and improve the profession. It involves, first of all, making sure that future teachers start by getting a degree in a subject and not in teacher education and also that teacher training itself takes place not in the universities, but in school-based sites.

The only problem is that there is no money for these reforms.

No money—and a lot of rhetoric about a renewed commitment to education. I can see how on a small scale you are doing some good and deriving some satisfaction from it. But your larger criticisms make me wonder where there is a basis for hope.

I have to survive too. I can't work if I see no hope. We would not have a writing school if I and others had not believed it could work.

I'm a kind of miniaturist anyway. I'd be lost in Washington giving out grant money and that kind of thing. But I can make things happen and help other people make things happen in this smaller sphere within which I work. If I can take responsibility for my sphere, then that's my way of addressing all the shit that is going down outside it.

Peer Teaching

The Writing Center is a new idea, but its use of student, or peer, tutors is an old one: allowing students to teach and counsel each other goes back to the one-room schoolhouse. It was effective then and may be again.

Peer teaching builds confidence in tutors and proves the old adage that he who teaches, learns. For those being tutored, there are the advantages of individualized instruction and, from what a number of studies have so far concluded, enhanced skills.

Another appeal of peer teaching is that it helps break down the idea that all answers rest with the teacher. When students work things out with help from their peers, they are active participants in their own education—a state that more and more teachers say is hard to achieve in the traditional classroom.

> "In my classroom there are no answers. At first the kids go nuts. They look at each other. She is not going to tell us 'the answer.' They can't believe it. 'My mom said you *have* to tell us the answer.' This goes on for months. But by the end of the year, someone like Joanna says, 'It's up to us. We might as well try and figure it out.'"

> GERI STERN
> elementary school teacher
> *Los Angeles, California*

No Right Answers

Joanna was one of 27 students in Geri Stern's second-grade class in Pacoima, a barrio in the San Fernando Valley in Los Angeles. Stern felt that Joanna had a great need to express herself, and she encouraged the child to do so. As the school year wore on, Joanna became more responsive, and finally she talked so much at home that her mother could not stand it. Unperturbed, Joanna left her house, walked outside, and kept on talking.

Geri Stern loved that. She saw it as a sign that Joanna was not only ingenious but also irrepressible—not the kind of child to "sit quietly, eyes front, hands at your sides, mouth closed—top lip on bottom lip."

Stern crusades against the "top lip on bottom lip" school—teachers who equate quiet with learning and who shut kids down rather than open them up. But she believes that such schools are the majority, and her three years as a teacher have been a very isolating experience.

Stern's future as a teacher is uncertain. It is hard, however, to imagine her in a profession that did not include children. Starting out as a painter, she found that even her artwork focused on them:

A lot of the art I was doing was becoming political about children, about their lives and perspectives, and I was also looking for a job that would give me time to do my artwork. That proved a great fallacy. Teaching doesn't provide you with any time to do anything.

The children go home at 2:30, but if you walked out the door with them, you'd be an awful teacher, a baby-sitter. Even though I was paid for the six hours in the classroom, I regularly put in at least nine.

The first year was completely overwhelming. I virtually, truly, had a nervous breakdown over it. The amount of work is never-ending, and emotionally, I got too connected with the children, much too close to them.

I have a tremendous kinship to children. I feel as if I understand the lives they lead, and so when things happen to them, I, too, get upset. If they lose their lunch ticket, it is not difficult for me to see why it is the most important thing in the whole universe that they have lost their little lunch ticket. In fact, sometimes I become overwhelmed because they have lost their lunch ticket, they are crying, and all I can think of is that things are only going to get harder for them. The lunch ticket is the easy problem.

The kids are Hispanic?

Most are Hispanic, and they are all very poor. They are all below grade level. None of them can read very well.

They do not have very many experiences, and that makes reading comprehension virtually impossible. The reader [reading textbook] refers to things they have never seen, and if they don't see it, they don't know it exists. Most of them have never been to the beach or the mountains or have never seen snow. Many of them have never left the neighborhood—*ever*. I took them on a field trip downtown to see the [Los Angeles] Museum of Contemporary Art, and I prepped them for months about what we were going to see. We got there, and at the escalator one of the kids would not get on. She had never seen or been on an escalator before.

I have to go back so far. High-level thinking skills about modern art won't work when a child is thinking about the escalator and is afraid.

It's a problem in all the subject areas. The children don't have the experiences. I was thinking about why they are so far behind in school and how they have lost time. Maybe they are going to be permanently behind because there is something that happens developmentally in the first five years. If you don't learn, don't have X amount of experiences, and you can't catch up. Some kind of learning process is destroyed, I don't know. It is a terrifying thought.

But if that were true? Why teach?

To give them the sense that what they do, they can do well. I can nourish their self-esteem, and that, more than anything else, is why I'm there.

I'm also there to listen. I'm an ear for them, not a baby ear, and I pay attention to their needs. That's something a lot of children don't get in their lives.

I have this philosophy: I don't believe that a child is a child and—poof!—all of a sudden he is an adult. There is a complete continuity so that everything you do to a child is being done to an adult. The very same body that sat in the second-grade class is sitting in front of me now. It's the same person.

Freud would agree with you.

But as teachers we are not taught to see the big picture. It's small—first graders do this, seventh graders do that. This week it's Thanksgiving, next week it's Valentine's Day.

Kids are given Valentine's Day activities that I remember doing at school, and that I'm sure you did. They are doing it all over the country: it is the same dopey ideas year after year to "get through" Valentine's Day.

Teachers are doing this dopey idea for Valentine's Day, or that dopey idea for reading. Then we have to think up more dopey ideas for the next day or find some new dittos to get through the day after. There is no larger picture, no sense of how a child—or the year—develops. There is talk about "unit planning," but it is too sketchy—and amounts to more dittos and dopey ideas.

Kids end up doing mountains and mountains of low-level work. That's what is available for teachers to buy…you can ditto up zillions of copies of low-level work—you know, they match yellow to the banana, and then you can say the kid knows what a banana is.

I can't imagine spending a year like that and not becoming a little batty.

Some teachers are a little batty, but mostly they cut themselves off from the kids and put a lot of their energy into keeping the kids quiet. Keep them quiet and control them—that's the program, and for some teachers I think it's also their motivation. Teaching can be a power trip—and not only for some loud, aggressive teacher. It can be a power trip for someone who is very meek and really has no control in her own life.

Teaching is a female power trip?

Very often it is. How come people don't value teachers? How come it doesn't pay? Because it is woman's work, and society puts a low value on work that women do. In the past women had few opportunities, or their income was seen as supplemental—so they let us teach. There's also the myth that we can do this job on mother love. Why get paid for biology?

There should be more men in elementary schools. It would change the status of teachers even if for the wrong reasons. It would also change children's impressions of women.

You feel that the status of teachers is low?

In Pacoima, kids would consider becoming a teacher quite a step up, but at Marboro—a private school where I taught during the summer—teachers are low-level people. I would love to interview the parents at Marboro. I'd say, "You're sending your child to the most expensive private school in the city. How would you feel if your child chose to be a teacher?" They would all *plotz*. That would be a horror, a shame, a disappointment. That is something I have never understood. If you don't value teachers, then why do you want them teaching your kids?

What's it like in a school in a place like Pacoima?

It is very stifling. It is in the Valley. It is very hot. There's no air conditioning. There is noise everywhere because the windows are open in order for us to breathe because it's so hot. The school is overcrowded. We have three recesses, two lunches. Most of the day there are children out in the yard playing, and so it is always noisy. It's dirty—not filthy, but dirty. But then there are 1,400 people in one facility. How many places have 1,400 people in one facility?

Jails, hospitals.

Someone once said to me that there is no other job in the world where you are in charge of 27 people at once.

Movie usher?

You might be in charge of 27 people, but you are not trying to coordinate their behavior all at the same time. It is very stressful, and there is no relief because the woman in the next room has her 27; and the next room, 27. There's no relief. You can't go out of the room, sit down for a minute, and put the children on hold, catch your breath.

I'm sure other teachers don't feel safe. I'm not afraid, but it is not a safe neighborhood, and I would not go there at night. You are supposed to leave by 4:30; most schools are run that way. Gang activity is pervasive in the evenings...the young kids are involved with the gangs on a superficial level. They dance in the park, hang out, and drink beer. By fifth grade the kids get more involved. Some of them have no choice. There is just no status in their lives.

No status for good grades?

There is status to getting As. But most of them can't–not without a successful bilingual program.

You're in favor of bilingual education?

I know there is an argument that the "Koreans learn English" [so why can't the Hispanics]"; but I support bilingual education because I think that this immigrant group is different. The economics are different, the numbers are different, the culture is different. The Mexican family doesn't value education. The family comes first. They have a shaky grasp of their own language, and now comes English.

Most of the parents don't speak English. They want their kids to learn English, but they are not behind their words in any way, and they rarely learn English themselves.

One reason these parents don't get involved in the school is that they are frightened of the school. They hold the school in such high esteem that they just don't think they belong there. I've had mothers backing out of the room because they have been taught not to turn their back on authority. Another problem can be if the parents are illegal and they are afraid to come and interact in school.

The result is no parental support?

Right, and no awareness of what goes on in schools. If the parents knew, then maybe they'd put more pressure on for change. In private schools parents are hovering everywhere. Everyone jumps in response to what the parents want. It could be like that in public schools also.

Economics makes a difference.

Yes. It's why kids from low-income families have difficulty learning languages. In low-income families they sort of bark language at the children–"Eat your food," "Go to bed." Kids are not given the time, the attention, or the language.

It's even worse in the next school over. The kids there are more disadvantaged. Almost all of the children there receive the government breakfast and lunch, probably the only meals they get. Some kids at our school are on the government meals. I get angry because for breakfast they serve them some sort of sweet roll, and then the kids come into class all hyper. They are very poor; they live in garages. I have one boy who lives in a house with 27 other people. He doesn't have quiet in school; he doesn't have quiet at home. When is he supposed to concentrate, do his homework, or do his thinking? There is no place for him.

Without a lot more money–not necessarily for raises, but for smaller class size, better facilities, and even more books–it's hard to see a future for that kid.

Do you think our society is ready to give a damn–to spend the money and change it?

No, there are too many conflicting philosophies about how children should be treated. My operating theory is that children should be taught to think for themselves and be highly creative. I provide very few answers for them. The joke among my students is, "The teacher wouldn't tell us. She is going to make us think of it for ourselves."

But the teacher in the next room might feel that children should be seen and not heard. She'll talk politicians' talk about "the basics." But unless kids know how to think for themselves, it is all useless.

On a basic level it's really pointless to teach information. I can't teach information. I can teach you how to find the book that has the information, I can teach you how to learn. The public schools are still teaching information. They are sinking ships of information, and they are all just drowning.

How do you teach the children to think?

I feel that each day I must use some high-level thinking skills, or I am wasting my life and their time. I am emphatic about not wasting their time. We are always doing something, learning something, even when we stand in line. Sometimes I'll say, "Think about a tree—how tall is the tree?" They are thinking all the time.

I also teach the children to be activists. I have all sorts of techniques to get them to feel they can make a difference. I teach them to take action about things that are important to them.

I taught the children the whole thing about boycotting and striking and sitting-in. I did it for months and months until they really had it. Then one little girl came to me and said, "My mom and I are boycotting." I said, "Great. What are you boycotting?" She said, "We are boycotting the clinic because they are giving out birth-control information." [Laughs] So it backfired on me, right? They need the birth-control information more than any other group in the city. But she got what I was teaching, the idea that you can act on your beliefs and make a difference. I can't tell her what to act on, that's not right.

Do you regard yourself as a radical-feminist teacher?

Oh, absolutely. People say the teaching profession is liberal. I don't understand that. I don't see it. School politics are conservative, status quo. Even the union, I don't think it is child-oriented at all. The union thinks that more money will bring more respect, and I don't think that's how it's going to work. Something else has to happen. The union doesn't support education; it's a business. I don't like their tactics. It's the union versus the administrators—you're supposed to turn in your paperwork late, make mistakes in your report card, slow the process down.

Why?

So that the salary hike, or whatever, is obtained. But the administrator has no more control over finances than we did. She's nothing more than a teacher who now sits at a desk.

Tell me about the kid who has meant the most to you.

It's Joanna. I try to get the children to express themselves, mostly to each other, and Joanna was a little girl who picked up on that. She appeared to need it tremendously. I would teach them all sorts of subtle words to express how we feel, not just *mad* and *glad* and *sad*. And Joanna would come to me and say, "I'm feeling sad, no not quite sad, but *pained*."

She also learned to think for herself, and she asked questions.

What happens to her next year?

Maybe she'll get a teacher who doesn't think *why* is a dirty word, and maybe not. I try not to think about it.

When we started to talk, you said you came to teaching through your art. I'm not sure I get the connection.

When I decided to teach, I felt I had some kind of unfinished business to do in the classroom. I was very shy in school. I never said anything, and I got all As. No one ever pushed me, no one ever wrote in my cumulative record that I needed to express myself.

I always thought I was not athletic. A couple of years ago I was in the yard with my fourth graders, and the teams weren't even; so I said I'd play. As a child I was always the kid picked last, the one about whom they said, "Oh, God, do we have to have her on our team!" So here I was on the team, and it came my turn to kick. The kids were teasing me, and I kicked the ball and hit a home run. As I was running around the bases, the kids were screaming, "Yay! Yay!" And it occurred to me that I had to come back as a 26-year-old to be cheered into home plate because I had never, ever, experienced that in school. That is what I wanted to do, to go back and be myself. I don't think I was ever myself. I was just a little doll who sat there.

My art, too, was about going back. Something about being back in a school environment again and seeing how children live is very important to me. But sometimes I will stand in the classroom after the kids leave and think, What am I doing here?

There's no social life. Even lunch hour is not a lunch hour. You get 45 minutes for lunch, and most of it is taken up getting the children out, getting them in; if you want to go out into the real world for lunch, it is virtually impossible. You are locked in all day.

At other times I think I'm hiding from the real world, the men's world. But I love what I do; it's my calling. I have a real knack for arranging information in a way that kids get and it sticks.

What are your plans?

I intend to go to Spain next year. After that I don't know.

Social Isolation

Geri Stern is a young teacher, and the camaraderie that is very important to some teachers (I think of Jill Marvinowski letting off steam in her school's lunchroom) did not exist for her. She saw the others as "old guard," and that made her feel very isolated.

It is hard, as many teachers remarked, to imagine the isolation of teachers. But I glimpsed what it must be like when I first met Geri Stern. Our interview took place in a publishing office, and it was enough of a change for her to remark on the fact that a man had spoken to her in the elevator.

There were no men in her school, and normally she was locked in a room with twenty-seven young charges for six or seven hours a day, isolated from the adult world. Since she did not like or respect most of the other teachers at her school, she found little con-solation in the lunchroom—a source of intense comfort for some teachers.

(Teachers see other teachers, and no kids, in their lunchrooms. These are the inner sanctums, places to share frustrations and achievements, and maybe even smoke a cigarette. Because there is no time to leave the school for lunch, there is nowhere else to go unless a teacher chooses to remain in her own classroom, as Geri Stern often did.)

Geri Stern felt alone, but her problem is a common one and rarely addressed by schools. To recruit bright young teachers, it is necessary to offer them a less isolated—and less isolating—world.

"There are days when I say to myself, 'The kids don't care, the parents don't care, the administration doesn't care. Am I the only one in this building that cares?'"

SHEILA SCHRAIER
high school Spanish teacher
Bronx, New York

We Are All Foreign-Language Teachers

Sheila Schraier has a small joke she tells colleagues: though she is a Spanish teacher, she reminds them that "we are all foreign-language teachers."

She reports that many kids at Truman High, where she teaches—one of the three top high schools in the Bronx—are functionally illiterate. Though she is considered tough and insists on such things as attendance and homework, it is a struggle to get her students to do any serious work.

Teaching at Truman High for 14 years and currently assigned a role as a mentor teacher, Schraier says she is "dedicated and burned-out at the same time." It's easy enough to understand the burnout. But her dedication—like that of many teachers—continues to amaze me.

Her large classes and unmotivated students represent an uphill battle. It is the battle Manuel Montalvo recently lost at that same high school.

What keeps Sheila Schraier at it? Her energy and a strong sense of humor probably help: when she tells some of her war stories, there is humor along with the exasperation, and there is always the hope that her next class may have one of the gems, a kid who wants to learn.

Her first teaching experience was at Evander Childs High School, also in the Bronx and her own alma mater. The time was 1968, and New

York City's decentralization effort was underway. At one point her school was on strike for three months. Chaos ensued—a lengthened school day and quadruple sessions. It was "rough," she remembered, especially since she looked no older than her students and had been given no real preparation in her education courses:

The education classes were nonsense. The only way to be a teacher is to teach. It takes experience: you have to get over your butterflies, get used to getting up in front of a group and thinking on your feet. There is no other way to do it. Reading a textbook about what John Dewey said about education is not going to prepare you for walking into a city high school.

I remember that first year at Evander: they'd stop me for my pass in the halls, and I myself found it very hard to call my ex-teachers by their first names. It was a long time ago.

Can you compare the kids you taught then to the ones you teach now?

Fourteen years ago, when I got to Truman, there were some rough kids, but by and large they were pretty motivated. What we now call an honors class was then a regular class, and what we now call a regular class was then a "G" (for general diploma) class, and so on. It's all gone down—skills, motivation, standards—and there are now very few outstanding students.

What do you think happened?

The sixties—all that freedom business—changed our society. Once you loosen it up and you lose it, you can't get it back.

The parents aren't on our side. In the city schools parents are either ignorant or disinterested. Maybe some of them just trust the schools to do the right thing; so you never hear from them. But when you call them on the phone, they act as if you are *bothering* them. If you tell them you are having a problem with their child, the attitude is "What do you want me to do about it?"

I have perhaps 170 kids. On open-school nights I'll get maybe 40 parents the first night and 10 the next. Where are the rest of those parents? I fail many of their kids.

You do? Many now talk about "grade inflation," passing kids who should fail.

I'm not like that. I'm fighting against it. I tell them at the beginning what they have to do to pass. It is very specific: you have to do your homework; if you miss three homework assignments, you will fail. And you must study for tests.

I expect them to be in school–even during first period. I'm getting up at the crack of dawn, predawn, in order to get there, and the student who lives across the street from the school is not making first period. I drive 30 miles, and they can walk out their door and be there in under 10 minutes, and they miss first period.

I remember I called one parent who said, "She has *such* a hard time getting up in the morning." *Click.* That's it. And I'm thinking, What is this? Help me out on this. Don't tell me she can't get up in the morning.

Then parents, as well as the schools, have become more permissive?

The schools had to become more permissive because the parents were more permissive. We do not rule society. Schools are a reflection of society. If you assign homework and the kid isn't doing it and you can't get the parent to make sure the kid stays away from the computer, the TV, and everything else and sits down to do the homework, then I can't do much in my 40 minutes. There's got to be somebody at home sitting on these kids if they are not self-motivated, and most of them are not. Somebody has got to be out there making sure that they do it. The schools cannot do this.

We have some excellent teachers, but what are we supposed to do? We can't learn it for them; we can't do their homework; we try to present the material in the easiest way we can, but they have to do the work.

When I give them a list of 50 vocabulary words on Friday and tell them to learn these words for the next Friday–a whole week– I can't learn it for them. I'm the teacher. They've got to have the self-discipline to sit down and learn the words–and not on Friday morning, 10 minutes before the quiz.

Very sad.

There is *nothing* wrong with the schools that some help from home won't cure.

Some say parents feel alienated from the school. Intimidated.

That's a nice explanation, but it's nonsense. They can come to our school anytime–I've been interrupted in the middle of class. For my generation and previous generations of immigrants, school was the key. You had to go to school, get an education and a diploma.

These parents, maybe they have eight kids and are working two jobs. You know, they can't handle it.

What are the students at Truman like?

They are narrow. They look at life with blinders. They live in the cultural center of the world, and many of them have never been to a museum.

Also, they make no distinction between talking to their pal out on the street and talking to a teacher. There is no sense that we're not their pals. I'm the teacher. I'm supposed to get a little bit of respect.

They'll walk in: "Hey, yo. Hey, Ms. Schraier, man."

How do you handle that?

"Hey, yo, Dow. C'mere, Dow." Then they get it.

Truman has a minority population?

They're mostly black and Hispanic kids who live in Coop City–a place that started out as a white middle-class haven in the Bronx. And it destroyed the Bronx.

My mother was the only one in her mah-jongg game who did not move to Coop City. It happened all over the Bronx. White people moved out of integrated neighborhoods into Coop City. Then these people became disenchanted with Coop City. It was not paradise on earth, and the flight of the white middle class from Coop City began. Now we're about 75 percent black, 20 percent Hispanic.

Do many black kids want to take Spanish?

Many of my students are not literate in English, and I am teaching them a foreign language. This is the irony of my life.

Very often their first exposure to English grammar is in a foreign-language class. How can I teach direct-object pronouns if they have no idea what a pronoun is? You ask them to pick out the noun in a sentence, and they tell you, "the," "in."

Or you say to them, "Wait a minute, what is a noun?" "Person, place, or thing." Very good. Then which is the noun? "Dunna know."

[Mimics them] "Why do I have to learn a language? I'm never

goin' to Spain. How come I have to learn a language?" I tell them it is a requirement.

What keeps you going? The situation doesn't sound too great.

I don't know. You know, I'm very cynical and very optimistic at the same time. I'm very cynical because I know what I'm dealing with. But sometimes you get a gem, and sometimes you get a really good class. You can have a lot of fun with them, and that makes it not so horrible. But I can't take ninth graders. I don't know how elementary school teachers do it. I just can't take that immature silliness. If I have three ninth-grade classes, I'm dead. I come home, and my teeth are permanently clenched. Then my own children get on me, and it's too much.

But when an older kid does well and I write a recommendation for college, I feel good about it. That's when it's all worthwhile.

You are white in a largely black school. Is race an issue?

White and Jewish. There is this latent anti-Semitism that comes out, especially around Black Solidarity Day. I don't believe Black Solidarity Day is a national holiday. Yet the worst students, who are looking for any excuse not to come in, ask me, "Do we have to come in? It's Black Solitary Day." Upon which I tell them, "If you can't say it, you have to come to school. If I thought there was a political motivation, then I would feel differently. But I say that it's not a holiday, and some of them, with chips on their shoulders, start mumbling and grumbling, "Well the Jews have their holiday." But of course on Rosh Hashanah, Yom Kippur, they're off.

Look, even Jesse Jackson talked about Hymie Town [Jackson's ignoble slur on New York City's Jewish population during the 1988 presidential campaign]. It doesn't make sense. We were the ones who marched with King. But these kids don't know that. They are ignorant, and they have to lash out at somebody. Who are they going to attack–WASPS?

Do black teachers have an easier time with the kids?

Depends on the teacher. A lot of times a black teacher is even harder on them than a white teacher. I know one who is an excellent teacher, and she doesn't take any crap–don't think just because I'm black and you're black, that we are cool. The black kids hate her.

Is there a drug problem?

As Bronx schools go, we're pretty good. They'll generally turn on before school or do it in little nooks and crannies around school. Actually, marijuana was a lot worse 10 years ago. There is some dealing in drugs and hard stuff.

Where do they get the money?

We're still basically a middle-class school, and some are dealing. You take a look at these kids. They are well dressed. Their wardrobe is newer than mine. I can assure you of that.

What percentage go on to college?

I'm not sure, but we rank among the top three high schools in the Bronx. Bronx High School of Science is number one. But they have drug problems too. That school has real drug problems because the kids are so wonderful in science, they can concoct some of the stuff in their own labs [laughs].

What about violence?

Again, not as bad as some other schools. Kids come to school with weapons—knives, which are easy to hide, and some guns. It was worse 10 years ago when there were gangs from our school who fought against kids from across the Parkway—it's called "the Valley." Now you have a group of friends, and this one insulted that one. They have to straighten it out, and what better way to straighten it out than with violence? You can't be verbal. You must strike out.

Girls too?

Girls can be more vicious than boys. Boys usually will use their hands, but girls come at each other with razors. The girls will use anything. Girls will scratch, bite, tear hair out—clumps of hair. I've seen this in the hallway.

The blackboard jungle? Are you ever afraid?

It's not that bad. I was once afraid, but the situation involved an emotionally handicapped kid, and they didn't warn me about him. I was on cafeteria patrol, and I don't take any nonsense there either. He wanted to leave the cafeteria, and I didn't let him out. He walked out another door, and I went after him.

I got him into trouble, and after that, he'd follow me to my car. I was told that he was harmless, but I wasn't sure. That's the only time in all these 20 years that I was actually afraid.

I'm usually pretty intimidating. I know it's hard to believe, but a lot of kids are afraid of me. [Sheila Schraier is about five-five, quite slim, and looks to be about 28.] I'm right in these six-foot-two guys' faces, and they know I'm serious. A sub [substitute teacher] once told me, "If you are absent and you have 33 kids in the class, you'll get 34 papers because I find myself doing the assignment too!"

Have you ever considered teaching English instead of Spanish?

I really don't think I'd want to be an English teacher. Now I tell myself, "What do I want from them? I'm teaching them a foreign language. They barely know English." What would I do if I was teaching them English, and they didn't know English?

To have lasted this long, you must have some kind of idealism, some kind of social conscience?

It's like I'm burned-out and I'm dedicated at the same time. I'm told that things aren't that great in the suburbs either. But in the suburbs I'd have 18 kids, maybe 25 kids, in a class, and that would feel almost like being on vacation. The pupil load is one of New York City's problems, and that's why New York City will never be able to compete with the suburbs even if city salaries improve.

Salaries used to be competitive; we used to call it "combat pay," as a matter of fact. But then with the budget crunch in '75—and salary freezes, layoffs, and so on—we fell behind. In Chappaqua [an affluent suburb in Westchester County] top of the scale is about $60,000. I could live on that.

Do you think your salary is fair?

I think it should be quite a bit higher.

Would higher salaries improve what goes on in the classroom?

We'd probably get a higher caliber of teacher. Some of the people we're getting now are really bottom of the barrel. They're not at all comparable to the people of my generation.

Why?

Why would you subject yourself to this? The hours are good—8:00

to 2:20—and the meetings are not that onerous. But the kids eat some of these new teachers for breakfast. Some of the new teachers are not too bright. I don't know how they got through college.

By taking education courses?

I have such a low opinion of those courses. They're useless.

That's what almost everyone says. So why don't teachers fight against education programs?

You see something is wrong, but it's not that easy to go out and change the world. I think there should be more student teaching. That seems obvious to me. Why isn't it obvious to the people running universities?

At the beginning it is so much work. You're just trying to keep your head above water. There isn't time.

How do you know the new teachers are no good?

Partly from what the kids say. If they call a teacher a jerk, he is a jerk. If they call him an SOB, then he's a good teacher.

I think the master, or mentor, teacher is a good idea. That's one way experienced teachers can help beginners.

And merit pay?

Sounds good, but who will judge? The administration? What if you are active in the union, and they don't like it? Or if someone just doesn't like you? It will not work.

Competence testing?

Maybe for new teachers. The time to get rid of teachers is in the first few years, when we're on probation. If the administration doesn't check up on teachers at the start (and they often don't), then it's too late. Once you have tenure, it's almost impossible to get you out.

Do you see any difference between male and female teachers?

I think many of the female teachers are tougher than the male teachers. Maybe we can get away with more, and we don't try to outmacho the kids—something some male teachers do.

I think, too, that more of the men work two jobs because they don't usually care for their own kids. I couldn't work two jobs—

I have young children. Nor could I work summers or live in the area of the school. I have to get out of there each day to avoid a nervous breakdown. I go there, and I give it all I've got, and then I come home. I couldn't be in it 24 hours a day. That's why summers are so wonderful. I'm totally out of it, and I am recharged in September. We all come back mellow and, of course, by the end of June we are all strung out.

Strung out?

What everybody sees is that we're at home by three o'clock and that we have the summer off. But they don't see any of the other aspects of teaching. Teaching is very mental; it's physical, and it's emotional. I say, "Five shows a day." That is what I'm putting on. I teach five classes, and that's five shows a day.

Do you put on a show?

This is the TV generation. I can be funny, and when I get on a roll, they love it. I have one kid, a real do-nothing loser. "Oh, we're having a midterm?" [Laughs] Or, "Today's the final?" He'll do that. They are supposed to bring pencils because the final is done with a Scan-atron sheet. They don't bring pencils, and I do a "booby count" on the board. "How many boobies came in without pencils?" Things like that.

You know, I have to do it with my mouth, and once I get on track, they enjoy it. It's humor—insulting but not vicious: for example, a favorite expression of theirs is *dis*—short for "disrespect." Kids say, "Are you dissing me?" and I respond with a long rigmarole on the word: "How do you spell it? Is it a verb?"

I'm not being mean and horrible and nasty about it. There is always a little smile behind all the insults. It doesn't work on everybody. Some of them do have a chip on their shoulder, and they take umbrage. Again, you have to know your audience.

What do these kids think their future holds?

They have very unrealistic expectations. They think they are going into these high-tech careers, and they can't even add—not to mention that they can't speak English properly. But then, who knows? Maybe the interviewer won't know how to speak English either. I don't know what is going on in what I call the "real world."

They also want the rewards without any effort. They want a 90 in the class, but they don't want to do any work. Somewhere along the line they have to be given a dose of reality, and I'm the wall.

A one-woman crusade?

I try. But you try to get something from the administration and, you know, they are not there. Sometimes I ask myself, Am I the only one in this building who cares?

What about the other teachers?

Some of the other teachers care. But many teachers are extremely burned-out. I will not tell you differently. They're just putting in their hours. You know, you bang your head against the wall for 30 years, and it's enough.

Do teachers talk about the differences between now and 20 years ago?

All the time. It's one of the major topics of conversation–how everything has changed and how it's hopeless unless society decides that education is important.

Maybe there is a little sense of turnaround–even *Time* magazine came out with a cover story that did not blame teachers. [In fact, *Time*'s November 14, 1988 cover story–"Who's Teaching Our Children?"–praised the teachers: "(They need) the patience of Job and the wisdom of Solomon" to work "under highly adverse, sometimes dangerous conditions."] But when push comes to shove and our allotment comes in from the board of education, we find they've cut an additional eight teachers from our staff. Do you know what that means? It means that classes have to be dropped and other classes will become even bigger.

It is outrageous. Don't cut teachers! Don't cut classes! If there are cuts to be made, let them cut nonessential personnel down at the board of education. We don't need them. We need more of us. We are the ones in the trenches. We are the front line.

In fact, I really don't know what they all do down there in Brooklyn at the [central] board of education. If you go down there, they are *always* having a party. There is nobody there. Call the board of ed., and you can be on the phone six hours before you get through.

So I've discovered when I've attempted to get information for this book.

You have to go there in person. In order to get anything done, you've got to make a pilgrimage to Brooklyn.

[She then asks some questions about this book and, as many other teachers have done, she tells me that you have to be there to really know what it's like.]

You know, it is very nice to be an author and sit on top of Mount Olympus and pontificate about what's wrong with the schools. I remember one book that was written by a woman who had taught for exactly one year. Then she quit to write the book, and that struck me as tremendously hypocritical.

People can tell me what is wrong in my classes, and it may be true. But teachers can't turn around the other 23 hours in a day. (Not in our 40 minutes with 34 students—what is that? A minute for each student?) We can't do it alone. We need some outside help.

"Maybe a lot of what we teach is not relevant, but then I do not know what is finally relevant. Is it to discuss the Oprah Winfrey show every day?"

MIRIAM SIMON
high school English teacher
Kansas City, Missouri

What Is Relevant?

Miriam Simon is a veteran English teacher in the Kansas City, Missouri, school system. When she started out in the mid-sixties, Kansas City had begun to integrate its schools. That was 10 years after the U.S. Supreme Court's historic Brown v. Board of Education decision but still in advance of other cities like Boston, where integration efforts (and riots) began in the mid-seventies.

Desegregation hasn't worked in Kansas City. Whites left the inner city for the suburbs and also crossed the state line into Kansas. The result was the same as it has been in many American cities—an even wider social chasm opened up between white and black than had existed before.

Miriam Simon's current school, Lincoln College Preparatory Academy, is an exception. Three years ago Lincoln was made a magnet school for youngsters who have at least a 2.5 (C plus) average and who plan to go to college. While the majority are black, more than a third of the students are now white.

There is a lot of money riding on the success of magnet schools like Lincoln, and some bitter ironies. Miriam Simon pointed out that Lincoln became a magnet school and improved its program in order to attract whites back into the inner city: "Did we have to wait for the need to attract whites before we improved our school system?"

Her black colleague, David Hutton (whose interview follows this one) said that some whites slipped in with averages below 2.5 when qualified blacks were kept out–affirmative action upside down.

Still, Lincoln Prep is a success story so far. It's won some awards and, said Miriam Simon, "I can teach here, and that is different from what I hear about other Kansas City inner-city schools."

She teaches an advanced class called the "International Baccalaureate" as well as regular English classes. There's a wide disparity between the two, and she finds her own patience and interest dwindling with the less-accomplished students. She wants to reach them, but only if she can maintain some standards that she herself can respect–a dilemma she has not been able to resolve.

But who can? What was nice about talking to Miriam Simon was her eye for contradictions. She gave me no answers, only raised some excellent questions. The question, or issue, that moved me most was why she became a teacher and why she may soon get out. She's traveled a long way and touched a raw nerve–the sameness and dead-end future of her profession after 25 years.

Her journey literally began after a trip she and her family made to Israel:

We had driven from Kansas City to New York and then flown to Israel. In Israel I realized what everybody had to do to make their country a livable place; and coming back to America, driving across the country and seeing its lushness–Ohio, Indiana–I realized that I had just accepted all of this as my birthright. I had not had to do a thing to make America a decent place to live.

It sounds sort of corny, but I felt I owed a debt to America. I figured one way to pay it back was to become a teacher.

You began to teach in 1964?

At Paseo, in midtown Kansas City. When I began, the school was pretty much white, and the idea was to integrate it. But by 1969 it was an all-black school, and it is now in the ghetto.

What happened to Paseo is typical. Despite a huge desegregation effort, most inner-city schools are now black. Millions of dollars have been made available to them, and many have become magnet schools in order to attract whites back into the city.

But desegregation didn't work?

It is working at Lincoln–but not at most schools. With all that massive effort only about 600 white kids have been pulled in from the suburbs–we have some of them at Lincoln Prep.

Tell me about Lincoln.

Lincoln has a good system, and it works. There are no discipline problems. We are maybe 60 percent black, the rest white. The kids must maintain a 2.5 average, and they want to do that.

They are motivated?

Right.

Why?

They are middle-class. They want to make something of their lives, and they believe that education will change their lives.

That is not a belief I hear often in the inner city.

You will here. But we do have some transfers from all-black schools who do not have the skills or the attentiveness, and I don't take the pains–it's too late for some of those kids.

How are skills in general?

I don't really understand it, but it's as if we have two populations: one-third of the school can be competitive in any college. They are gifted, ready to go to a good college, stay there, and benefit. The others are a question mark.

I have seniors who are not skilled, and by now they are turned off. They do want to graduate, and some will go to college for a semester and then drop out.

What accounts for the two populations?

Let's see. I teach five classes a day. In my International Baccalaureate class the kids sit on my every word. They write long papers, read *Othello*, the Greeks, and all that. It is getting to be pretty much all white. I have only seven black kids in that class.

Why?

I don't know. They are the really interested and willing kids.

Last year some of my advanced black kids told me that they didn't want to work that hard. The Baccalaureate program enables you to go to any school in the world, but they say they are not going to any school in the world–so why work so hard?

They don't have the money for any school in the world?

Last year we got $700,000 worth of scholarship money. A lot of money is coming to the school, and college is a real possibility. They're just not interested.

Yet you say they are motivated?

They want to go to college but with the least amount of effort. Most of the whites, though, put in the extra effort and are on the Baccalaureate track.

Is the difference social class?

Well, right. The white kids who are bused in live in neighborhoods like mine. Their parents are professionals and liberals.

Are there many black teachers?

The faculty in our school is about 70 percent white. We all think it is terrible, but they [the administration] claim now that there are no black teachers available. They've all gone where the better jobs are–for more money.

Has the degree of student effort changed over 20 years?

When I began, the consciousness of black kids was very high, and they were involved with politics. They understood racism. The first five years of teaching were very exciting. I still see those kids, and they have made something of their lives.

By the mid-seventies–when I taught for awhile at Southwest, a school near my home where my own kids had gone and which is now about half black–there was no way I could reach the kids. No way at all.

Why couldn't you reach them?

I don't know. Kids came in stoned. Nobody cared. Finally, in desperation I taught the Missouri driver's test guide. Most kids at Southwest were turning 16, and they had to pass the driver's test.

I understand the army uses some comic books to instruct our soldiers.

At least the army is clear about what it wants to teach. I would love to do what is relevant, but I don't know what it is—that I could respect. I had one class this term teach me their slang, their dance. There are smart kids in that group, but I cannot get their attention. They'll do whatever they have to, but they're not turned on.

Except in my advanced class, I'm not certain about whether there is any compatibility—the sense that I am doing what they need to have done. I don't know what they need. To write an organized essay?

The standards are there, but the gap between them and realization are wider. There's a sense many kids have that it's all meaningless.

Are they less skilled today? I don't know. They can't think.

Aren't you asking a lot?

[We both laugh.] I try to help them remain open and to make sure their mind still works. In those ways maybe I'm still making a contribution, although I don't know if America is interested.

In open minds?

Right. I think the kids are caught. They've learned how to behave and have lost their openness. I try to counteract that.

Are you a maverick?

I've had some run-ins and sometimes been surprised by what people find objectionable. Just the other day a parent and her minister came in to see me. They were upset because I had invited someone to demonstrate Buddhist meditation in school. The Buddhist used the phrase "empty your mind." The minister felt that if we did empty our minds, God would slip out and Satan would come in.

I remember when I was first teaching, how I had these Moral Majority types in my room all the time. The issues were the classic ones you hear about; for instance, they didn't want me to teach Salinger's *Catcher in the Rye* because they objected to its language.

I had the superintendent in my room checking out how I taught Salinger. That ended in a stalemate. I kept teaching Salinger, but they removed the student from my class.

If I don't overdo it, the administration seems to respect me—even if they see me as a maverick. I have usually found support, except when I got kicked out.

Kicked out?

In 1969, I supported the black students in a walkout. They had a list of objections—like being suspended without a hearing—and I supported them. I had worked with the police to make sure it would be peaceful—no stones thrown, and so on. It was peaceful, and I was very proud. But then I was transferred to the administration downtown.

The principal said I was a bad influence on the faculty because I supported students. You see, the kids' top demand—once he would not meet with them or talk to them—had been the removal of the principal [laughs].

How about your own kids? Would you have liked them to become teachers?

[Pauses a long time] Oh, dear...I'm probably going to say more no than yes. I just think it's really hard to teach.

Can you fill in that pause?

On a day-to-day basis I do not see that much gratification, even for the younger teachers. Gratification is important, and you really have to get that.

Teachers want to change kids' lives or they really want to matter in a kid's life. Maybe it's ego, but so many things affect kids that you can't feel your own impact.

After four or five years I got a letter that I saved and still read. This student at Paseo said, "I now know what you are talking about." Thank God!

Right now I have that excitement in my Baccalaureate class but not the rest of the time.

Do you feel teaching is rewarding?

That letter is my reward. Also, in my personal life I have never stopped learning. This summer I was in Cambridge, England, where I took courses in Shakespeare and Irish literature. Teaching organizes me, and it has an intellectual component that affects my personal life. That's a big reward. It gives me a platform on which to dance.

How do you feel about salary?

I'm at the top of the scale and make about $38,000. I think that is legitimate—and competitive—for nine months' work. I have no complaints, but if I were raising kids, I could not do it on this salary. I was fortunate because my late husband was successful and I did not need the income.

Most teachers I know do cry money all the time. They work two jobs—at the 7-Eleven or in sales. I know I'm in a different spot.

Your grown children went to inner-city schools before white flight. Would you send them to Lincoln today?

Yes, I think I would. A while back my students and I visited a local private school for a week. It was no better than my school, and I didn't see anything different going on.

But then the private-school kids came to visit us, and their behavior was very distant and superior. My journalism kids were taking a minicourse called the "Urban Safari," and these private-school kids—who also live in the city—treated the idea of an urban safari as a joke. Or worse. Nothing was said, but they made our kids feel that their safari course was for those who belonged in a zoo.

It's very stratified—public, private; inner city, suburb.

Our inner-city schools are about 80 percent black here, and the suburbs are about 80 percent white. When I go out to the suburbs and see all those fancy cars in the student parking lots, it makes me sick.

But then in our school, the Baccalaureate program—what you call A.P.—is practically a white track, and I can't really explain that either.

No ideas?

I established a rule that things have to be in on time. If it doesn't come in on January 8, it gets an F. Then the kids hand in an incomplete job and scream and yell when I don't give them credit. "What, aren't we going to get credit for trying?" There has been a lot of that—just try, that's all you have to do.

This comes up in suburbs as well as in the city.

It's a fascinating issue. My youngest daughter asked if I thought it was better to hand in a sloppy job than to be late and hand in a quality job.

What alternatives!

I know. Doesn't make sense. But do schools?

Schools are not organized to allow kids to think. How can a kid take seven classes a day—and go from class to class every fifty minutes—and think? The structure of school is impossible: math and science and two languages and social studies and a computer class all in one day!

What about less is more? Fewer classes for longer periods of time.

We did that in the sixties and called it "modular scheduling." Every day was different, and you would spend two hours in chemistry—enough time to set up the experiment and actually work through it. You had several English options, small groups for individual help and large groups for lectures and presentations. We had team teaching, and the kids liked it. They could never figure out their schedule, and so they never got bored [laughs].

We should have larger blocks of time. If you are doing Handel's Oratorio, then take the time and do it! Modular scheduling was marvelous, but the teachers couldn't stand it.

Why not?

It wasn't structured enough. I guess they wanted to know that they would do the same thing every day—have it all more predictable. I loved it, of course. But some teachers and administrators get nervous if the kids are even loose in the halls. They need it rigid, lockstep.

Is your school in favor of merit pay?

Everyone is afraid that it will come down to who is the principal's friend; there isn't a high level of trust. But I see teachers who do a hell of a lot more than I do, and I think they should get paid more.

What makes a good teacher?

You know, when I worked on my Ph.D., I studied how to measure teacher effectiveness. Did I know there was a hundred years of research and no conclusions at all? They couldn't even define an effective teacher. But the research did show that even though high school teachers claim they do not have enough freedom, they still want a principal. They want to be told what to do.

I compared teacher aides and teachers: the former had taught in the classroom as aides but had not gone to college. They were better teachers! It isn't only what you know; you have to want to see kids learn.

Do teachers feel stuck?

You are stuck. That's the reality. I was in Chicago this weekend, and a teacher I met told me that she is in the best district in Chicago and that after 18 years she is bored. But you don't want to become an administrator really, and there is nowhere else to go in the system. If you continue teaching, it is going to get boring.

What keeps people at it? Security and the benefits. It's all financial. I think there are a lot of non-risk takers in teaching.

When I walked out with the students in Paseo, two teachers called me at night. They said they would have been there with me, but they could not afford it. Then the other teachers got mad; they looked at what I had done and said, "Well, she can afford it."

How do you think society views teachers?

I myself do not regard teachers highly. I met this tall beautiful redhead, a young woman, who is teaching the fourth grade. I said, What are you doing? You could be anything.

She said, I am teaching because I am molding young minds, and so on, and I thought, Here I am a teacher, and I question all that.

Hold on. What happened to your debt to America and how you feel you are making a difference? When you meet a young woman who wants to teach, you cannot understand it?

I know! Maybe I question the monotony of it, the dead-endedness. I am considering changing careers.

What do you see in the future for our schools?

I'm not really worried—I don't focus on how the schools are in imminent danger or reveal a nation at risk. Let the country improve!

Give us some models of decent behavior in Washington. You know, we talk about cheating in schools, and the kids say, "Well, there is Oliver North and all the others. What do you want from us?"

Or they point out that all that really counts is making money. I get really crude: "Would you eat a cup of shit for money?" "Of course," they say. "Would you kill your best friend?" "Would anybody know about it?"

In real life they are mostly kind and caring. But making money is what they see our government is all about. They see that anybody will do anything—lie, cheat, steal, abscond.

Why is there such a low moral tone in the country? I don't know which comes first—the poor role models in Washington or a failing school system. I'm not worried about schools. I'm worried about the country.

Get the focus off the schools!

"I wanted to inspire young people to reach for the stars. That is a cliché, but I wanted to encourage young people to be the best that they could be, and I thought I could do that."

DAVID HUTTON
high school English teacher
Kansas City, Missouri

Reach for the Stars

David Hutton loves to teach, but he increasingly despises "the fill out this form and that form" of his job. He isn't alone. Many teachers feel drawn to the classroom and disappointed, if not repelled, by most other facets of their profession.

Their disappointment, moreover, grows. As they move toward middle age, the disparity between their salary and that of friends becomes more evident, and galling; that, too, has happened to David Hutton, who has taught for 26 years and makes $31,000 a year (with a master's degree and credits toward his doctorate).

But within the classroom it is sometimes a different story. Hutton says that he loves to teach, more so now than when he began. He is concerned not only about his students' academic performance but also about their self-esteem—an issue that was very much on his mind as he talked about his black students at Lincoln Prep.

Like his colleague Miriam Simon, Hutton feels it is important that the school hire more minority teachers. He himself is black, and he thinks his students' self-esteem would benefit from the added push of more black role models.

At the outset he struck both chords—the self-esteem of his students and the system's ill treatment of teachers:

I became a teacher because I wanted to help youngsters learn. I think I've succeeded, but even more than that, I think I have helped them to feel good about themselves. I have helped youngsters to have positive self-esteem and to feel proud of who they are.

My disappointment is with the system—not the children.

How so?

Teachers lack authority, and what we do is constantly questioned. (I myself am not often questioned, but I see how others are.) We should have a greater influence on the curriculum and on the evaluation of both teachers and administrators.

We are also not paid enough, and we lack community support. This school system has turned down all proposed increases in the school levy or tax since 1968. When the school tax was increased a couple of years ago, it was by a court order, not the will of the people.

Do you protest these issues?

All the time. I speak out on teacher rights and empowerment, which means I am considered somewhat radical. Most other teachers don't think what I say is radical, but they do not have the guts to speak out. Maybe they are brainwashed and feel teachers are supposed to project a certain bourgeois—or status quo—image.

Lincoln Prep is a magnet school?

With an emphasis on college preparation rather than on one discipline like other magnet schools. We draw students from throughout the Kansas City school districts and from some suburban areas. The purpose of the magnet school is to promote integration and excellence in education.

How is it doing?

On a scale of 1 to 10, I'd give it a 9 for integration and a 7 for excellence at this point.

The 2.5 average (C plus) that we require is not that high, but when I started, it was 1.6 (D plus)—if you can believe that. To allow 1.6 was a farce. That was the politics of education—trying to keep everyone happy.

In fact, even now some nonminority students are admitted with lower grade averages simply because they are white, and many qualified black students are not admitted because they are black. I am for integration, but I think sometimes the black students are pushed to the back and the white children are given a preference.

Also, we are hooked on everything being 50-50 at Lincoln, but we don't have enough black teachers in the classroom. When I bring it up, they say there are no minority teachers to hire.

Why not?

It may have to do with working conditions and salaries. Also, there are fewer male college graduates than there were 10 years ago.

Do you think it's important for black students to have black teachers?

Yes, it matters because of image and identity. Students can learn under any teacher of any color if that teacher is a good teacher. But they may be able to learn more—and to identify—with someone of their own color. Here, where 60 percent of the kids are black and there are few black teachers, it sends out a negative image. The reverse would never happen. You don't see schools with a majority of white students who are taught by a majority of black teachers. It would never happen.

Miriam Simon said her advanced class was largely white.

I don't have one of those classes. I don't know whether the students are more qualified or just steered into those courses. Their families may be pushing them more, and there might be a higher percentage of white-parent involvement.

Why?

Sometimes parents feel that whatever is going on, they can't do much about it anyway. Then there are also some blacks who still believe that white is right. You don't question the man.

Really?

Some things I'm not really certain about, but I do get that feeling sometimes. I think there is also a feeling that if you are going to school with white students, then that in itself is just better. My criticism of some blacks at Lincoln is that they just want to lose their black identity and become anything except black.

Nice trick.

[Laughs] I have many white friends, but everyone knows that I am black and that I know who I am. Many kids now do not know any history, and they have no roots. It's very different from 20 years ago, and the change shows up in the classroom and elsewhere. I don't think my black students feel that good about themselves.

Twenty years ago there was more black awareness. I never felt it was racist, but it was about learning who I am and doing what I can to contribute. It was a feeling that I am somebody. Today many black students think that if they can get a good education and some kind of job skill, then everything is going to be rosy.

They don't know about racism?

I don't think they do.

Then Kansas City must be very different from New York.

I don't think it is very different, but the youngsters have been very sheltered. Many of the students at Lincoln have what they want; things have been fairly easy—I am not saying that is negative, but it is part of why they think the way they do.

Isn't this the first generation of middle-class minority kids?

That's a good point. They are probably wealthier than in the past and less aware of the dynamics of our society.

Many teachers seem to think all kids are less aware.

That's also true. Part of my problem as a teacher is that I would like to see them excel, naturally, but I would also like to see them give something back to the community. They want to be engineers, doctors, lawyers. Very few want to be teachers anymore. I tell them they must realize that whatever they want to be, they must be taught it. It doesn't just happen.

What changed?

Teachers do not command respect—maybe because of test scores and the way standards seem to have gone down. I also don't think teachers as a profession have asserted themselves. They just take anything.

You mentioned wanting kids to reach for the stars. When you were young, what made you feel that way instead of wanting to make $5 million a year?

I got it from my parents, who valued education, and from teachers I had and also my church life. I was taught to reach out and help others.

Have you regretted the decision?

Yes, I have, especially in the last 10 years. I guess many people complain about what they make, but I have friends who have a high school diploma and make more money than I do. At one time that did not bother me, but as I grow older, it does.

Also, we teachers have no power, and then I see people in administration who have the power to make changes and who don't change. They keep the status quo.

What kind of changes?

I think our students are pampered too much. When there is a behavior problem—I think we should give students real counseling and then state what will happen: either they behave, or they will be transferred out.

Something else I see is the way many administrators forget about what it was like to be a teacher. They know the problems in the classroom but don't seem to want to resolve them until the problems become a burden for them.

Schools are often too permissive, and the administration does nothing about it?

Right.

Why don't the teachers do something about it?

They are afraid of losing their jobs or afraid of the way they might be looked upon. Many teachers go with the status quo.

Do teachers like the merit-pay idea?

I do, provided *all* salaries are raised first and provided it can be done without personalities being involved. Starting salary is now

about $18,500, and with a Ph.D. or equivalent it's about $38,000–
that's the range.

How about competency testing?

Should be a criteria, but only one. I would say that 90 percent of
the teachers in my school are good teachers.

How about your actual classes. Is homework a problem?

I don't give a lot of homework. Most of the papers they write are in
class. We go step by step in class so that I can help them as much as
I can.

In my class, if they do not do their homework, I try to get into
the child's brain and find out why it is not done. I will counsel him
and try to help before I go to the next step.

What do they read in your 11th-grade English class?

We have a textbook, and we're reading Steinbeck's *Grapes of Wrath*
and Richard Wright's *Native Son*. I will also choose others.

**Do you make sure some of the works are specifically targeted to a
minority population?**

Yes. I can't say about the other teachers, but I think most do.

**Apropos of the students not having roots, how do they react to
Native Son?**

Mixed. Some like it and some think it too cruel. Some do not like
the language and feel Bigger is distorted as a person.

They have no personal reaction?

They do not think it's part of their lives. It is a reading assignment. I
give them some background on Richard Wright, issues of social
consciousness, and so on. A few see it, many do not. It's hard for
them to make connections, and I'm not sure why that is.

What are the skills like?

I'm not teaching the top students. I have a range from sixth grade
to first, second year of college.

Would you consider leaving?

I have too many years in it. I will stay and try to be the best teacher

I can be. The problem I have is staying and keeping my mouth shut. I'm staying, but I'm raising hell with it [laughs]!

You are tenured. Can't you raise all the hell you want?

Yes, but sometimes I think my colleagues may feel I am beating a dead horse. They are tired of hearing me talk about empowerment, our salaries, and all the unnecessary paperwork.

Why not become an administrator?

I thought about it at one time, and I decided I really couldn't hang with it. First of all, I don't want to go back to school. I don't think I could take all the bullshit courses, and let's face it, you have to groom yourself for that stuff. You have to act a certain way and project a certain image. I have the feeling, even if I got the certification, that I'd be passed over because of my record as a hell-raiser.

People know me. They know I'll speak my mind, and if I don't like something, I will speak out against it.

The kids know that, and they like it. When they come to me, I try to guide them in the "right" way.

The bourgeois way?

[Laughs] Yes, for their sake, they must learn it. I don't think they could handle standing up for what they believe in. If they did [participate in a] sit-in, they'd probably be expelled, and they would feel it was not worth it.

Do you feel you are a bit of a social worker? Psychologist?

Yes. I do many things to try and make them feel good about themselves. I'll tell you something else too. It is sometimes hard to academically motivate young black male students, and I really work on that group. As a black male teacher I try to motivate them and to put them in positions of leadership in the classroom. I intentionally do that because I think it is needed—more so than with the other students who already have that push.

I have observed that many black male students are not given that academic push. They are pushed to excel in sports, and that's fine. I'm not putting sports down, but more is needed in the academic area. I think they respect me for the knowledge I have, and I think they are intelligent enough to see what I am trying to do.

Do your students come to you with their problems?

Not as much as they used to. I'm not sure why.

Do you feel you make a difference?

Yes, I do. Some may like my style, and some may not. Most of the time when we discuss a novel or a story, I'll respond to whatever questions arise, even if off the topic.

Why do you emphasize that you are trying to help kids feel good about themselves?

Many do not feel good about themselves. Maybe I should not say this, but I think many black students don't feel that they can measure up in academic competition. They don't know that they can do as well as someone else if they put their mind to it. They really lack confidence.

I believe in integration too, but I still feel something can be all black and have greatness [laughs]. There are some black people who do not feel that way.

How can you make them feel good about themselves?

I try to draw things out of them. I try to encourage. I give compliments. If they don't do something well, I just tell them, "I know you can do better than that. I have faith you can do it." Just simple comments.

The celebrated Los Angeles teacher Jaime Escalante tells his Hispanic kids that math is in their blood, their Mayan roots.

It is very important to have pride in who you are. Some teachers have lost that.

Do you think in the long run that Lincoln Prep has a chance to become truly integrated?

Yes, I do. Race relations are good at the school, and I think most of the parents who send their kids there fundamentally believe in an integrated multicultured society. The teachers also feel the same way, and the administrators do too.

People look to Lincoln: we are trying to prove that we can have a very excellent school in the inner cities.

And?

And we most certainly can! If we all work together and agree to enforce the same high standards, I believe that the students at Lincoln have it in them to compete with the very best. It's in them; if the self-esteem is there, then they can go very far.

"Hispanic kids are taught to respect the teacher. To them I'm a god. But teachers are human. We can be sexy. We can go home and have a few drinks and then throw all the papers on the floor and refuse to correct them.

The image of the teacher for all these years has been back in the 1800s in the one-room schoolhouse. But now it's begun to change. Take the movie *Looking for Mr. Goodbar*. Here's a teacher who goes to bars and looks for men. No bun in the back anymore.

Teachers are human, normal, with problems. That's why they have these employee-assistance programs for teachers and clericals now. They didn't open up those clinics for teachers on dope and alcohol for just a few people."

LINDA PRESCOTT
elementary school teacher
Los Angeles, California

Teachers Are Human

Linda Prescott has taught for 20 years. She spent 6 years at an all black ghetto school and the last 14 at a largely Hispanic and Korean school, Hobart. Both are in Los Angeles.

She is not the "bun in the back" type of teacher but very much a contemporary woman. She says that people think the grade school teacher is only one step ahead of her kids, intellectually and socially.

She knows it isn't true, but it bothers her. So does the lack of an adult structure.

"You know, the thing is I'm still in school. I'm not a kid, but the walls are there, the bells are ringing. That bothers me. I'm still doing what I did when I was eight. I'm still going to the yard, I'm still going to the classroom," she said.

We didn't really talk about the clinic for teachers with problems—what mattered was that they exist, as do teachers who need them. Instead Linda talked about her profession, and her first words were emphatic:

I wouldn't go into it again, the way it's going. Not because of the kids—I love the kids—but the L.A. system—I think probably our whole school system—stinks.

What's wrong?

Five years ago there was a push for integrated classes. But walk through my school now, and you'll see an all-Mexican room, an all-Korean room. We teach bilingually, *and* it's segregated.

I am against bilingual education. I say put the kids in a room, segregate them for a year, and really teach them English.

How does bilingualism work?

It doesn't. Now we are teaching social studies, and it's half in English, half in Spanish, and it is too much for the teacher. That's what is going on in my school, and no one is happy.

Hispanic parents don't like it. They want their kids to learn English—*their* English is very poor.

White parents are pulling their kids out and putting them in private schools. I don't blame the white flight, not when we are giving all of our attention to the children who are coming from Central and South America—Los Angeles is over 55 percent Latino and Mexican. We cater to them, and the rest of the children are getting what I would say is a half-assed education.

Who are the children at your school?

Poor kids. About two-thirds of them qualify for free lunch. They are Hispanic and Asian—mostly Korean.

As a "Title One" school [one that qualifies for federal assistance due to its disadvantaged population], Hobart gets special monies. To get the lunch, kids fill out an application, and if they qualify as below the minimum family income they get the free lunch.

Yet these children have candy in their pockets; they have money in their pockets. Most of them could be fed at home. Instead, we feed them. It's your money and my money.

Is any of the money going into making class size smaller?

Our school operates year-round. We are so big that there are three shifts during the year. But our classrooms are small. I'm embarrassed to tell you that I have only 17 in my class.

Why does a small class embarrass you?

We need the small class, but it sounds as if we have it easy when you hear I have 17 children to teach. When I started out, it was 36.

Are the kids learning?

Everybody asks about basic skills. Basic skills! Now kids know how a submachine gun works, how a knife cuts you open, that a man can put his hands over a woman's breast...you can't just look at the educational system. Look at the media, at TV. What is it doing to these kids? Kids can't speak English, but they can curse.

You know, every so often some politician somewhere fights to make sure the Pledge of Allegiance is being recited in the classroom. The Pledge of Allegiance! Shit, much more than that is involved. [She is very agitated and goes to her kitchen to get us both some soda. When she returns, she laughs and says she knows these are not the "basic skills" I have in mind.]

The kids in my class are learning the basics. But most of the kids in my school don't know *how* to write, they don't know *how* to speak, and they don't know *how* to read. They don't know *how* to really examine a paragraph and cull information from it. We need to work on *how*.

Also, children need to feel some self-worth and to learn about self-respect. They'll get math again and again. But being able to listen to each other and to know that there are differences and similarities—these are prime concerns for me.

It is one of my main goals as a teacher: to help give kids some self-respect.

You sound as if you're very involved with your students.

A lot of teachers come up to me and say, "My God, your kids are always hanging onto you." That doesn't mean I'm a good teacher, but I do think a lot of teachers forget that they can really enjoy their kids.

I pay attention to the kids' feelings. My own parents were alcoholics; so looking at what I had as a child and what I grew up with, I try to give these kids something they are maybe not getting at home.

These kids have to handle a lot. Our school is in Little Korea. We are surrounded by a very bad area, and there are gangs everywhere. About three months ago, in fact, one girl died while being chased by a gang in our yard. Our teachers' parking lot is locked at eight o'clock, and we hold parents night in the daytime. Otherwise it is too dangerous.

We have a party at school, and the kids want to know if they can bring the drinks. You know, "I'll bring the beer." [Laughs]

Third graders?

Sure. Look, we are considered a good inner-city school. Our kids, they are beautiful kids. There are problems but not headaches. They are manageable.

You should have seen my first school. I yelled so much, I developed nodules, and the board of education had to pay for my speech therapy.

You screamed for six years?

Off and on I had to scream. My God, you don't know what it is like. I got hit three times in the stomach and eye. I was an abused teacher. You constantly had to be on top of it. They are either verbally aggressive or physically aggressive. They are constantly on top of each other, either yakking or getting into a fight. It's like the blackboard jungle, you know, the chaos.

At first, I thought, I'll do the best I can. But what an introduction for a new teacher! It was rough. It took a few years before I settled down, developed my discipline, and figured out how to reach the kids.

How do you reach them?

I let them know that I care about them but that I am not responsible for their actions. They are.

In all my years, I guess I like working with kids who need a little more help. But I don't want to go back into the black ghetto. I could make more there—it's called "combat pay." But I put in six years, and I don't care about extra pay.

It's bad enough where I am. There is so much pressure on the teacher. They come in to evaluate me, and if I'm in the corner blowing my nose, they want to know why I'm not with the kids.

Yet they don't come to us and ask teachers what we need and what would be good for our kids. The whole system should be rehauled. We need to question what we teach and how we teach.

Last question. What do you think the future holds?

I could go back to school and become a lawyer. I've got the application on my desk. It would be nice to go out for lunch and sit down and have a nice lunch with a glass of wine and relax for an hour without hearing the bell ring.

But I genuinely enjoy children. I'm thinking…I don't know.

Postscript

Self-Esteem

Listening to teachers like Linda Prescott, one has the impression that the point of an inner-city education is to nurture a child's self-esteem. Because she has seen so many children whose self-esteem is low, she spends a great deal of her class time trying to turn them emotionally around.

No one can quarrel with her compassionate instincts. Like Geri Stern, Prescott is a teacher who feels very close to her students and who tries to make up for what she believes they do not get at home.

Nonetheless, when teachers feel responsible for their students' emotional well-being, they undertake a difficult and complex assignment. Keeping a child's academic, as well as emotional, needs in mind cannot always be easy.

There are strategies that seem to strike this balance: Jaime Escalante, the mathematics teacher at Garfield High School in Los Angeles who became the hero of the movie *Stand and Deliver*, sometimes uses his weakest student as the tutor in an advanced-calculus class. He feels that all learn with this arrangement, and the tutor's self-confidence is given a needed boost.

Attempts to recruit more minority teachers and to offer a curriculum that includes the contributions minorities have made are also methods of positively tackling the low self-esteem of many inner-city children.

These tactics make sense: self-esteem *and* knowledge are both allowed to grow.

"All these other teachers said, 'Give them an F for the day, and tell them they will fail.' Assertive discipline–that's what the teachers call it. It's a new concept: at the beginning you post your rules in writing on the wall, and you set down what the consequences of breaking the rules will be. But the hard part is sticking to the consequences. Everything the kids do is breaking the rules. I finally said, 'The heck with it' and just tried to teach through the disorder and pick up the kids who were anxious to learn."

MARY WILLIAMS
high school ESL teacher
Norwalk, Connecticut

They Call It Assertive Discipline

Mary Williams sees teaching as her life work, but at 45 she is reluctant to begin. When she received her teacher certification 22 years ago, she was "appalled by the whole thing of having to get up in front of a classroom of kids and control them." So she put off teaching until a few years ago, when she got her feet wet as a kindergarten aide. Then this last year she dove in headfirst–by teaching English as a second language at Norwalk High School in Norwalk, Connecticut.

It seemed to me that she'd been given an impossible assignment–the classic case of a first-year teacher who takes on what nobody else wants to touch. But she is slow to blame or censure and has struggled to make her class work. That struggle made me think of her as a kind of Gulliver in Educationland. Without the armor of an experienced teacher, she is naive enough to record what others no longer see.

At the start, she announced:

I ran into my old control problem when I taught last year at Norwalk High. I am very nurturing, and I'm very patient. I'm a good teacher, but classroom control is not my strong point.

111

What was your class like?

They were just very active, constantly talking and moving around the classroom. I decided I did not want to spend all my time telling them to sit down, be quiet, and pay attention. I kind of let the noise go on, and with time it got worse and worse. One of the problems I had at Norwalk High was that I was down in the industrial arts section, totally isolated. There were no classrooms near me, and I had no telephone in the room. If I had a problem, I was stuck. If I said, "All right, you are going to the office," the student said, "No, I'm not," and eventually I would back down.

Were these tough kids?

Let's put it this way: I got the kids nobody else wanted. The ones who had a bad attitude or weren't too smart. Some had learning disabilities. They got weeded out from the entire ESL group and put in my class. Last year there were too many kids; so they hired me. And when they divided up the groups, I got the problems. I had 11 to 15 kids in the class. It was a good size. Most classes were 20 to 25.

How did the half year go?

Ultimately it was successful. But three months into the job I was ready to quit because I was so frustrated by the kids' lack of motivation and by my inability to make them behave. I tried to get help from the guidance people, and they said, "We can't talk to those kids. They all speak Spanish. You'll have to take care of them." When I told them [the guidance counselors] it was their job, they again said, "We can't talk to them."

I got very frustrated, particularly by being in that room and not getting the backup I needed. I'd go up and talk to the headmaster, and he'd say, "Just call me." I'd remind him that I did not have a phone, and he'd tell me to just send them up to his office. I tried to send them up to his office, but they would not leave. If they did leave, I didn't know if they actually went to his office; and even if they did, they couldn't talk to him, because he didn't speak Spanish.

I was very frustrated, and my husband wanted me to quit. One really bad day I had to go down the hall and pound on another teacher's door and ask for help. That teacher went to the principal and demanded a room for me. There was no room, but they moved me to whatever room was temporarily available–each period I was moved to a different room. That wasn't too much fun either, but it made a big difference. I had a phone, and if a kid started something, I threatened to call the office and–*bam*–it would stop just like that. Latino kids in particular seem to have a fear of authority, at least on the upper levels. They don't fear a teacher very much, but when you talk about a man–the principal's office–then they care. They know it is going to get back to their parents, and they are all afraid of their parents.

Did you have much contact with parents?

It made a big difference when I did. I probably should have gotten on the phone a lot earlier than I did. I didn't call the parents, because I was in an odd position. I didn't feel I was truly in charge of the kids, because when anything major happened, I had to get the approval of one of the other teachers. You see, the kids were still on the other teachers' rolls. I gave them the grade, but some other teacher would list the grade. It was a strange situation. I was technically a long-term substitute.

But what you really were, if I may say so, was a dumping ground for the kids the other teachers didn't want.

I don't know how to explain it really. I was never listed as the teacher. Most of the kids were 9th grade, some 10th and 11th. There were a couple who had learning disabilities. I tried to get help for them, but I still don't think the school has done anything. We had a big meeting in April about one kid, and by the end of the year nothing had happened. That kid was up for psychiatric evaluation: he was like a little kid; he could not control himself at all; he'd roll around on the floor, constantly talking or drawing pictures. His guardian said that the kid was not in control of himself at home either.

Now you are waiting to see if there will be the funds to rehire you? And it will be the same situation?

Yes [laughs, embarrassed]. Possibly some of the same kids. But by the end of the year I felt much better. I felt I had really crossed some bridges and was ready to go ahead. The teachers did offer to trade classes with me when I was very upset. They'd take my kids, and I'd get the top group. But I refused. I knew my kids; I knew where I was and what I was doing. I wanted to succeed with them.

You say the kids are not motivated?

No. I don't think many of them wanted to learn English. At least they didn't pay attention and wouldn't repeat things out loud–they were embarrassed to do that. Also, they wouldn't study at home at all. I would give homework assignments, and they would not be done.

At one point I just said, "Those who want to talk English come over here, and the ones who want to talk Spanish go over there." That's what I finally had to do. They would never stop talking, never. When I gave them a work sheet to do, they had to come up and ask about every question on the sheet. Is this right? Is this what I should be doing?

What was the matter?

I never did figure it out. Some people said I was just too soft. I should have been stricter. I should not have let them talk; I should not have responded to them when they came to me for help; I should have changed the whole structure. But these suggestions didn't feel right for me, and I couldn't follow them.

Would the students have learned any more if I'd been able to adopt the assertive discipline other teachers recommended? I don't think so. My kids did pretty well on the final exams; ultimately they did learn. But I'd like to know now how they are doing and how firm a basis they did get.

Why didn't they want to learn English?

I don't know. Some were unhappy and wanted to go back to their own country. A lot of them were from Colombia, all from Medellin –where the big drug cartel is.

You wonder. I think some of these kids were doing drugs, but I never saw any evidence in the school.

Did you get to know the other teachers?

A very small number. We were tucked in with the foreign-language teachers, and when I left the classroom, I'd go to their lunchroom. I met math teachers too because I was tutoring in math.

The teachers seemed to be competent and care a lot. They'd been there 10, 12, 15 years. It seemed to be the younger ones who got really frustrated.

Will you look for another job if Norwalk doesn't rehire you?

I don't know [laughs, embarrassed]. I want to be a teacher, but I'm not yet 45–the age at which I promised myself I'd begin.

People have been trying to get me to teach for years. All the time I was working as an aide at Silvermine [a local elementary school], they urged me to teach. But I didn't feel ready, partly because I knew I would give 150 percent. I didn't want to do that, because my family comes first.

It's what happened when I took this job. I did give 150 percent, and I was just gone from January to June. I was not a mother. I was not a wife. I was just a teacher. This room [her dining room] was filled with my materials. I was constantly working, looking over teaching materials, and making lesson plans.

Everyone says the first year is the worst. You go in kind of blind and are just groping around. But if I go back, I've got a base, and I hope I've learned how to manage a classroom–though I'm still not too sure about that.

What kind of high school is Norwalk?

About average, I guess. We had only one merit scholarship this year, and that is not too good. There are about 1,000 students, and there's a large minority population–a lot of Haitians, Hispanics, blacks.

We read about how minorities are falling behind in the schools. Is that true at Norwalk High?

Yes. From what I have seen, it does come down to the home environment. These people move constantly. At the elementary school someone would arrive in mid-September with a bunch of kids and plunk them down in the school. The school would have to search for medical records and the rest of it, and then two or three months later the family would move somewhere else. Then they'd move back and again move out. Or they'd leave for a year and then return.

There was no stability in the kid's lives. Also, there are an awful lot of broken homes, a lot of single-parent households.

At Silvermine I was very involved with parents, both as an aide and as a volunteer coordinator with Spanish people. Mothers wanted to know why their kids were behind in class, but when the kids would ask them for help, they didn't know what to do. Most of them haven't been to high school themselves, and there are no books at home.

I grew up in a practically all-white world, and I don't have too much to go on here. But I think that kids who have two educated parents do better in school. I can see it with my own kids. We have reference books all over the house, and Joe and I are both academically minded. My kids ask a question, and they know they are going to get an answer.

Teachers don't have anything to do with it?

Not very much. Every once in a while a teacher will turn on one kid and make him want to learn. But in general it doesn't really matter.

Perhaps teachers and schools might be able to do more—or at least work differently.

I don't know. I think they are doing the best they can. There has been a real change over the past 20 years as to who takes responsibility for students. More and more, people are saying that the children are entirely the school's responsibility. They want schools to teach morals, ethics, health, all these things that parents used to teach. The kids are coming to elementary school with no moral values, and that's scary.

Kindergarten kids with no moral values?

The first kindergarten class I worked with was just incredible. Out of 18 kids, 14 had no father at home. Many lived with grandparents; they moved in and out constantly. The kids would come in wearing gold chains around their necks, and they would talk about the drug deals they had seen in the housing projects.

There's not so much home structure now. Nothing is settled and secure. They are shifted around a lot. I think about it all the time but cannot come to any original conclusions. More and more, people seem to want other people and institutions to take on the responsibility for every aspect of their lives—for themselves and their kids.

A tall order.

Impossible—no one appreciates what teachers do. I think many teachers are really frustrated. They feel they are not appreciated by the parents and they are not appreciated by the administration, and it doesn't really matter what kind of job they do.

In Norwalk a lot of teachers were ready to throw in the towel because they felt they were not being appreciated. New teachers were hired at a new, higher pay scale, and they were getting more than people who had taught for 10 years.

Also, parents will often call and support their children with really lame excuses: "She didn't feel well"; "She didn't want to go to school"; "She had to go and get her dress for the prom." There is an awful lot of that, and it makes teachers feel very sad.

Do you think the key to making teachers feel appreciated is money?

It would help. I was watching a TV show in which a waiter pointed out that he would have liked to be a teacher but that it didn't pay enough. That's why he was a waiter.

A lot of people think that it's an easy job and we have the summers off, but being a teacher is very stressful. It would help if there were more ways for teachers to get a mental shoring up—psychological counseling or just support groups. That's really how our lunchroom functioned. We would all come in and just moan. There were lots of days that I was in tears, and one teacher would tell me that she understood and, yes, it is frustrating. Another would tell me not to worry about it. That was a big help.

I felt isolated down in that industrial arts section, not being able to motivate the kids and trying to teach a lesson while they jabbered away. I was teaching American history or drilling them in verb tenses, things like that. They don't care about American history or English grammar.

Some are really motivated, but it was hard to work with them when the rest just wanted to sit with their friends and talk or to put on their makeup. I'd be talking and writing on the board, and I'd turn around and they'd all be talking: somebody would be fixing her hair, someone would be putting on her makeup, and they'd be passing the perfume bottles back and forth or throwing spitballs. They were like little kids, and then it finally dawned on me: they were mostly freshmen, and they *were* little kids.

I remembered what I had been told years ago: if all else fails, lower your expectations. I did that, and it worked. It made it easier to accept what the kids were doing, and the funny thing is that when the teachers in the lunchroom would describe what was going on in their classes, I'd sit there and say, "That's exactly what is going on in my classes, and I'm on the opposite end of the spectrum."

What did you do to unwind?

I didn't. It took me about six weeks to recuperate. I don't know, but I suppose a lot of teachers do drink. Talking to other teachers in the lunchroom was important. We talked about whatever was a hassle —sometimes the kids or an upper-level administrator or other teachers who didn't understand what we were trying to do.

I think the material for my book is waiting in that lunchroom.

A lot of teachers had a hard time understanding that our Hispanic kids were different, and they'd get very impatient. They expected these kids to just sit down and listen. But the kids could not understand what they were saying.

When I started tutoring them in math, it helped a lot. A lot of kids came way up in their math scores because I took the time to explain what was happening.

The Norwalk ESL program is supposed to be transitional and last no more than three years, and we do get a lot of flak about it... you know, "My parents learned English..." But I think the bilingual program works. Without it kids will never get into the mainstream.

What is your answer to critics who use the "My parents learned English..." argument?

Many parents did not learn English. A lot of them just dropped out. The ones who did remain in school also had parents who were much more interested in education than parents are today. The parent or parents don't follow through on homework or supervise their kids at all anymore.

Also, student motivation is a huge problem. I can see it in my own kids, and they are closely supervised. My kids ask, "What good is it?" and "Why must I study?" We have to keep making them understand how important it is to get an education. And my students —who are not reminded at home that education is important— don't care at all. They don't understand the real value of an education. They would rather be out working, and many of them do work. I tell them that they will be in the car wash for the rest of their lives, and they say, "That's okay. I make a lot of money."

It's just a different atmosphere. Half the time they are hanging out in the girls' room. When I went to school, you went to classes.

What made you become an aide when you were certified to teach? Was that part of the wait-till-you-are-45-before-you-plunge-in plan?

Being an aide was my way of figuring out whether I wanted to teach or not. It was a position that was open, and it is a nice way to be in the classroom, be responsible, but not really be in charge. I didn't have to do the planning, and I learned from other teachers.

I know this is what I'm going to do. I'm really certain of that. It's my life work...but perhaps not yet.

Postscript

The Good Old Days?

When veteran teachers reflect on their careers, the change in the way the profession is seen always receives a good deal of attention. So radical has been the shift in public perception of the profession that now many teachers don't even like to admit that they *are* teachers.

Yet they all remember a time when they felt people saw their work as important, perhaps even admirable. They miss that respect now—even within their own families: it is a sign of how much times have changed that many veteran teachers were urged by their own parents to become teachers, and now those same parents commiserate with them because they are still in the classroom.

Teaching—once a safe, secure, and respectable profession and a sure sign of one's firm foothold in the middle-class white-collar world—now looks to all as if it is a profession built on sand. What prestige can there be in a profession that cannot financially compete even with nonprofessional occupations and where the intangible rewards have begun to slip away? Where is the prestige in work that signifies white collar but can now even be physically dangerous?

Teachers say there is none, and they point to social change and the erosion of family life to explain what happened. They offer us reports of kids who are adrift, unsupervised at home, and responsive to television soap operas, the local shopping mall, and far worse.

And how, they ask, can our teachers be valued when we have no time for even our young? What respect will they receive in a society that signals with each new budget that it does not value education?

These questions reveal how our teachers think. Teachers strongly believe that their role in society has changed and that the profession has lost ground.

They *have* lost ground, but I think that what they have forfeited is their position as authority figures. When we look backward, it is difficult to find a golden age of respect.

Each generation of teachers seems to think it was better "back then." Here, for example, is what a renowned study of American life, *Middletown*, said about the world of Midwestern teachers in the 1920s:

> Few things about education in Middletown today are more noteworthy than the fact that the entire community treats its teachers casually. These more than 250 persons to whom this weighty responsibility of training the young is entrusted are not the wise, skilled, revered elders of the group. In terms of the concerns and activities that preoccupy the keenest interests of the city's leaders, they are for the most part nonentities; rarely does one run across a teacher at the weekly luncheons of the city's businessmen assembled in their civic clubs: nor are many of them likely to be present at the social functions over which the wives of these influential men preside. Middletown pays these people to whom it entrusts its children about what it pays a retail clerk, turns the whole business of running the schools over to a school board of three businessmen appointed by the political machine, and rarely stumbles on the individual teacher save when a particularly interested mother pays a visit to the school "to find out how Ted is getting along." The often bitter comments of the teachers themselves upon their lack of status and recognition in the ordinary give and take of local life are not needed to make an observer realize that in this commercial culture the "teacher" and "professor" do not occupy the position they did even a generation ago.

It sounds familiar. Teachers in the twenties had much the same complaints as teachers do now. Both reported a fall from grace and remembered how people used to respect teachers—once upon a time.

But when? Governesses in the nineteenth century suffered a status that was just above that of the parlor maid, and the nineteenth-century American schoolmaster, who boarded with the town's prominent families, was not exactly a social lion. He was a dependent, the poor relation at the merchant's table—about what you would expect from a nation that built an empire out of the wilderness in record time, too short a time to worry over much about "book learnin'."

What has changed, I think, is the teachers' corner on the culture-and-education market. Even if teachers were never high on the social scale, they were the nominal guardians of cultural life. (Think of Sinclair Lewis's portrait of the spinster schoolteacher Vida Sherwin in *Main Street*. The poor woman works for all forms of cultural betterment—the debating society, a dramatic club—and lives in a boardinghouse. She does not get invited to meet the doctor's new bride when she arrives in Gopher Prairie. That honor is reserved to the town's leading citizens, its merchants.

(But now there are far more book clubs, museums, magazines, television, and even ship's cruises to take on the roles that the Vida Sherwins once dominated.)

A second change is that teaching was once a poor second to a husband, and now it's a poor second to a dynamic and lucrative career. (This point was also caught by Lewis. When a shoe clerk proposes to her, Vida Sherwin hotfoots it out of the classroom and, at 39, is ecstatic as the homemaker. Meanwhile her younger counterpart, Fern Mullins, is driven out of town when falsely accused of seducing one of her students. If she does not find a husband, Fern Mullins will be finished.

(For both women, teaching is a poor second to a husband and places very definite limits on their social importance. Teachers are tolerated, even liked, as long as they know their place—like any servant.)

Now, of course, women do have more options, and so why teach? The economic incentive has lost its teeth and that, too, influences how much people respect the teacher. (A parallel problem exists for colleges as well: the dean of the Law School at Columbia University recently wrote that his school could not compete, as it had in the fifties, with private law firms. The economic chasm is now too wide, far wider than in more innocent, less money-mad days.)

It may also be that even 40 years ago, when far fewer people went on to college, an education was seen as special. People who did not have much formal education had a certain awe of the teacher and the classroom.

Some of it I remember—people whispered about my own mother, "She's a teacher," and I think it meant you were to watch your manners or your grammar when you were around her. My mother was the first in her family to go on to college, and there are still many veteran teachers around for whom that is also true. For their parents, many of whom were immigrants, the classroom appeared to be a step up the social ladder.

Now there isn't even a ladder: everyone talks about how there is nowhere *to* climb, and all mourn the loss of respect. But as I've suggested, it may be authority, more than respect, that teachers have lost, and this, too, seems part of a larger social change—authority figures in general are not very popular or credible in America right now. Indeed, if parents themselves haven't much authority, then how can teachers? The whole idea of the teacher as being *in loco parentis* sounds pretty old fashioned—the true good old days.

"If you are looking for teachers who 'vent,' there are plenty of them. But we don't vent anymore. It's gone beyond that."

JIM GRUNBAUM AND SAM STERN
elementary school teachers
New York, New York

Why Fight It?

Jim Grunbaum and Sam Stern are pals. Between them, they have nearly 40 years experience as elementary school teachers in Harlem, the South Bronx, and upper Manhattan—too many years, both said, "to vent."

They did not get excited when they talked about school corruption, violence, drugs, low student achievement, or any other aspect of inner-city school life. If Manuel Montalvo was emotional, then Jim Grunbaum and Sam Stern were both quite flat.

I spoke to them on different days but found it hard to tell them apart. They are very alike, and their attitude—whether you want to call it laconic, realistic, or perhaps something more negative—makes them virtual doubles.

They had both become teachers more or less by default. Grunbaum started out as a science teacher to avoid the draft, and Stern, who called himself an average college student, said he lacked direction and so did what his father suggested—become a teacher.

Neither thought it worthwhile to get excited about the poor performance of their students. Jim told me he had undergone an est transformation.

"Five years ago," he said, "I realized that the kids are the kids. They

124

haven't changed. Everybody always complained, 'It isn't like it was; it's this; it's that'—all complaints. And I said that the kids are the kids, the school is the school. Why fight it?

"If you take an attitude that it should be different," Grunbaum explained, "you are just going to be unhappy. The assumption is that the parent should be, the kids should be, it should be the way I want it to be—this is the attitude, and that attitude is irrelevant and without meaning. It is what it is."

His friend Sam Stern felt the same way. When I pressed him, Stern said, "I used to get excited, but now I just accept it as a way of life."

Both Sam and Jim showed some life when they spoke about corrupt school boards or the unions; and both, it seemed to me, had learned how to make the system work for them. They knew and were very open about how to collect every possible dollar from the system.

They have perhaps 15 years to go before retirement, and both will see it through. For Jim Grunbaum, who currently teaches in a Harlem school for the gifted and talented, his situation is a welcome change from most of the inner-city schools he has taught in during the past 19 years. Jim began by telling me that "teachers teach. Kids learn. That's nonsense. Doesn't work."

Why not?

Learning is active. It's not passive. Kids are just along for the ride and think if they show up, they are going to be educated. That's not true. Education goes beyond the classroom. Education needs reinforcement at home. The kids who are ignored—like they are supposed to know what is right from the day they are born—kids who are never spoken to, who are just sent away and not dealt with, are going to be at a great disadvantage.

Are you saying you have largely taught the kids who are ignored?

Yes, in upper Manhattan. These kids have tremendous problems. The last couple of years I've had students whose parents were my students.

How are these kids doing?

They get to a level, and then they start acting out. Some of them barely get by, and there are the kids who are so thoroughly afraid, they act out to protect themselves.

Afraid of what?

Of the other kids. It is all posturing. Everyone wants to prove they are tough, or they get stepped on. Unless the teacher dispels that fear, sets up an environment for learning, nothing happens. Outside the classroom the kid goes home, and he needs a place to do homework. Is there anybody going to tell him he has to read a half hour a night? Or say, "You are doing poorly in a subject. How can we help?" Parents don't know. A lot are new immigrants coming from a poor rural economy like Puerto Rico, the Dominican Republic, Latin America. They don't even speak the language. Their kids speak some English but think in a Spanish syntax. They are going through a translation process in order to carry out the schoolwork.

It is a total effort. Learning does not go on in the classroom from nine to three. That's not it. It's the total picture—the homes where parents speak no English and don't know how to help the children. That is a social issue that nobody is going to address. I mean, how are you going to address it?

Then why aren't schools doing more to involve parents?

They are, but some of the parents have their own political agendas. It is a power struggle, and the education of children is secondary. I don't even know what the parents want. They talk about the power struggle and having a say, but I don't know whether it is an attempt to buy into the money, which has happened. And then, again, some are making trouble just to make trouble.

Buying into what money?

When the New York City schools were decentralized, the power went to the local school boards. They run the schools and the neighborhoods. You have patronage, paybacks and buyoffs. Maybe a parent will get a job in the district as a teacher aide, or he'll do somebody a favor, and his kid will be placed in the school of his choice. Also, parents get elected to the school board. The board channels money out of the schools. Who knows where that money finds its way? An oak school table shows up in somebody's dining room, a so-called plumber gets the contract to retile the bathrooms. There is corruption there too.

There are some parents who do not line their own pockets. They are truly interested, but there are not enough of them. The poorer the district, the less parents are involved. They just try to hold on.

Ninety, ninety-five percent of my kids were just very nice kids—below grade level for the most part. Maybe 3 to 4 percent are real troublemakers, and they can cause a lot of trouble. Some of them are victims who need help, but the social services are not provided. School cannot do it. I'd be in the district office and say to them, "This kid is crazy. He needs psychiatric care." The administrators would agree, but there are just so many things you can do.

The teachers who survive in New York are good. Some are good disciplinarians and good teachers as well. Sometimes that is the mark of a good teacher—that the person is a good disciplinarian.

[I cannot tell if he is serious, but as he continues, I realize that for all his cynicism, Grunbaum has thought about what makes a good teacher and judges himself rather severely.]

I've run the gamut. I was recognized by my peers as being very good. Then at one point I looked back and asked, "Why is it that I'm good? I can see I'm not getting across a lot of stuff to these kids."

Am I a good teacher? Or am I standing up here, with the kids sitting quietly, and going through some motions—all doing work. I think in my Regents classes I was good. But was I effective in my other classes? Was I a good teacher or just a good disciplinarian? In these self-evaluation sheets that the schools distribute, when I thought I'd become more liberal, more understanding, I'd fill them out and find out that I was "ruthless" and "dictatorial."

When there are 35 kids in a class, you're going to lose some. The back row—they're gone.

But some students learn?

I used to call my district "Home of the free, land of the stupid," but that was kind of a joke. I spent a year at the district office and saw that some schools do work. You go into them, and someone is in control; you know that there are things going on, you see kids who are involved and teachers who are teaching. The teachers are really moving forward, and they're making progress. Is it the greatest progress in the world? No. Last year our district [Six] showed the greatest progress of any district in the city. Considering that it was still the bottom district in the city...

Still, is it enough? What made you become a teacher?

Vietnam. When I was finishing my degree, my lottery number was low. I thought, I'll go into teaching, and I'll see; I can always get out of it. After the first three days I said, I will finish this year and I will not come back. The kids had my mind. Definitely, they had my mind. I was in shell shock.

How did they have your mind?

I'd sit in my car and stare straight ahead, my mouth open. Here I was, 20 years old, and they were 13, 14. How was it that a group of 13-year-olds could possess me like that? I was just in shell shock. I took over a classroom from a very strong, experienced teacher. He had quit, and I came in knowing nothing. There were a lot of very hostile kids. I didn't know how to control them; they went off on their own.

It takes three years to make a teacher, I think: one year to learn the kids, one year to learn the curriculum, and one year to put it all together. The probation period before tenure is three, maybe five years–I've forgotten. But probation doesn't mean anything; being tenured is almost automatic.

I'm not sure I understand why you decided to remain in the classroom once you saw what it was like.

I started to make certain investments in things, and I said, "All right, I'm here." I bought a condominium. I was making these investments, assuming the salary level would be at a certain point. I'm not sorry. I was for a while, but I'm not now.

What are the rewards and frustrations of your job?

The kids are great. I have a lot of fun. I laugh a lot; they laugh. We see progress. Frustrations? The total resources are not there. The school I'm in needs work.

But being a magnet school for the gifted and talented makes a difference. It's a much more relaxed atmosphere. The kids have problems, but they're motivated. They have a good attitude. The parents' association meeting was very well attended–maybe it's the parents. And the school is right in the middle of Harlem. The kids do have a tough environment–it's the drug capital of the world up there.

In my last school there was crack–that's a bad thing. Kids on crack can be totally dysfunctional–and dangerous. Fortunately I didn't have to deal with it directly. It just gets passed off: the kid gets bounced on from school to school; he's just moved around, and nothing is really done. He needs institutional care but will not get it.

Sounds terrible.

It is. One of the reasons I couldn't go back to my other school was that I couldn't stand the negativity anymore. Even some of my closest friends, people I've known 20 years–all I heard from them was constant complaining, moaning, groaning. I just couldn't take it.

So why don't they get out?

Good question. After some years you get locked in. At this age am I going to get out of the school system and make the same money? No, it's a financial consideration.

You don't feel underpaid?

Not now. Underpaid is if you don't have enough money to do what you want to do.

A lot of teachers seem angry about the lack of acknowledgment.

I would agree that there's not enough recognition, and it bothers me. Some of it is the teachers' own fault. If you bad-mouth it and say this job stinks, who is going to respect it? And I'm guilty of doing that. You don't hear lawyers talking that way–or doctors.

Also, there's a whole other ballgame. The custodial function of the school has become so great as to equal the educational function. No one has addressed the fact that we should separate the educational function from the custodial function. Schools are open now from seven in the morning to seven at night. The kids are there, they come in; they are cared for in the morning, they have breakfast, they go to school, and then there is a latchkey program till six at night. They have these programs all day long. [The latchkey program is designed for children of working parents. The school functions as a safe place for children to be after school, and activities, such as sports and arts and crafts, are offered to them. These programs are not limited to the cities, but are more and more prevalent in suburban schools as well.]

But isn't that better than the street?

Certainly, certainly it is better than the street. However, there's a lot of money coming out of the budget, and they are doing all this custodial work. Then there's the food—they are feeding kids three meals a day.

But that's a different budget.

Look, there is only one pot. What's the difference where it comes from? There is not a separate facility to care for the kids and for the schools. It has all become one. These schools will never close for snow. The custodial function is too important.

No snow days in New York City?

The last day we were closed for weather was the threat of the hurricane. I have gone into work because I knew that in a school of 130 to 140 teachers 60 could be out; so I knew I could pick up some extra classes and make extra money.

You mean you get paid according to how many kids you're watching?

No. Your program says you are supposed to have so many classes. Anything extra they pay you for. I have a class; then I'm supposed to be relieved. I know I can come in and pick up a hundred dollars a day sometimes. If I can make an extra hundred dollars a day, it pays to come in. It's not necessarily a good situation though; when you have 60 people out, you don't have enough people to cover the school.

Are there many male teachers in your current school?

The school is only grades four through eight, and there are not that many men. I don't know the percentages. What I do lack is the camaraderie. I can talk to the women—have no problem with that. Even in the district office there were only four men, and one was the superintendent; you couldn't talk to him. I said to him at a meeting once, "It's all women." He said, "We'll fix it. You're fired." That was his idea of a joke. There are no men. Who am I going to talk sports with? I found one, an administrative assistant, and I'd come in Monday morning and say "How 'bout those Giants? All right."

What would you say are the three biggest issues facing education today?

Money, money, and money.

Money, certainly, is a problem. We need money for more teachers and smaller classes. School buildings need maintenance and repair. Facilities and equipment are inadequate. Social services as well as health services are not there, though they have made a start. There is some movement, but in my district we don't have a school board. Once a new board comes in, probably everything will grind to a halt as the members begin to exert their power. There are buyouts–principalships are bought. This is true absolutely. Can I prove it? No. Do I know it has happened? Absolutely. The rumors and the evidence are very strong.

But rumors–

It's more than that. Knowing the situation, the way it is, you know that it's true. I know it's true. I have seen things that convince me that it is true.

Could you give an example?

I could, but I wouldn't. I'd rather not.

In my district the school board was removed because it was corrupt.

Then that is public record.

It was stated that the school board was removed because it was ineffective and highly political. They couldn't prove it was corrupt. Now there is a trusteeship with three people from Central [District]. [School Board Six was dismissed in March 1987 by then –NYC Schools Chancellor Nathan Quionones.]

Now those three people run the district. Teachers should have more say in all facets–hiring, decision making.

Is teaching better now than it was 15 years ago?

Teaching is much better now.

The kids are better now?

No, it is me that has changed. I don't expect much, and I just accept that it is what it is.

"It's not worth it. I do not want to get upset."

SAM STERN

Sam Stern is in his early 40s. He has taught elementary school for 17 years. All told he has been in three schools, all of them located in the South Bronx, where he grew up. His neighborhood was once white, largely Jewish; it is now black and Hispanic. He doesn't believe anything internal—or any amount of money—can change the schools in the South Bronx. The kids here are "consumed" by the streets, and their parents "are not working, not striving the way my parents did and I did."

He characterized his students as "generally far behind the country in terms of reading skills, math skills, social skills." I asked him why.

Immigrants who came to this country were behind at first and had to catch up. For the Hispanics that is partly true. For the blacks I think it is a combination of things: many have come up from the South in the last 30, 40 years, and I almost believe they have been held down by liberal policies in the past—there is a lack of incentive to enter the mainstream. The welfare system has not encouraged people to become part of the mainstream economically; people work the system.

Why would that affect a little kid? Why wouldn't a little kid want to learn?

Because they have to deal with all the other problems in the area: parents who are alcoholic drug abusers, parents who will beat each other and who consequently will beat their own children. They see the norm as being filth in the streets; the homes—I've been in the homes, and there is garbage all over the place. Not all—there are some of them who keep very nice houses. But you go into the houses, in the hallways, and there is the stench of urine. You walk down the streets, and they are dirty and dangerous.

In my class most kids come up anywhere from a year to three years. But then what happens next year? I really believe that no matter how good and nice they are, the kids are going to regress. I know some of the nicest kids who are in jail for murder. I believe the streets consume them.

All right. Then what can be done?

I have a simplistic answer, but no one seems to want to hear it. Just drop ADC–Aid to Dependent Children. In other words, let it be known that these girls cannot have children at 14, 15 and have the government take care of them, give them the apartment, food, health care.

Is there anything that schools can do internally?

I really believe that the streets are much stronger than the schools can ever be.

Is race an issue?

Not now. It was 15, 17 years ago when the blacks and Hispanics made a big push to get the white administrators in the district out. As soon as the whites left, and they left in droves around 1971–from principalships, district offices–the blacks and Hispanics were at each other's throats for the power.

They still are. They all say, "This is for the children," but it is not. It is a power base that district politicians try to grab; and the school-board members wield a tremendous amount of power now because they have divided it up in terms of principals, assistant principals, extra jobs. For example, I need an extra job; so I have one that pays me $25 an hour, fairly good money, and I make an extra $500, $600 a month. And in order for me to really keep that job, here's what happens. The school-board member who is in charge of that program–it's called a "continuing education pro-gram"–will send me invitations to various functions: "You are cor-dially invited to a Christmas party in honor of so-and-so (I don't want to use the name). Recommended donation–$45." And you walk in the door there, and there is a big jar, and you stuff $45 in the jar. And you are entitled to one drink; so it doesn't cost him much.

Who's the money for?

The school-board member.

Him personally?

I don't ask that many questions; I have to do this two, three times a year, and since I'm making an extra $3,000 or $4,000 dollars from October to May...

Here's a cute story: it used to be that to become a principal, you took the credits, got certified, and were placed on the board of education's list. No more. You still have to pass the test, and you are still on a list; but appointments are now up to the school board, and they can do what they want.

The school board works like the godfather. Each has a number of schools. The godfather of my school has our school and maybe four or five others in the district. When the principal needs to get more funds or something, he goes to this board member, the godfather. A couple of years ago, supposedly in this district, three or four black teachers were vying for a principal's job, and out of nowhere the board member brought in this white Jewish guy to be principal. The rumor went around that he had paid the school-board member $12,000 for the job—well worth it because principals get about $65,000. [Later, when Sam's friend Jim shows up, they make a joke about this "power base" that I don't understand, and Jim concurs: "There are sellouts, where jobs are sold."]

I used to have my problems with administrators. I resented them, thought they were stupid.

Were they stupid?

A lot of them were stupid, but if I had shut my mouth, I would have done better.

In my wife's school, they just appointed this guy A.P. [assistant principal]. And he got up the first day of school in front of the board members and said, "You know, we are going to turn this school around, we are going to work together and turn this school around." So everybody looked at each other thinking, This guy is full of shit.

Then, as it turned out, we were at a dinner gathering with another principal and some teachers, and my wife mentioned this new A.P. His name is _____ and he is really terrible," she said. They all cracked up. "He used to be at our school," they said, "and he always did the minimum required, never anything extra. Unless it was written in the contract, he would not take a step up the stairs." And now he is asking teachers for detailed lesson plans, things he never did. And this is fairly typical.

[Sam's story brings to mind what happened when Victor Herbert, the new head of NYC's high school division, addressed all the principals before the start of the school year in 1988. He, too, said that he thought the year would be different. After a brief pause everyone in the audience laughed. I mention this incident to Sam, who has many more stories about administrators to relate.]

Another principal at the dinner gathering had retired. Very nice guy—whatever you asked him the answer was yes. You have a problem? "Sure." He gave one teacher permission to leave, and she came in to ask me to cover her class. She said she had to go home and do the shopping [laughs]. This man thought of himself as a great liberal. He cared about the children and wanted to protect them; but in protecting them, he was actually keeping them down. He talked about these poor people, how they were—what do you call it?

Deprived?

Right, deprived—and how they had no opportunities, how we had to love them, and so on. But we don't have to love them; we have to give them the skills so that they can go out there and join society. You know, guys like this principal, they don't give a kid a sense of responsibility. A kid could be terrible, he could pull a knife on another kid, and an hour later you see the kid come out of the principal's office, the principal will be patting the kid's shoulder. Maybe the kid picked up a piece of paper, and the principal is giving a certificate for the "War on Waste." The kid pulled a knife on someone, and he's getting a certificate. You've got to protect the other kids, the good kids, and suspend him.

And protect the teachers. I know this one teacher who quit after her car was vandalized eight, ten times. Everyone knew this one kid didn't like it when someone made him do things like homework. He would tell other kids, "We are going to get the teacher's car." What happened? Every time this took place the principal would come out with his hand on the kid's shoulder. The teacher quit; she felt she was being abused, and she quit. She no longer teaches. Now she sells books to schools.

What keeps you at it?

The money isn't that bad at this point, though I feel we have been screwed by the union. In 15 more years I'll be able to retire with—the way I'm planning it—at least my full salary. And if that gets eroded by the time I'm 67, 12 years later, Social Security should kick in and kick it back up. Also, we get many benefits—though the health coverage isn't great—and I love the time off. I like leisure time even if I'm not doing very much, and the school day goes very fast. I enjoy being in the classroom; I like the kids. All those things add up. It's very difficult—

You don't feel frustrated that the kids are not learning very much?

No, I've given up on that. Some do; some don't. I give it my best. I hold the kids responsible for homework, for keeping the room clean, keeping themselves out of trouble, and I'm responsible for giving them the best education they can get. So I enjoy it, and they seem to enjoy it. We don't have any kind of discipline problems.

I know a woman who is an excellent teacher, you can tell. Her career has spanned 40 years now, and she thinks that if in a class of 35, 5 get the point or stay interested that's pretty good. Now I ask the kids, "Who understood what I just said?" and maybe half—16 or 17—raise their hands.

To please you perhaps.

No, if they don't understand, they don't even hear me, they are day-dreaming.

You said you were screwed by the union?

I'm not as bitter as I used to be. I was chapter chairman in 1975 when the city realized it had a big fiscal problem. There were going to be 2,000 teachers laid off, and we were up for a new contract.

They called a meeting at a big auditorium and [AFT president] Shanker gets up in front of the chapter chairpeople, about a thousand of us (the rest of the union was in Madison Square Garden waiting for Shanker to come out), and he says, "Listen, the city is going to rehire the 2,000 teachers that were laid off, and we are not getting anything else. No raises. Times are very very tough for the union."

And people were very upset because under the Taylor Law they were losing two days' pay for every day that they were out. So he tells us all this, that we are getting nothing, that we are being pulled back to two preparation periods a week instead of five, and that those two preparation periods will be retained by letting kids out early. [Usually, preparation periods are carved out of the regular school day. They are meant to give the teacher some time off from the classroom in order to work on lessons and other school-related matters.]

So basically we are getting nothing and giving up a lot, and Shanker says, "Are there any questions?" A woman raised her hand–I am sure to this day that she was a plant–and said, "Al, I don't understand why we should accept this. But I love you and I trust you, and I'll follow you into *hell* if you want me to. [Sam is actually animated here, the one time in the interview he will show that kind of energy.] And all of a sudden everybody around me gets up and cheers–"Yay!"–and claps like this man was God or something. He's just told us that we are getting sex Greek-style, and everyone is up and cheering. So Al says, "Take this message back to your people in the Garden, and let's move on from here."

A week later they laid off another 2,000 teachers. That was 4,000 layoffs all told, and the union never said anything. I should have seen it coming: if they are giving up preparation periods and letting kids out early, that's even less teachers they need. Classes at that point went to 40, 45 students.

What is class size now? Have the schools changed much since 1975?

They are the same. Maybe there is more of a feeling of accomplishing things now. One thing the city has done that is really excellent is reduce class size in the lower grades. Kindergarten through second, third grade is supposed to be capped at 25. (There are ways to get around it though. The district is supposed to "average" 25 per class.) And certainly, having fewer children in the classroom makes it physically easier. I once timed how much individual attention each kid in my class got, and it turned out that the average kid in my class got about 15 seconds of personal attention a day.

Do you remember certain kids?

A few have made it. One, a nice kid, never gave me any trouble, did his work. The biggest trouble he was ever in was maybe telling a joke and smiling. When he was fifteen, he shot six people. He was a black kid, and he shot six Chinese. Had them lie down, and then he robbed them and shot them.

I had another kid named Jesus who I was sure would be consumed by the streets. Way below grade level. Jesus went on to open his own auto-body shop, and he's now making six times what I do a year.

A girl came back last year. She was pregnant, and I knew she was in lots of trouble. But she told me that she had her life together now and she was off drugs. She had met an Italian guy, and he loved her very much. They were buying a house in Spring Valley, the whole American dream, and she asked me to come to her wedding. So I looked up her address and called her aunt's house. "Where's Rosemary?" I asked. And the aunt said, "I don't know. She is crashing somewhere." So I said, "What happened to the guy?" The aunt wanted to know what guy, and when I explained, she said that Rosemary had just made the whole thing up.

Another girl I had—just the best girl I ever had, beautiful, very smart. One day in April her brother comes to school and says, "Raquel won't be here. She had to go to Puerto Rico. Her mother was murdered over the weekend."

The girl came back to visit me a few years later. She was on drugs.

It's discouraging, it really is. The best kids get consumed by the streets.

There is a message here. I can't think of these things.

Do you have contact with the parents?

No.

Have you tried?

Parents have their own problems. They can't straighten themselves out. It's just repetition—generation after generation after generation. It's the kids who, if they don't get something immediately, give up.

But if you could involve the parents and break the cycle?

I don't believe that. The parents will lie to you as much as the kids do. In general they are ill-prepared to face the world. They are on drugs or are rowdy; and if a kid is 14 and gets pregnant, it's no big deal. I have the kids of my former kids in classes now.

Talk-show question: What do you think are the three biggest issues facing education today?

I don't think there are issues facing education. There are issues facing society. Get people off welfare; don't make it easy for people. Challenge them; don't let them think they are going to get it for free. There are no easy answers, and you have this tremendous problem where you have parents who don't know what the right thing is to do themselves.

Let's say you have all the money in the world to put into education. Then what could you do?

I don't think all the money would make a difference.

New bright classrooms with 10 kids in a room, great teachers, counselors?

I do not think it would make a difference.

What do you think about merit pay?

The concept is great, but who decides who is an excellent teacher? The principal who is getting laid by an incompetent teacher? Or someone who buddies up to the school board?

What is your school like physically?

The schools have been terribly run down in the past 20 years, especially with the fiscal crisis in New York City. Tremendous problems—windows would be broken, doors, locks, and you couldn't get them fixed. The roof in my other school leaked terribly for years. On the fifth floor you would always have floods in your room. You'd come into some rooms, and the ceiling would be buckled three or four feet. You'd tell the administrator, and he'd say, "Okay, just make sure nobody sits underneath there." [Here, as in the union story, Stern is animated. In fact, at this point there is a bizarre note of hilarity about our discussion.]

With the rains, the ceiling would collapse. You'd move everything away from that spot, and it would dry up and be okay until the next time.

You'd finally get a contractor in—they were working on low bids —to do a tile job in the bathroom. A classic example: tiles should be lined up in rows, right? Well, these tiles curved, went sideways. You'd be in the bathroom washing your hands, and these tiles would just pop off the walls.

My school now was built in 1859, and sections have been added on since. No one can ever find their way; people get lost there. I work in what they call "the penthouse." It is the attic. It has no working windows—one window is just an opening (I hope it gets replaced before winter), one doesn't open, and two are boarded up. But at least I have windows; the other sixth-grade teacher's room only has one window—inoperable—to begin with. [Stern narrates a few more stories about New York's dilapidated schools and then shifts back to the poor administrators he has encountered.]

I was saying that in my last school I was fairly disrespectful of my principal and assistant principal. I considered them idiots. What cured me of showing them how I felt was the last time my car was stolen—my car was stolen three times in 10 years, plus all the break-ins. I told my principal that I wanted to be allowed to park in the school yard. There are some principals who do allow that even though it is supposedly against the rules. But this man essentially told me that he didn't drive and he didn't care, and I told him to f— himself. That was just as the school year ended.

When I walked into school the next fall, a woman teacher who had also been on his nerves and I were plopped into the gymnasium—they didn't have enough classrooms. And all we had were some movable blackboards, benches from woodworking shop. Acoustics were terrible. Her class went crazy, and then my class went crazy because her class did. Just terrible conditions. I realized how crazy all this was, and I just shut my mouth. The next thing I knew, I was made the science coordinator because I had not opened my mouth for six months.

So if you are a good old boy...and, truthfully, they need male teachers. They need people who can do things like lunch duty. That is another thing I did last year [Sam has told me, as have others, that his previous year's special assignment as "reading specialist" actually meant that he was the principal's private gofer. When not driving the principal to meetings, he'd "get lost in the bathroom and smoke a cigar. Then there was lunch duty, breakfast duty, gym, and some other crappy jobs—chauffeuring, testing, ordering supplies."]

You tell me that kids don't learn much, cars get vandalized three or four times a week, classrooms have no windows, jobs are bought, and you are very cool about it.

I used to get excited about it, but now I just accept it as a fact of life. I realize that there are innumerable break-ins and thefts. You get insurance coverage, and that's it. It's not worth it. I don't want to get upset.

Postscript

On Power, Politics, and School Boards

Other New York teachers also spoke about corrupt school boards who use their schools as power bases; and even though it is very clear that schools are not ivory towers, I was surprised to hear that they are sometimes mired in the mud.

That rapidly changed when a New York City school-board scandal erupted on the front pages of local newspapers in the late fall of 1988. It all started when a Bronx principal was arrested near his apartment for allegedly buying two vials of crack. Soon after that his eight-member school board—one of thirty-two local boards that run NYC's elementary and middle schools, choosing principals, allocating money, and ruling on educational policy—was suspended. Charges included drug use, theft of school equipment, sexual harassment of teachers, extortion of money from principals and teachers, and—as Stern had said—the use of schools as political clubs.

This particular school board, District 9 in the Bronx, had charge of 34 schools and 26,000 children. Like most city school boards, some of its members were politicians. Now there is a movement to bar political leaders from serving on school boards and to tighten financial-disclosure requirements.

Reforms to tighten controls over local school boards have an ironic side. New York's school boards were created in 1970 in order to give more control to neighborhoods. But decentralization did not empower communities so much as it did school-board members—with often questionable results.

Nor is the problem limited to New York. Increasingly, school boards—long ignored in the school-reform movement—are coming under scrutiny. While corruption is not an issue for many of them (especially in the suburbs), it is still widely perceived that the more than 15,000 school boards nationwide need help with the intricate problems they face.

Calling attention to these problems and highlighting the importance of school boards are many recent events. Among them is the decision in Illinois to abolish Chicago's Central Board of Education for the city's 420,000 pupils. In each of Chicago's 594 schools, control will be turned over to committees of parents and school officials. In New Jersey what was cited as "grave instances of patronage and misuse of funds led state officials to take over part of the control of the Jersey City school system. Now the state controls all contracts over $5,000 and all personnel decisions. And in Massachusetts the Chelsea School Committee has asked Boston University to help it run its poorly rated system of 3,300 students—a direct appeal for university help on an unusually large scale.

> "Building self-confidence and learning to
> take risks are what schools should be about.
> Once kids have learned how to take risks,
> then I think they are pretty set in life. But
> the big problem is that we don't let them."
>
> RICHARD STERNBERG
> elementary school teacher
> *New York, New York*

Taking Risks

After 19 years Richard Sternberg is still encouraging kids to take risks.
But he hasn't many illusions left about New York City's public schools. He
thinks that they are managed by the wrong people and haven't the resources needed to do a good job. Also, like many others, he has seen decentralization turn into a scramble for power that has shortchanged students
even more.

Sternberg may soon leave the city system. Nineteen years on an ob-
stacle course is a long time. If he does, it will be to teach elsewhere under
"better conditions."

Better conditions—not money. Like many other dedicated teachers,
Richard Sternberg did not enter teaching for money, and it isn't money
per se that will drive him out.

He said he believed in doing work you enjoy. For him that means
teaching. His first schools were in his home state of Michigan, and since
then he has taught in New York City. When we first talked, he was teaching on Manhattan's East Side and had just begun the year with a class of
fourth-grade children that he had also taught two years previously:

I have the same group of kids that I had when they were in second grade. I just loved that class. Then they increased the size and gave me all the behavioral problems, the kids who have just been pushed along. So here I have these bright, sensitive kids and these disturbed kids who need help. If I were a parent, would I pull my kid out of this class fast!

I can't be of any real help to the disturbed kids, and all I have been doing so far is disciplining.

I know how to do it. I spent one year in Harlem, and I can take the toughest kids and make them behave. But that's not what I want to do.

You went to the principal?

"Oh, you can do it. You're wonderful," she said. She's not going to do anything about it. There isn't much she can do.

I will have to be extraordinarily tough for the next two weeks and do things I haven't done in years. I feel sorry for the other kids, I really do. But I haven't a choice. I'll track the parents down, even if I have to call them in the middle of the night. Either they'll pull their kids out of my class, or they'll be so sick of hearing from me that they will make their kids behave.

You have a lot of contact with parents?

Yes. Either they respond because they are so inconvenienced or so embarrassed that they have to get rid of me, or they are so thankful, they will do anything I ask. Often they don't understand what is going on or don't believe me. Then I say, "Come in and see it for yourself." I had a parent who came in for two weeks. I told her to come anytime, don't make an appointment. After she'd sat in class for those weeks, she was ready to kill her kid.

What do you mean you can "make" a fourth-grade class behave? What if they are disturbed or don't want to?

You set up routines. You don't do anything until that first routine is followed. If it takes all day to go up the stairs, you spend all day. It reaches a point that is extreme and absurd, but I know that until routine things are done without conflict, nothing will be done. I hate it, but if you do this for three, four weeks, then the next thirty-four weeks will be far better.

What kind of mix of children do you have at P.S. 59?

We have open enrollment and get kids from the neighborhood,

which is upper-middle class, and kids on welfare who are bused in from a Bronx project. There are also diplomats' kids [many foreign embassies are located in the area] and the children of neighborhood supers and janitors.

Is your school considered a good school?

By whom? I don't consider it a good school. There aren't any good schools in NYC [New York City].

The classes are too large, and the teachers are fighting each other just to get materials. I don't have enough books for every kid in my room. There isn't adequate preparation time. I'm very good at teaching science–I've done it for the district. But you can't teach science if there are no materials and no time to prepare.

The rooms are too small–kids shouldn't have to sit in such rooms. Some people can sit at desks for six, seven hours, but small children can't.

Even the best schools in Manhattan are built like prisons. You walk into these small rooms that are awful, ugly.

I think that schools should be beautiful places. The first place I taught, a school in Michigan, was gorgeous. Each class had its own door to the playground. Kids just came in; they never lined up.

Then I came here and asked to teach in Harlem. I thought it was important to do that. That school was shocking–when you walk into these small rooms built like cells, what does it say to people about where they are? In Harlem, I was told that if I made it up the stairs, I had it made. It took me about an hour and a half.

Why?

The kids were all fighting. First of all, you don't build schools where kids have to climb up five flights of stairs. No kid should have to climb up five flights of stairs. And if you have kids with the potential for conflict, you ought to know what will happen at the back of a line when thirty kids are climbing five flights of stairs. Elementary logic. But NYC doesn't work that way. NYC asks, "What works for the budget?"

I was given the 14 worst fourth graders–typical for a new teacher. (It happened again this year because I had been out [taken time off]. Then you push and lobby and fight for what you need.) And we were in the middle of the great decentralization conflict.

Remember decentralization? It became in part a black-Jewish conflict. In my school a black West Indian replaced a Jewish principal, and all over there were fights for power. I thought decentralization was a good thing then, and I didn't realize that we'd end up with a black district, a Puerto Rican district—all these different power groups making trades.

When a strike was called, I didn't go out. I decided I had to teach, not politicize. Anyway, the new principal hated me, and the other teachers didn't trust me. When the year ended, even though they gave me rave reviews, I was fired because they said I would not fit into the new program. Parents started to fight for me, but I knew the principal would be on me all year, and I left.

But while I was there, I spent a lot of time with the parents. I talked to them and knew that sometimes when I asked them to help me get their kids to behave, they might brutalize their kids. But I thought, The kids need some order in their life and in the class. And so I went up into those tenements. Some of them were terrible, and the parents *were* brutal to the kids. But after a few visits the kids behaved, and they learned something. As a result, I became a demonstration teacher and helped train other teachers about some classroom basics.

When I came here, I thought it was the worst system in the world and that teachers didn't have a clue what to do. The teachers were used to ethnics who were competitive and succeeded—not because the system is good, but because of the kids themselves. That is still going on—at special schools like Stuyvesant or the Bronx High School of Science. You could put an idiot in front of those Jewish and Asian kids who've been tested as very bright, and they'd still learn.

I'm disturbed because here is a tale of a teacher in Harlem who reached parents and apparently made a difference. Then you left after a year.

Yes, but I'd learned that what counts in NYC is how much power you can accumulate. That's what the principal cares about. Even the mayor: the mayor doesn't care how good an education kids get; he cares about how good it looks for votes.

Where I am now has one of the best staffs I have seen. We got rid of all the bad teachers—one died, one retired, one they put in the computer room where she only sees kids once a week. It's a great staff—even the teachers in my school whose own kids go to private school feel our staff is far superior to that of any private school's. What a shame it is that these kids are not getting the education they deserve.

Why?

Because classrooms are small and ugly, and the classes are far too large. Because there are no materials. The teachers resent the principal, and also they resent how if you are really incompetent, you can get an out-of-classroom job—like running the open library or the computer room.

It's hard to fire incompetents. The principals have to supervise teachers during their first three years—the time allotted to get rid of the incompetents—and really see what is going on. But they don't. The principals have all this paperwork, and they've gotten out of the classroom because they hate to teach. I think it's a terrific idea to say you can't be a principal unless you've taught all grade levels, and even after becoming a principal, you should have to go back in the classroom some of the time.

Also, you know, some principals become principals because they like authority.

And teachers?

Yes, some. I find authority, control, a difficult issue. Early on I had a class that I talked to a lot about independence and the need to question. By the end of the year they were so good at questioning that when I asked them to be quiet so that I could fill out the records, they said they didn't see why they should be quiet just because I had all this busywork to do!

I think they had learned an important lesson—one that schools rarely teach. We run the show, and as we all know, schools are terrified of any threat to their authority.

The state has these ideas about what kids should learn. But that is not the issue. What are we really teaching them?

Half the time education amounts to being socialized in very traditional ways. We teach kids to conform, and they learn how *not* to take a stand.

We need to set up situations in which kids take some risks. We should be teaching them to take stands and to question. You don't like something, say, the lunch program? Then what would you do about it?

John Holt says the schools are set up to make children stupid.

That's true. There are all kinds of programs in schools to make kids fail. For instance, there is this kid in my class who virtually cannot read a word. Rather than talk to the parents and figure out the problem, the schools establish a program. For two years they say we can't expect anything because he is from a non-English-speaking background—which is nonsense. I've seen kids learn to speak English in three months.

Then they get him in a program with a few other kids, some form of individual tutoring for 40 minutes a day. But the rest of the time he is in the class of 30 and doesn't understand. He moves very slowly, but they keep pushing him along. By the time he is 11, 12, he has been in many so-called programs. He has been pushed along and is so frustrated that he drops out of school. He fails because the programs are a charade, a way to move him along. He progresses a little, but he is always in a group, always behind everybody, and always feels second rate. Those are the kids who drop out.

Not that self-respect is enough. Self-respect and this new buzz word *empowerment* are not enough. That is a cop-out. If you have not learned anything, you are not going anywhere. If you don't learn to read and write, you cannot have self-respect.

[Pauses] I could go on and on. Actually, even the union makes some of these points. And remember I was the scab in Harlem. The union wants teachers to have more power over decision making, and that is crucial—I've seen how awful administrators can be, whether they are laissez-faire or autocratic. Teachers should elect their principals, and by and large, teachers should run their schools.

It's true that unions protect some incompetent teachers. But if teachers had more decision-making power, they'd force the incompetents out. Teachers can make it miserable for an incompetent.

Have you seen many new teachers?

I was on the board of examiners for NYC teachers. The principals did not want to fail them, but I wanted to fail almost all of the candidates we examined. Their English was awful, virtually illiterate. Their grasp of materials was inadequate; even their methodological grasp was weak—though you can teach them that. Often, I felt it became a racial issue; principals would try to pass them, to find reasons to pass them. Once you had decided on one person, then you couldn't very well change your standards. So the mediocre—and they were bad—came in.

Also, there is something called "charisma in teaching." There was one black guy who had terrific charisma, and his English was good. I would have taken a chance on him. He could be a good teacher. But they failed him for what they called his "poor data base." Another woman, with a "great data base"—and what I thought was a terrible teaching style—we passed.

My school has two Mount Holyoke graduates, some [University of] Michigan graduates—very few of us majored in education. Lots of us have subject-matter backgrounds. I think this education major is awful, and it's a bureaucracy set up to perpetuate itself.

Let's talk about males in elementary school.

When I began to teach, I think about 25 percent of all teachers in all grades were male. Now I think it is about 7 percent. There are very few male elementary school teachers, and sometimes you feel exploited. I used to be very good about moving heavy things; I wouldn't do that anymore. Then they often assign the worst classes to men because they think men can "handle" them; and that's why they put the men into the upper grades.

When I taught science, the deal I made was to teach kindergarten through sixth grade. I hated grades five and six, and I loved one and two. Men are not supposed to like the lower grades. I fact, I was programmed and thought it would be boring to teach the lower grades. Just the opposite is true. As a teaching assistant in a Western civilization course I found the students' questions boring. There was nothing profound or interesting about teaching college freshmen—they were not exciting or interesting or enthusiastic. But little kids—you get to see them grow and blossom, and it is just wonderful. Little kids are very honest and very funny and enthusiastic.

How does being a male teacher in the lower grades affect your social life?

Socially, I am a bad catch [laughs]. I go to a cocktail party, and someone says, "What do you do?" I say that I teach, and they think, Oh, my God, maybe he teaches at a university. And that means I am barely a possibility. Then I say that I teach in the lower grades, and you can see them thinking, Bad catch. They also think that most of the men who teach are gay, and I'm not sure that is true. In fact, most men will avoid teaching in the lower grades even if they want to in order to avoid being branded gay.

Some elementary school teachers are gay, and some are not. It shouldn't make a difference. Also, single men are the ones who can afford to teach. If you have a family, even if you like kids, you can't afford to do it.

Usually, parents are terrific about my being a male and a teacher in the lower grades.

How about society's view of teachers?

Americans do not value education, and they do not like or respect teachers. It used to bother me; it doesn't anymore. I just figure that Americans don't value education, and so we are going down the tubes. All the rhetoric I hear is rhetoric. We're told, for example, that the next two years are going to be the best years for education –the salaries are going up. Then we'll have a recession, and the first thing they'll cut is education spending. It will get worse. These things are cyclical.

England is in the same boat. Education for its poor is worse than it has ever been. Regardless of what anyone says, people have to be taxed to get a good educational system, and people are not going to be taxed.

It's very serious. Without well-educated people, democratic institutions cannot function well. What we'll have is an oligarchy. The few who are well educated will rule the many, who have no real education–just as you have in England right now.

We are becoming an oligarchy now, and people don't even know it. Formerly, when New York's population was made up of Italians, Jews, the Irish, people voted, and eventually politicians had to respond to them. But those groups have left, and the people who stayed do not vote. Politicians do not have to worry about responding to them–something they realized very quickly. The establishment does not respond to black and Puerto Rican educational needs. That's true throughout the U.S. but is magnified here. In Scarsdale [an affluent N.Y. suburb], where people understand why it is important to get an education, the kids are getting one. The parents run the show.

My view is bleak.

I have put in enough years that I can retire. In fact, I may retire and go to a suburb or a private school in order to have better conditions. Better conditions more than anything else. There isn't anyone who quits just because of the money. (I knew I'd be underpaid; this country is about money.)

You're saying that the educational system is going down the tubes; it's the haves and the have nots; the few will rule the many. Yet you might retire and teach in a private school. A vicious circle?

Right. It is very hard to stand up for what I philosophically believe in. If I had a kid, I'd look very carefully, but I would try to put the kid in public school.

I think what I would do if I were a parent is set up a foundation. Call it "public-private." You recruit parents who want their kids to go to public school, and you raise money so that you can hire extra help. I would like my kids to be in school with black and Puerto Rican kids, but not in a class with 32 kids. So what you do is set up a foundation and hire extra people for the public schools. It would cost, but so do private schools. It could be done.

So you are saying we should spend more money for education. But what about those rotten teachers you were interviewing for jobs? Is that who the foundation hires? Where do we find the teachers?

I think there are lots of women who still want to teach and men who would come back too. For women in particular, teaching is still appealing—it's terrific when you have kids. Of course, if we can change the attitude, men, too, might want to stay home with kids. I have a friend who is a physicist. He's going to teach and be home. And my dad is terrific with kids. He would be terrific in a day-care center. But "real men" don't teach, and so he is an engineer.

Do you eat quiche too?

[Laughs] I enjoy my life, and do what I can in the classroom. My thing about some teachers is that they don't have rich lives, and if they don't have rich lives, they don't have anything to bring to their school.

It's not that schools should be all "fun." But schools should help people select the life they want and one that is meaningful for them. Children should understand that some things are hard—not all things are fun—but that it is really important to do what you like to do. You should do in life what you enjoy.

"I really like teaching, but I think there is a lot more pressure put on teachers than society recognizes. To move every kid along at a steady pace is a lot to do. You have to guide each individual child, and all children do not learn in the same way—that is the biggest reality I've had to face."

JANINE HOPLEY
elementary school teacher
New York, New York

Each Child Learns in a Different Way

It sounds obvious enough—each child is different and learns in a different way. Yet when she student-taught, Janine Hopley found that often an entire class was asked to open their books, turn to the same page, and begin work. Now she wonders how many did not know what the lesson was about? How many did not learn?

Paying attention to each child is easier when there are fewer of them. At the Lenox School, where Hopley now teaches, there are about 15 children in a class, often with more than one teacher in the classroom. She has been at this private school for four years.

We met while she was working in a summer camp, the kind of job many teachers take in July and August. There was a terrible heat wave, and I was struck by Hopley's patience when faced with a roomful of five-year-olds who each had some urgent need for her attention. But when I remarked about it to her, it was clear she had not found the children at all difficult. She enjoyed the chance to work with kids who were younger than the ones she teaches during the school year.

Janine Hopley is in her 20s, one of the youngest teachers I interviewed. For her, teaching still feels new every day. She is absorbed by what she does, and by the fifteen second graders in her class. She says the

152

eight-year-olds "have pretty much mastered the basics. But they are still children. They have that awe of learning new things. Their eyes light up. When they become excited about something you were not sure would interest them, it is a great feeling. You know that what you are doing is reaching—and affecting—them."

Her experience as a teacher has been largely positive. For her, working in a private school has clearly made the difference:

I interned in a New York City public school, and it was one of the nicer ones. But I feel there is not as much parent involvement—or the wealth of materials and resources—in the public schools as there is in private schools. I feel fortunate with my children because I can do pretty much anything I want to do as long as it is consistent with the curriculum. There are fewer constraints: to set up a field trip, for example, is straightforward. [To do so in public school is apparently a tangle of red tape.]

Also, when compared to public schools, I think private schools have a lot more administrative and faculty cohesiveness. In public school I felt that we were each in our own room, and that was it. Whatever happens within your four walls is it. You follow the state-mandated curriculum, but there isn't any sharing of ideas, parent help, or teachers talking together.

Of course, a really dedicated teacher can give a quality education even without good resources. The woman I worked with in the public school was a very good teacher. She worked hard to give all 30 kids in the kindergarten class the basics.

But in public school class size is a problem. You have to spend a lot of time dealing with management issues—making sure everybody is sitting, standing—and if you're spending time on those things, then education has a tendency to slip.

There are only 15 in my class at Lenox, and it is a lot easier to manage 15 than 30. The children at Lenox also come from private nursery schools. What they learn in nursery school is probably more than I learned in kindergarten. They come to us ready to take right off and read. It's amazing: at five, the children have the skills of seven- or eight-year-olds. They are ready to go.

These kids start with many advantages.

They do. But in some ways a lot of privileged kids are like disadvantaged kids. Both are neglected but for different reasons. With disadvantaged kids, maybe they are from a broken home or their parents work two jobs. With privileged kids, the parents may have high-powered jobs and are not around. It comes up at conferences that the child will do things for the housekeeper that she wouldn't do for the parent. And the kids are materially spoiled.

What kind of relations do you have with parents?

Consistent ones. Each year we schedule two written reports and two conferences. There's also a "meet the teacher night" at the beginning of the year and a lot of phoning back and forth.

The only time there is a problem is when the parent is hearing something about his child that he doesn't want to hear. But it's part of my job to help the parent understand that I'm not making a derogatory remark. We need to work together to help this child overcome either a learning difficulty or a behavioral problem.

You mean parents challenge your view of their child?

Parents have different expectations from the ones teachers have. Teachers see kids in a group—emotionally, behaviorally, academically—but parents only see their individual child. If I tell a parent that his child has trouble in a particular area, the parent points out that the child has moved forward. I may agree but still point out he has a way to go to catch up to the group. (By the second grade—a transitional time—we do begin to measure kids by the group.)

Are you comfortable with the parents?

It took me a while to get comfortable with the parents. I felt a bit intimidated, and I thought that whatever I'd say, they'd look for a deeper meaning or think that I was not really paying attention to their child. You know: "That is not what our child is really like."

Being a new teacher, I found myself taking notes and saving work to support anything I might say about a child. It's also easier for a parent to understand what is really going on when it is documented in black and white.

I understand that it's difficult to get into a good New York City private school.

Admissions to New York City private schools are very high pressure—for kids and parents. The parents go on all these school tours, and some of them are uptight: "Is my child good enough for the school, and if not, why not?" They want to know everything about the school. If they are going to pay the price, they want the best for their child. In the lower grades the price is about $7,000 a year.

How do you think the parents see you?

For the most part parents respect the teacher because they are paying so much money to get us. If they didn't respect the teacher, I think they would try to do something about it.

But society in general doesn't have respect for educators and, of course, from a teacher's point of view that is amazing. Teachers give the next Einsteins of the world their start. It's amazing that teachers are looked down upon so much. "You just work from nine to three and have summers off"–that's how a lot of people see teachers.

Is it true?

I don't think so. A lot of times I'm in school from seven to seven– just preparing and getting ready for the next day. Then I'll go home and be on the phone for two hours with parents I haven't been able to reach during the day.

This may change. As I get more experienced, I probably won't have to put in so many hours on simple things like what to do for homework or for the next lesson. It will come more automatically.

Still it surprises me that some people are close minded and think that teachers don't do anything. My family is very supportive of what I do. Except for an aunt, I am the only teacher in my family.

I remember how when I got out of school, my father said, "You're going to be a teacher, and then what are you going to do? Are you going to be a second-grade teacher forever?"

That's supportive?

I guess he thought I'd teach for a while and then go into administration–keep moving up within the field of education.

Do you plan to remain within the private-school system?

I don't know if I can see myself teaching in a New York public school and having to overcome so many of the barriers of disadvantaged schools. Perhaps after I become more comfortable with myself as a teacher, I'll consider it. For now, having the support to do what I need to do is important.

At Lenox there is a lot of input from the teachers on what is learned. Both teachers and children have a chance to grow; it isn't like a state-mandated curriculum.

I feel that I've learned a tremendous amount in the three years I've been there. Every year you learn—whether it be a new curriculum or a different type of child.

You sound like you're down on the public schools.

Well, when you're new, they naturally put you in the more disadvantaged schools. During the half year that I interned in the public schools, I saw a lot of people get pushed around in ways I would not want to be. One kindergarten teacher I know was pulled out of her class after a week of school and put into a Harlem school. She went from a middle-class West Side school to Harlem. I don't know if I could handle that: not so much Harlem, but that she had everything set and ready to go and then was pulled out.

How do you feel about the training you got?

I think it was pretty well balanced. As an undergraduate, even though they talked about being innovative and creative, most of the training was pretty traditional; but then in graduate school I got a more progressive orientation. I've learned to use it all—from work sheets to a more one-on-one approach.

Are there men teaching in your school?

Two in the lower grades and three gym teachers. There are few men teaching in elementary schools, and we need a better balance. My education classes were also mostly composed of women. Everything was from a female perspective, and that made our discussions biased.

Did you have role models?

I remember some good things teachers did, and I also thought about how I do not want to be the negative role model—a teacher who puts a child down and humiliates him in front of everybody. That's one thing that I try to be conscious of not doing, even though I understand it. It's quicker to single out "You in the back of the room" than to quietly go over to the child and talk to him.

I've had kids who rubbed me the wrong way, and I tried to overcompensate. Because children pick up on it very easily when you don't like them. What's nice in a private school is that I often work with an assistant teacher. I'll find out what the other teacher feels about the child, and if it's a personality conflict, the other person will take over and look out for the child, so to speak.

When I consider the kids I really like, I see that each child's situation involves a whole family. The parents are real supportive, and we work together as a team. I think that it's very important for the school and home to work together.

It must take a lot of energy to face 15 small children each day.

The biggest reality I've faced is that children don't all learn in the same way. It's not that you stand on this podium and present what you have to present, and children just smile at you and learn. There's a lot more work in it than just going through your time blocks each day.

I remember when I student-taught in a very traditional school. The teacher told everybody to take out their math books and work on page 10. Everybody seemed to do it. But obviously not all were learning, because I see that if I give my kids an assignment, there are some kids I have to guide, step-by-step. Others can do work more independently, and some need no help at all.

Each student receives some individual attention?

Very much so. We also try to draw them out. It's very exciting when you have a kid who at the beginning of the year will only do drawing, and at the end you see him at the science table using the microscope, observing. He has become a more-rounded person and will be less limited as he grows older.

What about burnout?

There was a big turnover at my school last year. Some teachers had been there for 15 years, and they really needed a new and different environment. Teaching is very demanding. It's the kind of job that could be your whole life: there is always something more to do, a child to think about, a paper to put together.

It's important to keep some balance in your life. You have to take it personally, but you can't take it too personally if the children don't meet the expectations that you set for them.

Are you strict?

Some people have said to me, "You're a real softie." But I see a softie as someone who lets things get out of control. I don't like things that are out of control. When, for example, I give my kids some space and I see them going beyond the limits, I'll pull them back together again. There's a period during the day when they can do what they like in the classroom—play with blocks, draw, whatever. When that gets out of control, I pull them back and tell them what we will do, because they can't handle the time on their own.

I guess I see myself as pretty controlling.

Control seems to be an important issue to teachers. It comes up a lot.

It's complicated. I think for children to learn effectively, they have to feel that they have some control over things. If they have some control over what they are doing and learning, then they will be more receptive to what you are actually saying to them.

A lot of times they will test the limits, initiate a power struggle. It's easy to fall into a trap and be ready to argue with a seven-year-old child. But I catch myself, and I'm pretty firm: "This is what we are doing, and you are going to do it."

For me it is important to establish that I am the teacher and you are the children, but I am going to be fair to you if you are fair to me.

What advice would you give a new teacher?

I was very nervous when I started. To a new teacher my advice would be, "Be yourself. Don't try to be somebody you're not." You know, teachers can get into a high-and-mighty position. They think they are the power in the room; but I've watched the children in that situation, and a lot of times they are intimidated by the teacher and become defiant. When children feel dictated to, they become defiant, and they are not going to learn.

But if you build rapport and respect, if you establish who you are and who they are, they will learn. I see it every day.

"Schools are going to have to function like families. Whether we like it or not, we are the community."

LARRY DILG
high school English and history teacher
Los Angeles, California

We Are the Community

Larry Dilg says he was 35 when he started to teach, and "I guess I came to it with a mature point of view. I knew I'd be a good teacher though—I learned that in Mississippi during the Civil Rights movement."

In Mississippi and later in Ghana as a Peace Corps volunteer, he reflected the social activism of the sixties. Afterward, when he returned home, he was involved in theater and also worked for a long time as a rock 'n' roll musician. But even when he worked once more as an actor, Dilg still tended to measure what he did with a social yardstick. Recognizing how many people cannot read, he decided he wanted to learn how to be a reading tutor and combine that work with theater.

Dilg went back to school to take education courses, and soon he had a chance offer to substitute at L.A.'s Oakwood School. He found that he liked working at the private school, and when he was offered a full-time job, he took it. He has now taught for five years and likes doing work that makes a difference, if not a fortune.

He knows that the public schools, which are often a child's only stable community, could use more good teachers, but like many private-school teachers, he thinks they are impossible places to work. As a student teacher he observed the public-school system up close and decided that it prevents teachers from being able to teach:

When I taught at a public high school in Los Angeles, I was supposed to be the student teacher. At first I was an observer, and I was horrified by the teaching, or rather the lack of teaching, that was going on. The man assigned to teach me how to teach was doing so little teaching that I was shocked.

He was a popular teacher and a nice guy—a good male role model, I suppose. A muscular male role model at least. He read all these muscle magazines and had some sort of health-club business on the side. I guess he was trying to compete with Jane Fonda. But in his composition class there was nothing happening except a weekly vocabulary test. He used Wilfred Funk's *Five Steps to a Better Vocabulary* as the only text. It's a good self-help book, but he would assign a chapter to "learn" each week, and that was it. There was absolutely no teaching involved.

Every few weeks there was also a book report or a trip to the library where the students would take out books. Most of them didn't take out books. They would do a book report of perhaps four pages, and he would speed-read these reports in a minute or less. Then he would write on the front, "B—technical errors." What technical errors? Obviously he'd see a spelling mistake or a grammatical mistake, and he'd figure, I can say this. Then he'd hand the reports back. It was outrageous to me.

Was his teaching typical of that school?

There is a lot of bad teaching—and no teaching—around. In this man's composition class many of the girls spent their time doing their hair. That's in a fairly good public high school—not an A.P. class, but not low level either. There were just no demands made on the kids.

In that high school I urged the teacher to let me begin teaching in the second quarter rather than second semester, and I taught there for about a year.

I found it very difficult to do my job in a public high school, and later, when I fell into the Oakwood job, I took it. I had gotten over my guilt about having to serve the people by teaching in public schools. Actually, I still feel it, but so much works against education in the public schools.

What works against doing your job in a public school?

Bureaucracy works against it. We kept really complicated records and were constantly being interrupted for the most ridiculous announcements—things like, "The third-grade class is holding its cheerleading tryouts in the gym."

Attendance was the main order of business, and once it had been taken, a student was gone for 10 minutes while he delivered the attendance to the office. It was chaotic. People came in and took students out at will. Then there was the book situation: there were not a lot of new books available at school. The class I taught was restricted to books they brought themselves.

The mix of students was wide—from people who were barely literate to people who were quite smart. That may be nice, but it's difficult to design a curriculum that will really serve them. Also, there was a critical mass in the classroom that was not interested in learning, not interested in education at all, and that was difficult.

At Oakwood, do the kids want to learn?

Whether they want to learn or not, their parents want them to learn, and so they do. They study a lot, they do a lot of homework, and they get excited by the work. They get excited by knowledge. Whether they would really rather study than watch television, I don't know, but they make the sacrifice. They are not watching television.

At the public school I taught 75 kids, and only two of their parents came in on parents' night. At Oakwood we set aside a day for parent conferences, and we are booked solid. At least 75 to 80 percent of the parents come in and speak to you in the lower grades, and maybe 50 percent in the upper grades. There are also phone calls and all kinds of contact.

Any problems with parents at Oakwood?

Sure. Some push me too much. Either it's "My child is special, and he needs extra work" or "My child should receive a B instead of the C."

The parents just want to see their child succeed. They sometimes want more than the child can deliver, but I can understand that. We send our own child there; so my wife and I relate as parents as well.

As a teacher and parent, how do you react to charges that private schools are elitist?

I think it's true that kids who go to private school are part of an elite. But what is the tracking system in public schools if not a way to separate the elite from the rest?

I recognize that we must serve the whole society. Public schools are a political and social necessity. But I still don't like most of what I've seen of public education in California. If the public system were better—more like the public schools I went to as a child—then I might have sent our child to public school.

I went to Hewlett High School on Long Island. There is very little difference between the education I got there and the one I am giving now. The community wasn't that different from Oakwood, and there were heavy demands placed on kids. There are almost no demands being made of kids in public schools now.

The kids at Oakwood have been sheltered. In some ways that's good. They can afford to be open to culture and sensitive about issues of social conscience. Kids who are on the streets and concerned with survival don't have that breadth.

At Oakwood there is a lot of public-service work and work in affirmative action. Community service is required, and there's a high level of global and community awareness. There are kids involved in forming the L.A. Student Coalition, demonstrating with and for the homeless, fighting against apartheid in South Africa, going to Nicaragua to plant trees, and so on.

They can't shed their whiteness, their elitism; but there is quite a bit of attention focused on their position in society. We are trying to show them that along with their advantages come responsibilities to their society.

Sometimes, too, they are at a disadvantage. There are only so many As at Oakwood, and so when kids there apply to Berkeley or Stanford [University], they often have a lower grade-point average than lesser students from a public high school.

But they are getting a high-quality education. And these are important years—at 14, 15, when they are still at home and under parental supervision, a lot of energy can go into school. I know that at 19, when I was away from my parents, school was a low priority.

Do you have many black kids at Oakwood?

Our school has difficulty keeping blacks in the school. We try to maintain a certain number, including some scholarship students. But they are being mixed with much more affluent kids; they have to establish an identity where they are the clear minority; and they have to develop study habits that they have not acquired before. Try as we may to give them extra help—tutors and extra teachers—it is hard. There has to be a very high motivation to succeed, and many of them drop out. It's easier to go back to their own community than to work against so many things.

It is a problem we address every year and have not been able to fully work out.

How do you feel people react to your being a teacher?

I don't feel snubbed by parents, though I make less money than most of them. I think we deserve more money, and I'd like more money in order to buy a house. But I don't feel strongly about it.

Socially, being a teacher is okay with me. When I was an actor, if we went to a party and I wasn't working, I'd have to give ancient credits. Now at least I know what I'm doing.

You tell people you are a teacher, and they tend to want to talk about "what is wrong with education today." But my particular bias would be to talk about what I'm doing this week, what is really in my head. I guess any profession gets that: if you are a writer, then they ask what you have published or if you have anything under contract—not about your thoughts.

Do you think you will stay in teaching?

I don't know. I've done it for five years now, and in some ways I feel I'm burning out. I never minded criticism before, but now I feel more defensive about it, and I'm not sure that's a good sign.

But I know I'm not complacent. To stay fresh, I change what I teach every year. I also change the grade I teach and the books. Last year it was *The Canterbury Tales*, and this year it's *Light in August, Look Homeward Angel*. A lot of the summer has been spent reading the works again and planning how to approach the kids with works they will be reading for the first time. It's important to help them develop ways to respond and not overburden them with what critics have said.

Did your years as an actor help you as a teacher?

The teacher as entertainer? There's some of that, and also, there is a similar process involved—making something active out of knowledge. My instincts as an actor are to find things to do with what is there and not just say it. When you learn and understand, you act on what you know.

What do you think of the training you got to become a teacher?

I was well trained as an undergraduate, but my teacher training was ridiculous. It was more or less a waste of time. We had to follow the "right" form for a lesson plan or take a silly course in other cultures. It was all just very superficial.

I wanted to teach reading because if you cannot read, you are stuck in our society, and schools don't always reach kids. A one-on-one relationship might work though, and I needed training and insight into how a person reads—it fascinates me.

In the education classes they gave us a nice gray view of the difficulties of teaching reading—but no training at all. We didn't even study phonics! In order to even get some books on phonics, I had to write to this organization of true believers in Arizona.

The other people in the education program felt the same way. They had no respect for what we were learning.

You started out as a substitute in Oakwood's lower school?

Yes. Then they asked me to teach reading from January to June, followed by the offer of a permanent job. The lower school has few male teachers. It is a much more feminine environment than in the high school, and that was awkward for me. It wasn't the femininity, but the sheer banality that bothered me. When you're with little kids all the time, you become a little immature. You start to sound like a little kid. You can't help it. That's your life; that is what you are doing for eight hours a day.

One kid had a little trick. He had tied a dollar to an invisible fishing line near my desk. I took my scissors, and I cut that line and kept the dollar for a few hours. I guess that is pretty juvenile. You get like that!

You prefer teaching older kids?

I think so. I love the kids, and I love the subject matter. I'm learning about Africa this summer. I finally read David Sugar's book about the Arabs and the Jews. I've wanted to read it for a while, and my classes are a good excuse.

Teaching is interactive. You give all day long, and that is the joy and the delight. I love talking to a class, seeing them after school, and having someone come over and say, "I think Job is really messed up." That's the kind of thing I love—digging into the Bible or a book about Africa or a good novel.

Are you in the union?

Yes, we have a small local union, though it's part of UFT [United Federation of Teachers]. I think it is very helpful because teachers don't feel that they are alone when negotiating their contracts. Left to themselves, some teachers would not say anything at all.

You don't work in the summer?

No, I study, and I play with my kids, who are six and three. They want me, and I want them. It's great.

I'm curious what issues in education you think are important?

We have to help kids learn more [laughs]. Kids are not learning enough in their schools, and not enough people are being well educated. We need better readers, better writers; and we need more people to stay in school longer.

Right now kids see no reason to stay in school. Until we provide better jobs in the inner city and provide a correlation between going to high school and getting a better job, there isn't going to be that motivation.

Who will motivate kids? It's up to us. I think, in fact, schools will have to function as families because the family structure has broken down. Despite all the Republican worship of families, the truth is, basically, that families are falling apart.

But can schools function as families?

Who else is going to do it? Are you going to send men back to one of the women whose children they fathered? You can't mandate families. They either happen or they don't, and meanwhile, kids are in school for a long time.

I see the family issue as a school problem: we are the community whether we want to be or not. To a large extent schools have taken the place of the religious community. That's a problem for schools. What is our responsibility? Now we teach the Bible in ninth grade. We teach Genesis, some Esther, Jesus, the Gospels. Why? Because that is part of a liberal education, but also because we have to nurture the spirit that is not necessarily being nurtured in the home.

Is there a God? How do you live the good life? It is the school's place to examine these things and hope children will take these questions home. Do some research. Talk to their rabbi, their pastor, because that is what education is all about. If, because of some twisted sense of the First Amendment, the public school avoids such questions altogether, then I think that society is the loser.

But back to square one. We have to improve the education in the public schools and do more teaching. It can't all be done in the classroom though. Kids have to do their homework in order to learn. They have to be independent, and that is where the school has a community function. What if there is nobody at home? What if there is no place for the kid to study?

What if?

There is school. Schools should open up at night so that kids can use them as places to study. There are also churches and office buildings that could be opened up at night. We need to work with parents and people in the community. There are all sorts of solutions.

If we don't have enough teachers, then we need to bring them in from other professions. Obviously, we need better teachers. My teacher-ed. classes were by no means the best and the brightest. There were some nice people but few intellectuals.

Some teachers just seem dull. I found that many prefer Tupperware to Tolstoy, and in fact, when I tried to join in the conversations in public school, I was barely tolerated. I'm not sure why. Maybe because I was not a teacher they met at faculty meetings, or maybe because they were very closed people.

Your background is a somewhat unusual one for a teacher.

Yes, although I did teach in Mississippi during the Civil Rights movement. It was 1967, and I was teaching seven kids in all. Two black kids in the group were going into a desegregated high school the next year.

It was catch-up time for them and also their chance to get to know each other because they were going to be the only black students in the school.

We were with them all day and did a lot of music, singing those great songs. But we were a group of privileged white kids. By the end of the summer, as black power got big, our position was really very tenuous. We were friends, but there was distrust. We whites were going to leave, and we were also the enemy.

Of course I felt guilty—you know: "Yes, I am the enemy." But on the other hand, I thought we were doing some good things there, and people were learning some good things.

[We go on to talk about black-white relations in and out of the classroom. I praise Jonathan Kozol's book, *Death at an Early Age*, and Larry Dilg exclaims, "What a joke! Kicking Kozol out of a Boston school for teaching Langston Hughes. Hughes and the Harlem Renaissance! Not exactly radical stuff." Then we returned to the public-private school question one more time. He does concede]:

You can get an excellent education in the A.P. track of a public high school. Bright students can do very well. In fact, if you are very gifted in science, you might be better off in a public high school because they have more money and resources than do private schools. But for average kids I'm not so sure. My limited experience suggests that midlevel students were offered a lot of nothing.

Last question. Do you have other friends who are teachers?

I do not have a lot of friends. [We both laugh.] I have too much work, and I have two little kids. I have so much work to do, you know, that when the weekend comes, I just hope my wife will take the kids to the park for a while so that I can grade the papers, do the reading, make a lesson plan. I keep changing what I teach so that I am always working; and still the kids always complain that the papers come back two weeks late. There is only so much you can do.

In the Suburbs

In the Suburbs

Suburban teachers face a different world from the one their urban counterparts see. The difference starts in the parking lot—rarely guarded and no physical threat—and carries over to the classroom. Usually the classroom is also safe and while it is no Taj Mahal, chances are it's in better shape than the late-Victorian relics our city kids attend. Wherever the teacher turns, at school or in the surrounding neighborhood, it is familiar ground and not a quasi-war zone.

Suburban students are pretty much like the teachers' own kids (except they are often richer), and teachers know what to expect. With these kids, no one talks about "filthy" apartments, over-crowding, or raucous noise. Instead there are bemused, often critical references to a juvenile high life: from island hopping to Gucci loafers, Colorado ski trips to orchestra seats at the theater.

Not all suburbs are this prosperous, of course. Nor are all city schools so mean. But very often the distance between them is as wide as Andover and the ghetto, and no one questions that it is far easier to teach in the suburbs than in our cities.

In the suburbs everyone is more or less engaged in playing

school. Truancy is less of a problem; the kids show up, and some work gets done.

Parents are more visible, and their presence is felt. In fact, sometimes teachers complain of parents who "nag," are "too pushy," and are no real help. But although ambivalence, rather than wholehearted cooperation, seems to characterize teacher-parent relations in the suburbs, no one claims—as they do in the cities—that parents are uninterested.

The problems that exist reveal the cracks in our culture from the other side of the tracks. There are three areas, all of them intangible, that deeply concern teachers. The first is what they see as our skewed value system. This is the generation, remember, that has been raised on double-speak (Irangate, insider trading), the Baker religious ministry scandal, and the importance of looking out for number one. According to their teachers, these children have little understanding—or interest—in anyone different from themselves and are generally short on solid values. Where, too, are their heros? The family doctor and rock musician both drive BMWs, and they are both on the way to the bank.

Teachers also feel far more children are emotionally at risk. Stories of needy kids—who not only succumb to peer pressure (only nerds get As), but to drugs and alcohol—are common. There is the perception that many are disturbed and hunger for close relationships—unavailable within their families and bought outside their homes at high cost, such as pregnancy.

In this connection the common thread was "too much money, too little supervision." And while most teachers are too liberated to want to put things back the way they were and send mothers back inside their split-levels, everyone worries about how the school can pick up all the pieces once held by parents.

A third huge area of concern has to do with student attitudes and is not limited to the suburbs. Many teachers feel that today's children have higher and higher expectations but are willing to exert less and less effort: kids expect to be rewarded with high grades and lavish careers, but they do not want to work for them. There is a tendency to believe that "thinking makes it so," or "I tried, and therefore I should be rewarded."

This issue is a tough one. It calls into question current child-rearing practices, and any discussion of it can easily end up sounding like the death knell of the West or "why Asian kids are beating our kids" (something I heard rather a lot about).

But I think it is real. The same culture that can hold a workshop on "How to Be There for Your Child When You Are Not There" can also encourage kids to believe that wanting something is almost enough to make it happen. (This workshop took place. I was in a private-school gymnasium where it was announced by the headmaster.)

Other issues were raised, but these three headed the list. They were mentioned, moreover, by people in some of this nation's top schools. (These are the schools that are highly rated by all the usual indices—test scores, college acceptances, scholarships, and so on. Unfortunately, I cannot identify these schools or their teachers by name because it was on that basis that the schools, and teachers, opened their doors to me.) At top schools teachers feel that even though kids are learning, it's getting harder and harder to reach them or, put another way, the teacher is doing more and more of the work.

"I work in a model school. It's a really good school with a very strong principal, an extremely strong teaching staff, and children who have what all children in this country could have—the brains, the money, the resources. Yet I am questioning myself: What is the matter with me that I'm tired of it? It's really a puzzling question."

ELEANOR BLAINE
middle-school French and Latin teacher
Westchester County, New York

It's Games All Day Long

Eleanor Blaine is a French and Latin teacher in one of the most highly rated school systems in the nation. She started out thrilled by her work and now is wondering whether she can go on teaching.

This interview found her thinking aloud and trying to understand her change of heart. She was genuinely puzzled and too intelligent to find any easy answers.

She sees the way any job can turn stale and her own need for a vibrant intellectual life. But the social milieu of her students—the affluent children of fast-track professionals—also emerged as part of the picture. Why did her students leave their books at home? Fail to make up tests? Expect "games all day long"?

Eleanor Blaine thinks it may have to do with the way the upper-middle class lives now. She said an art-therapist friend, who sees many of these same kids professionally, suggested to her that young couples acquire material things and then they acquire kids. The kids are very privileged; and they are also programmed to within an inch of their lives. But as they streak through their fun-filled days—from tennis lessons, to Saks Fifth Avenue, to French 101, to karate class—no one really listens to them or takes the time to get to know them.

175

No one suggests that some things call for effort, not just a credit card or tutor; and that there are reasons to learn other than to rack up As and go to Harvard.

That troubles Eleanor Blaine.

She is now 57 and has taught for 10 years. Her own four children went through the same school system, but at that time she was at home—like many other mothers 25 years ago.

Will she continue? Her husband is too successful for her own hand-some salary—$45,000 in a school minutes from her home—to be much of a consideration. This past year she took a leave in order to write a French language book. As she told me, she can write this book with one hand tied behind her back. That gave her a lot of time to think about her profession and whether she wanted to continue in it.

I don't know what she'll decide. But I can see her dilemma: like her pupils, she is caught up in a system that reflects the problems of affluence just as much as an inner-city school mirrors the social problems of the poor.

(Not that I equate the two: better, no doubt, to be a "poor little rich kid" and suffer in comfortable homes and cheerful, well-designed, well-endowed schools. Still, as Eleanor Blaine and some of her colleagues all told me, suburbia is in trouble too.)

The way Eleanor Blaine got into teaching is characteristic of the woman:

I love foreign languages. When I was first married with four children, if I got sick, I would lie in bed with a French grammar. That's how much I loved languages.

I used to tutor neighborhood children in Italian and French. Eventually I put a sign up in the middle school and was called by the principal. He offered me a permanent substitute job in Latin and French. I said I could come on Monday, Wednesday, and Friday. Of course, he said it didn't work that way.

What did I know? I went back and told the principal I was interested in that job, and he pointed out that there was no job, only a permanent substitute position. That was what they would call it—in case the teacher whom I replaced got well. (Unfortunately she did not.) The semantic distinction mattered, and it taught me not to be so wide open in this world outside the home. You have to think before you speak.

Anyway, I got the job, and I had to resurrect my Latin. I'd had five years of Latin, but it was a long time ago. That first year was like my first batch of cookies—not so great. But it got better.

When I started out, it was the magic of teaching that was in focus. I was really willing to do anything as long as I could teach, but now, I must say, I've become increasingly annoyed with the details of the job.

Details?

It's the detail that comes into a teacher's job—much of it perfectly reasonable to ask us to do but increasingly onerous to me. There's the child who comes in and interrupts when you are talking to another child, the having to track down why a child is late, the calling of parents. The fact is that mothers are mostly working, and you don't want to call them at night; so you get hold of whoever the housekeeper is, and that's another detail.

It's true we don't have to make lesson plans (though I gather there is a state law that a lesson plan must be in your desk drawer at all times), but there is so much else: the careful grading you have to do on chapter tests, and then when you hand the papers back, the students are concerned not about understanding their mistakes, but about upping their grades. A good deal of grade grubbing goes on. "Why is this wrong?" they ask. "Didn't you take off too much?"

You teach both French and Latin?

I like teaching Latin, but I also have to teach basic French.

In New York State every child has to take three years of a foreign language by the time he gets to tenth grade, and so the middle school is taking the brunt of it. We are teaching seventh- and eighth-grade basic French to kids who can't really learn a foreign language. In January they are still spelling *oui* [yes] "W-E-E," and in June they still mix up the verbs for "to be" and "to have." They should probably just be having an oral experience and no written work at all. I know I lack the patience for it, and I don't feel it's what I was trained to do.

Most of the kids in basic French cannot learn a foreign language?

I should distinguish between the Regents classes, which are three-quarters of the kids, and the Basics classes. The Regents classes are so smart, able, and very attentive. Children in the Basics course just have to be present in the classroom for three years in order to pass. But there is a social stigma to the Basics course, and that makes it difficult too.

About a fourth of each Basics class are very learning-disabled. They have some auditory problems, some speech problems, and no attention span. Some are on Ritalin, a drug for hyper kids, and they call out in the middle of a class. [I've seen this. Having observed classes at Blaine's middle school for several days, I was surprised at how free the students felt in most classes to blurt out anything while another child or the teacher was speaking.]

Classes start out being very angelic. They're thrilled that they are going to learn a foreign language; but after a few months, when they see they will have to settle down and work, some of them get pretty nasty with each other. They call each other "retards," and their speech is inappropriate. In the middle of class a child will tell me his brother is an "asshole." When I say that is inappropriate language for a class, I'm told, "But I'm mad at my brother." Whatever is uppermost on their minds comes out—never mind the lesson. We are really teaching the near-handicapped, but unless a child is designated "handicapped," they must all take a foreign language.

Perhaps the children are just not interested?

No, they are unable. At first they sing the alphabet. As long as you play games with them, they love it. It's games all day long, and that is as it should be. But I'm tired of it.

We also play games in my advanced classes. We find they must get up every 20 minutes. We play relay races at the blackboard, Simon Says, and so on. That's why my school is good; we do all that.

An ex-teacher in your school system said that there was too much emphasis on fun.

It's possible. We sometimes complain at the middle school that the kids coming up from elementary school are not disciplined enough. I don't know if that is the fault of the teachers or the parents. But television has also helped create the so-called fun mentality. The kids expect that in a half hour you are going to show them, there will be a conflict, and it will be resolved. They want a lesson and entertainment all in a half hour.

I think perhaps these grades are the hardest ages to teach because the kids are not lost in wonder anymore and because they are not worried about college yet. Also, our principal pointed out that every 20 minutes they *have* to move. They are itchy, scratchy.

I've noticed that.

The kids march through the day kind of breathlessly. That's to accommodate all the subjects the state curriculum mandates, and it may well be too much.

Too much and therefore too little?

Exactly. There is too much going on in *and* out of school. I heard someone say, "Who is that streak of lightning that just went by—*whoosh?* That was your child." The kids' every moment is programmed, and with all that, there's no self-discipline.

In fact, I believe the students in our school are getting more and more disorganized. I've asked other teachers in my school, "How do you feel about the pen, pencil, paper situation?" It doesn't sound important, but when you get five kids who forgot their textbooks, and five more who didn't bring their workbooks, and a lot of the class didn't bring in any lined paper, and many didn't bring a pencil, you find yourself wasting time while they are reaching around borrowing from a friend. Then you try saying that there will be no borrowing, and you encounter students day after day who just sit and can't do anything because they haven't the materials. That's a big problem. It's a self-discipline problem, and it probably extends into other areas of their lives.

I don't know if this happens because there aren't people at home to stand over them, remind them, and get them organized. It's also partly the age group I am teaching, but it is nonetheless a big problem—getting themselves *ready* to learn and receptive to learning.

I don't think there's anything wrong with the teachers. I really wonder if the general permissiveness in society is something teachers can lick. The children want entertainment; they don't want to knuckle down and get to work or get to classes on time and do the homework.

Are you talking about the Basics class?

No, all of them. Before you fail them, you call home, and you also make them stay after school to do their homework. We have late buses on Mondays and Wednesdays.

Kids who don't do well on a test retake it, and we average the two marks. But we can't get them back on Mondays and Wednesdays. They have tennis lessons, Hebrew lessons, CCD [religious instruction], singing lessons, football, piano.

It's hard to get them back for detention. You call the parents, and they say, "Oh, I know, but he has got his tennis lessons. Can I write him a note?" No, they can't write him a note. I think it's this kind of thing that is driving me crazy. We are not the center of life anymore. School used to be the center of life. Now we are just one more acquisition, one more activity. [This is an epiphany for her, a new realization, and she immediately comments on it.]

This is good for me, to really think about what is irritating me. I have a friend who teaches Latin in a Rye [another New York suburb] high school, and he said that if I'm tired of playing games in a middle school and want the intellectual stimulation of a high school, then I'd be good for about three years. They're playing games all the time, he said. "You have to play mind games with these children. You can't even come at a high school kid and say, 'Do this, learn that.' It isn't like that in high school. It might have been that way when you were a kid. But now," he said, "we have to jolly them around. The don't meet their obligations."

Middle school, high school, it's pretty much the same thing. It wouldn't be that different in high school, and maybe it would not be any more of an intellectual challenge. You push them over and over again.

You sound very tired of it.

Yes, but what happened to me? Ten years ago I was so excited to teach. It was such a thrill. I had just come out of the house bringing up four children, and now, 10 years later, I feel irritated all the time at work. It must partly be me. After 10 years at a job, though, a person may just get tired of it.

I've had some incredible glimpses into the soul of a 12-year-old. When the students illustrated Greek myths, some were so sensitive that I asked myself, Why don't I want to go back for more?

The detail is part of it. Also it is hard to change your level or make any changes within teaching itself.

I don't follow.

Despite my friend in Rye's warning, I have tried for about five jobs teaching Latin in high school. I haven't gotten any of them, which may be partly my age–57–but is more likely my salary, which is $45,000. Because I earn so much, the school system would rather take a young woman and start her off at $20,000. There is no progression for me, and that's a problem for teachers: I feel stopped at the pass.

I have been told that teachers in this area are never hired at above a step six—about $30,000—no matter how experienced they are.

I think that is true, and it is a frustration: you can go just so far, and then there is nothing open for you. And it's hard to get out of the teaching profession. It's hard to find ways you can use these skills. I guess I could work for a travel agency, but I don't call that a profession like teaching.

There was a group of teachers at school, and they got people from business to come in once a week to talk to them about what skills from teaching would apply in the business world. But not one of them was ever offered a job. There are many teachers who want to get out of the teaching field.

Because they are burned-out?

Yes. You have that roomful of kids and classes and report cards and papers to grade, and you are dealing with children all day long. Intellectually it would be nice to deal with adults sometimes. You are always helping, helping.

[She catches herself and explains that she is not always this negative.]

What I say may be misleading. No generalizations really apply, and when I talk about fighting the pen and pencil business, we do fight it, and they do learn.

But you seem to be saying that the kids are not learning all they could.

There are more children in our Basics courses getting special remedial help than there were. The numbers of students in those Basic classes are growing—imperceptibly. The numbers are growing, and so are the numbers of learning-disabled kids. One woman who heads a special-education division said that part of the problem was that the kids were being raised by foreign-born housekeepers. These housekeepers were not raised in the system we're all trying to perpetuate. It's hard enough keeping after your kids. But why is someone from Jamaica or El Salvador going to keep after them?

[She tells me how to contact the administrator in charge of special education for the district, Mrs. J.] Mrs. J tells it like it is. Most people speak advisedly. I never hear prejudiced remarks, but the flip side is that I rarely hear any frank expressions of opinion, and no one generalizes. All talk is guarded.

But what's going on? I don't know.

I get the feeling that the teachers in my school tend to blame the parents, and the parents blame the teachers. There's a real generalization!

"As a teacher I think I went through the best years of education—that rainbow that went across there that was the best in the world—and I do not think we will see it again. Sputnik helped everybody, not only math and science. If it is going up, it is going up for everybody; if it is going down, it is going down for everybody."

BERNARD ROBBINS
retired high school math teacher
Yorktown, New York

The Rainbow Years

Like other veteran teachers, Bernard Robbins is nostalgic for a lost time— the rainbow years for education in the fifties and sixties. He sees the last 20 years as a time of decline, and like most, he puts his finger squarely on "society" to account for what has changed.

"All the changes in education are changes in society. When I first start- ed teaching in 1957, there was a great deal of interest in education, and communities were much closer to the children. But in the seventies every- body became a world traveler, and the community wasn't there.

"Parents' attitudes about what you have to do to educate a child have also changed. People are more interested in themselves now. They want their children to succeed but are not willing to make the sacrifices that are necessary. They just don't put in the time. There are reasons for this—it is hard to survive on one income—but it exacts a price.

"They give kids all the material things, the computers and the books, but not their own time."

Robbins and his wife raised three children in the community where he taught high school math for 30 years. When he retired, many felt that the school had lost a first-rate teacher and a man who understood kids.

We talked of the rainbow years and of the present and what has changed in 30 years:

Social attitudes. Now people think the educator will do the job. But kids have so much more now. They are just not interested in education, and the teacher is only an adjunct. It is the family that has to educate in the use of leisure time.

Kids have so many alternatives and ways to do the wrong things. Drugs are one problem, and so is peer pressure. Kids draw very rigid lines. If your group says you must not do homework, then that is final. Children can't get beyond that kind of peer pressure. It's too powerful.

Nor can schools. We can't solve the problems of peer pressure or drugs on our own. We can dodge and sidestep some problems, but with some children and some problems we can never put enough time into it.

It is very difficult. I've seen people—people removed from the reality of it—put in mountains of time, energy, and money on these problems. But again, education starts at home, and an environment must be provided there to make education work.

Then why don't teachers talk to parents more about what is not going on at home?

You make a valid point. On open-school day maybe six parents come. Parents go in the early years but not when their kids are in high school. We do need better communication between parents and schools.

How about the classroom itself. Did you have control over what and how you taught?

In my classroom, when I closed the door, I was the boss. I did exactly what I wanted to do. But there were so many other things we had to do that, as far as I was concerned, there was not enough time to educate.

There was the paperwork and also the general politics of the school: you had to do things that smacked more of public relations than of the children's education.

We spent a great deal of time talking about the curriculum. After five or ten years we knew the curriculum, and it was a good one. But then instead of actually teaching the curriculum, we spent more and more time selling it. That was time taken from the classroom and the children.

When push came to shove, we often opted for what shines, the new: we really went after the computer and sold the public on computers. Computers are an important tool, but what really counts in education is the response that the child gets from the adult. When the child has a question and is provoked or encouraged to ask the question, that is when education takes place. Right there. There is less and less time and emphasis to do that.

And we really didn't talk about *that*, about what happens when you really educate and the teacher responds to the child. Instead we kept stretching the curriculum, adding more computers, more materials.

At the same time we made the curriculum easier. We kept taking out more and more of the things that we had once put in. I think we took out the heart of the material, what really provoked learning. We no longer made the child try to do something that he thinks is beyond his normal capabilities.

Why are schools making it easier?

Because the public wants success, the kid wants success. It isn't just the school districts. The state has created a less-difficult mathematics curriculum as well.

We used to have a phenomenal mathematics program for the advanced learner. When students came out of the high school, they had really gone through advanced mathematics, and that set a standard for all students. But because of numbers and money, we phased out the tougher, more-advanced program.

Now more and more time is being spent remediating and working with children who have very low skill levels. I'm not knocking that. Those children must also be taught—and with the same level of intensity as the others. But if you apply the energy and time to the children who *don't* have the mathematical skills and if you don't seek out also the kids who can do the advanced mathematics, everybody loses.

When you have the more-advanced program, it has an impact on what everybody does. It sets a standard and adds to the overall level.

So success replaces real accomplishment?

Right. You have to have success; so you make it a little easier. Kids get very little homework now, and then a lot of them don't do that homework.

They also watch a lot of TV. Quiz shows are okay, but watching them is not the same thing as using your mind. You should be able to sit down and try, try to solve a problem that you have never solved in your life because you have been given the necessary information and now must try to put it together. If problem solving is not what it is about, what on earth are we talking about in education anyhow?

Skills are supposed to be taught in schools, and I think that is what parents think is being done. It is, to some extent, but not enough.

Why not?

It is hard to educate now. Children are very busy people. They go to school because they have to go. Some enjoy it, and some go to play ball. That's okay with me as long as they also do the schoolwork.

But what about the children who are not ready to learn, the discipline problems? We have been through it a hundred million times, and we don't know what to do with those kids who don't really belong in the classroom and did not come to learn.

Why not kick them out, suspend them?

We did that; we did that. It just doesn't help the kid or the school. There is no easy way to handle this problem; but if you keep at it long enough, you can eventually motivate children to start problem solving. Society doesn't function well now because people cannot solve their own problems.

Can teachers? Many of them seem stuck to me.

I think that's true. It would help if teachers took a break and worked for a while in other organizations—in industry, in the government, in research, and in service organizations. Maybe industry and government could reciprocate by putting some of their people in the classroom for a year.

Young people can be difficult. I felt it. But I worked my way through it, which is what everybody does one way or another. And I took early retirement at 55. Teaching is in my blood; I still tutor. But I needed a change and wanted to do other things.

What do you think about the caliber of new teachers?

The people coming in today are a product of this society; they don't look at education the same way as we did when I started. Maybe they're in better touch with the children.

If you were starting over again now, would you become a teacher?

I think I would. I'd be ready for it because I'd be a product of this.

But you'd be a product of the easier math and so on.

But I wouldn't know that, would I?

Postscript

Public Relations

Bernie Robbins is not bitter, and he still believes that "there is a great deal of elasticity in the school system. If you get the right leadership and enough people who will address the correct problems, schools can do a lot."

Nonetheless, he is disturbed by the way schools cater to image, not substance, and allow what looks good, rather than what is good, to dominate their classrooms.

"Public relations" is what he called it, and he was not alone. Many teachers made the same point, and their examples were things like distorting attendance figures by making sure kids show up in homeroom, even if that is their one appearance of the day; lowering standards so that the numbers who pass remain respectable; not sending all the minority students who need help to the remedial program because the quotas will be awry and people will cry "prejudice," or, conversely, shutting out some gifted and talented white students because a district must show at least a 40 percent quota of minority students; and juggling class-size figures by "averaging" the numbers in an entire district.

188

To show some concern for the schools' public image is inevitable. But for the rest, maybe schools will tell us what is really going on when the air is less polluted by distrust and hostility.

"You really have to look at what you do in a historical perspective. Does it have a moral function? Does it jibe with your heart?"

VICTORIA VICKERS
high school English teacher
Los Angeles, California

What Jibes with Your Heart

Victoria Vickers has been teaching English in a suburban L.A. high school for three years now. She came to the classroom from a very lucrative job in an advertising agency where her big account was a pizza chain. Teaching pays her far less but has that moral dimension she missed in sales. "Would I be proud telling my grandchildren that I sold a lot of pizzas? No!"

She loves teaching and is proud of her work at Eagle Rock High School. In only three years she's learned a lot about the classroom and her students. At first she was "aghast" at some of their home lives, and she probably became overly involved. Like many new teachers, she had to learn to draw back a little, and she has. But her enthusiasm has not diminished. "I love the learning process—with people growing, changing, learning more about themselves, and reaching out."

We talked during the summer, when she was home and pregnant with her first child. She expected to teach that fall, and this is how she described her school:

I am very fortunate to be in Eagle Rock. I love my school and its students. They're predominantly Hispanic and on the whole, fairly

190

poor. But our parents love their children and are pretty supportive.

Where we are, in the suburbs, the problems are just starting. What happens in the inner cities comes out to us in waves. The drugs come out in waves, and now we are starting to have the gangs and the violence.

The press says Eagle Rock is one of the places where a lot of money is spent on guns. In my classroom–maybe because of my teaching style–I don't see it.

I don't follow.

When you teach writing, as I do, you ask people to reveal themselves, and that is a lot to ask. Because the kids are vulnerable, I have to work to create a safe environment and make sure criticism is constructive. We make judgments, but they are judgments to help each other. I have to work to create and enforce that atmosphere, and therefore I lose a lot of the negativity that you see in some classrooms.

What are their skills like?

I hate to be judgmental, but if you apply the old framework that we all used in college, you'd be appalled. On another level–experience, creativity–they are wonderful. They're uninhibited by what has happened to them in the past or by any particular format–which is a wonder.

But in terms of college proficiency or the standards that were applied to us, their skills are very poor. My school is trying to correct that. We do our very best to turn out kids who are literate.

Are they?

Coming out of my classroom they are. But I was taught how to teach by some of the best in Berkeley's rhetoric program. I don't know if most writing teachers are as well trained as I am.

You must get to know the kids very well if they are writing personal stuff.

I love that. That's what I look forward to. I wake up every morning, and I think, What am I going to learn from them? That's why I come back every day. I think any good teacher feels this and wants to get involved and become a part of their lives.

During my first year of teaching I made the mistake of taking their problems personally. I am very good at being poker-faced, but I was shocked by the ones who were living eight in a bedroom. I don't think that made me as effective a teacher.

My second year I decided we would stick to the business at hand–education. When their personal life pertains, I deal with it, but I am no longer aghast, I no longer ask explorative questions. If they want to tell me–and they know I am a sympathetic ear–then that's fine.

Does your not being Hispanic make a difference?

I don't think it matters as long as you are a caring human being. But there are certain things I would not attempt to do. For instance, I don't make any Hispanic jokes, because that only works from someone of their own ethnic background. It's similar to the way people in your own family can get away with ribbing you, but for an outsider–forget it.

What's your feeling about the other teachers in your school?

Here, too, we are just starting to have problems. Our older teachers are very good, but the new teachers are much less impressive. They are hired because the school is growing, and teachers are needed. Schools have to hire what they can get, and that's not usually top people.

How could they be? As we all know, teachers are sorely under-paid. A starting teacher can make about $23,000. Or she can go into an MBA [master of business administration] program and manage people–a very similar skill–and start at $45,000. Or there's sales, and educating the public–another similar skill in which salary is unlimited. When I first went into sales, I made over $40,000 in six months.

Yet you decided to teach and have accepted an inferior salary.

That's true. I feel very much the same way as a friend of mine does. Before she went back into teaching, she was a real-estate agent. She said that she woke up one morning and thought, They're going to put on my tombstone: "Sold 15 houses a year in Van Nuys [a community in L.A.'s San Fernando Valley]."

She couldn't stand the idea that her work had no real value, and that's how I felt about advertising. You really have to look at what you do in a historical perspective.

You are pregnant. Will you teach after your baby is born?

I'm going to teach until I'm very uncomfortable. Mostly because I work in a great school. When our principal became ill, she relied on the staff. That has kept us together, and people here have been very supportive of me. I live for them.

Are you a member of the union?

I'm not a union person, but I broke down and joined once I was at the school and saw what the union was trying to do. Right now it's the best, or the most effective, way to bring about important changes. I don't know about the long run.

Unions are working to improve the conditions of teachers. The problem with teachers is that we are separated. We each go to our own individual classrooms, and we don't come together. We cannot have power unless we come together; and the union has brought teachers together, which makes us a lot stronger.

You can't have a good classroom if you have an unhappy teacher—I think you'll find that if you interview people who don't like their teaching jobs. Just as unhappy parents communicate that environment at home, unhappy teachers do too. If teachers are happy with their job, their pay, the work, they will be more effective, or at least they'll have the opportunity to be. Then you really are justified in getting rid of some of the dead wood that has been around the school too long.

Are you allowed to strike in California?

Yes, and we did strike. It broke my heart. The first year I didn't go out. I felt that I was supposed to be there for the kids and that my job is to teach.

But it didn't work. During the strike the school stayed open, but there were only a few teachers around. They rounded up all the kids and had them out in the football field or in the auditorium watching movies. There was no education going on, but attendance was taken. They counted heads so we would not lose any funding. [Schools are funded according to the number of students they serve each day.] I could not teach under those conditions.

Aside from the strike, what conditions seem to you to most affect education today?

Number one is problems in the family. We cannot teach unhappy, unhealthy children, and we have a lot of them. We cannot fix the problems in the home, and yet we are constantly faced with them: kids who are pregnant, on drugs, bitter. These are not classroom questions, but you cannot teach an unhealthy child. [I don't interrupt her but make a mental note to ask her why she earlier said that these children have involved and supportive parents.]

Number two is the decentralization issue. They make ridiculous decisions in Sacramento that affect the L.A. Unified School District. Schools should have local autonomy and with that, the responsibility to educate. The people of Eagle Rock should not be obliged to send their kids there if it is not a good school.

The third issue is the quality of teaching. Teachers are undereducated, if educated at all, and it seems to me that people go into the classroom without really having been trained.

You distinguish between being educated and being trained?

"Educated" in subject matter and "trained" in how to teach it. I had both, I think, but I didn't go the standard route. They hired me to teach in a public high school and to be responsible for 151 moving bodies each day even though I did not have a teaching credential.

You do now?

Yes, I've earned it. I was fortunate because I managed to take courses and workshops taught by teachers–the in-class training and work under master teachers were very valuable. Also valuable were the workshops on topics such as "How to integrate literature into a writing course."

What do you mean when you say that teachers are undereducated?

The quality of the teachers they are pulling in is not that great. When I was brand new and had no experience at all, a ghetto principal offered me a position in which I would have run the school newspaper *and* all first-year teachers, along with teaching creative writing and A.P. English. The offer made me realize that the quality of teachers he had must have been really miserable.

Or that you are very good.

I think that it would have taken a fool to believe I was good. Everybody who has been in the education business knows that your first year of teaching is the worst. It's really the school of hard knocks; it is boot camp the first year.

The only way to learn how to teach is in an apprenticeship situation, where you are doing it and where a master teacher is giving you advice.

But I could see a good private school offering you the same job that the ghetto principal did. Private schools often look for educated people, not necessarily teaching credentials.

But they would also offer me the support and backing to do it. In public schools, administrators are burdened with paperwork up the wazoo, a lot of burned-out people, and a system that is not responsive to new ideas.

I've been lucky. My school is supportive, and in my classroom kids write about their thoughts and about books that reflect on our society. They write about what they would do to change things if they were in charge. I try to empower them as much as possible.

The other thing that works and that I try to do is to make their peers their audience and to have them share their work with their friends. We try and publish as much as we can and make public their ideas.

Is that what you mean by "empower"?

Yes. Why write if no one is going to read it? If it is only for the teacher who sits behind the desk, who cares? But if your pals will read it —and, hopefully, the school—you will spend a little extra time on it. Not too much—you'll worry more about what you're going to wear to the dance—but you will spend a little extra time.

I hear about empowerment from teachers who feel their students are ignored at home; and earlier you spoke of unhappy, unhealthy children. Yet you also said that their parents were fairly involved.

I think I contradicted myself there. From what I know of the inner city and what I've seen of other schools, our kids are loved. I think that is a basic requirement for human existence. But they still have problems; more than half of our kids come from a broken home or single-parent home, and that's tough. Nobody comes to watch them play baseball at all. Teachers go. We make an effort to come watch them play at basketball games because there are no parents. Nobody minds the fort at home. It's just tough.

The parents are doing the best they can, and they love their kids; but it's not enough. Nobody is making sure they do homework. Nobody is reinforcing educational values. Nobody is helping them set goals.

Do you contact parents?

When I can reach them. It's very frustrating for me because you call, and nobody is ever home. I can't substitute for that love and support. There's no way.

But I can encourage them to learn how to help each other. In my seventh-grade classroom it's hysterical. They organize panels. I say, "When Mrs. Vickers is out of your life, you will have your friends to rely on." In fact, I think the gangs exist because they are the only source of support the kids seem to have.

The drugs make things a little nasty too. Last year we had an undercover drug bust that took in a fair number of people who were 14 years old and selling cocaine. That freaked me out.

The undercover bust?

No, you expect that in a public school. The youthfulness of the ringleaders freaked me out.

The school has tried to deal with the drug problem. But the battle is with our whole culture. It's very difficult to make it in this day and age, and we're constantly being told that you have to drive a Mercedes or BMW and wear designer clothes in order to be happy. Material expectations have replaced a spirituality that went out long ago. You're told that you have to be rich to be happy, but that is a fallacy. You get rich, and you are not happy.

Look at TV; look at the rock stars who are glorified. A lot of my kids have heavy-metal heroes—Iron Maiden, Poison. They are into music; in fact, their only source of spirituality and of culture is music. I think we should swing back to a more spiritual community that doesn't equate money and happiness—but then I'm a philosopher.

A philosopher who does not seem to have any status problems about being a teacher.

I've worked that out—my parent's dreams for my life and society's expectations. I've finally come to a place where I'm happy, and that works for my husband and our whole situation.

Is your husband a teacher also?

He could be. He has that sensitivity, and there are teachers in his family. But he has chosen a different avenue, fortunately a more lucrative one.

Is your choice predicated on your husband's making more money?

Absolutely. I couldn't do it otherwise. I probably would have gone on to teach after college had it been more lucrative, and I also might have gone on to get excellent teacher training. But why spend ten grand on a teaching credential? How long would it take me to recoup?

At $23,000 a year, too long. To return to your school, is bilingualism an issue?

Sure it is, and I do what I can. I could go crazy worrying about grammar. But my primary task is getting them to think and to be able to articulate their thoughts with a certain audience in mind. If that audience happens to be their peers, they can use one type of language and grammatical structure. If it happens to be a job interview, they use another language. They understand that. Or if it is for college—only a small percentage of them go to college.

Then what happens to them?

I am probably responsible for half the quick chefs in McDonald's. I don't know. I hope they go on to lead happy, healthy lives and do a better job than we did.

If the best job prospect is to be a chef at McDonald's, I think we have to do a bit more.

Yes. People forget that the key resource we have is a human resource. Ours is underdeveloped. Hopefully, children have this wonderful way of healing themselves and surviving, but it would be nice if we could help them along a little bit more than we have.

"Under the right kind of leadership, the right kind of inducement, the right kind of environment, I doubt that there is a teacher anywhere who couldn't or wouldn't do more *if asked*. In the classroom, out of the classroom, that's the bottom line—to be asked. If asked and then of course acknowledged (not necessarily with money), teachers can move mountains."

DR. JULIUS APPLEBAUM
middle-school social studies teacher
Westchester County, New York

A Bittersweet Life

Maybe Julius Applebaum would have moved a few mountains if anybody had asked him. But to hear him tell it, nobody asks teachers for their opinions or their help—a situation he says he has accepted after thirty-four years at the same highly regarded middle school. ("Middle school" is the new name for junior high school; a middle school generally includes grades six through eight.)

But who can forgive being ignored? In our interview Dr. Applebaum returned a number of times to the ways in which teachers are slighted and their views unsought. He was affable about it—very much the easygoing elder statesman who has seen too much to get unduly ruffled—but I felt his disappointment as he recounted various views and projects that had not received serious consideration.

Ironically, Dr. Applebaum's own principal provided me with a classic example of what angers teachers. Before I interviewed Applebaum, I asked permission to observe classroom life in his middle school. I was surprised to gain permission within an hour of my original request. But when I showed up to walk through a "typical" day, I soon learned that, as the principal put it, "Applebaum and the others are a little upset, but don't worry about it."

The teachers had been told, not asked, about my visit and were very angry about my intrusion by executive fiat. I didn't blame them; they were right. But it did mean I spent half the day selling myself and my interviews, time taken away from the classrooms I wanted to observe quietly.

(This was not my only run-in with teachers who were wary of a classroom visit. The bad press teachers have received may explain it, but it still seems shortsighted to me: if the rhetoric is that nobody understands or cares about our schools, then why turn away the few who come to find out?)

In the end, Dr. Applebaum did welcome me, and for this interview he stayed on after school for a few hours to talk to me. We had barely begun when another teacher walked into his classroom. They talked about a cocktail party given by the school to honor its teachers. It was set for the following week, and neither intended to go. Dr. Applebaum gave this explanation:

Teaching has been a bittersweet experience. I look at myself as no better or worse than a lot of folks here. I am certainly a very experienced teacher. I have taught at all levels, from kindergarten through college, and I've had a very comfortable career. But I find that I have hardly ever been asked what I can contribute unless I volunteer it myself. This is quite typical of my experience with what I call teacher/educators everywhere in the country.

It's pathetic, especially since most administrators started out as teachers. It's nice to go on an outing with colleagues and to be flattered—oh, what a wonderful faculty we have here—but it isn't what we need.

Last year I told a white lie. This year I will say I choose not to attend. In this small way I want to convey that something more ought to be considered. We're sensitive to the issues in education, but nobody consults us.

As a social studies teacher, what issues strike you as important?

I believe we need to really focus on human relations. Prejudice—racial, religious, ethnic—has not disappeared. It continues to grow and simmers just below the surface. Our children see few Americans who have a different outlook, and we as a country have problems on the international level because we see the world from our provincial point of view.

We also need to give our youngsters a much firmer understanding of our economic and political system. Before they become greatly disenchanted with our system, our kids better understand it, and right now they just don't.

Disenchantment can lead to great bitterness and then to conflagration. I don't think we've seen the end of the protest we saw in the sixties. Principals were distressed when colleges like Berkeley and Columbia protested, but someday we may see it in our junior and high school levels. We are not immune.

Another great concern is, of course, peace. This is not an original idea, but I think that to keep the peace, each year we should exchange 10,000 students between the Soviet Union and the United States and encourage them to stay for three years. Then we will keep the peace.

Lastly—and this is more personal—if there is one thing I regret in my lifetime, it's how little talk or thought our generation devotes to what we owe future generations. The so-called independence generation talked about "posterity," but we do not.

You've spoken about our provincial outlook. You are known in this school for trying to increase the children's social awareness.

It's a small first step. There are visits to hospitals and kids who raise funds for a school in India and for a poor American Indian school.

I want to question how deep this runs. Are these projects just another little number in the curriculum, or are affluent kids really changed by them?

I agree with your point. The only way these kids are going to be changed is if they are permitted to experience what kids in their age group in other areas and other economic strata know.

Peace Corps for the nation? I ask about this because teachers in private schools usually point out that yes, their students are privileged, but they are active in various good works. I'm a bit turned off by that approach.

You could well be; I agree with you. You can correspond; you can exchange videotapes, but that isn't enough.

What about a short-term exchange program?

That is the wrong question to ask me, because that's the dream I had many years ago when we were on double session and didn't have the money to build a new building. I proposed securing the funds, charting a plane, and taking 150 kids to another culture for a yearlong interdisciplinary program—history, geography, language, you name it.

They laughed.

Many years went by, and I again recommended a similar program. We had the chance to establish a direct exchange program, not with a school, but with a few ideally suited communities in China, Australia, New Zealand, and Indonesia. Correspondence and direct visits took place; a committee was set up. But nothing happened. This community did not want to undertake the commitment, and that—together with other issues where I have made recommendations that did not get off the ground—is why I am bittersweet about my experience here.

Have you considered changing schools?

I'm always looking. It isn't so much the job—I'm well paid here—but a new challenge, something that will give me a zest for living that I seek. At interviews I usually interview *them* to find out whether or not a real challenge is involved. I had one interview for a post as director of curriculum in Rhode Island. One young woman told me she didn't know what the rest of the group thought of me, but she wanted me on board right away. I told her that she was the kiss of death; she was the one classroom teacher on the interview committee—a token representative whom no one would heed.

Does that bother you?

Sure it does. Certainly it does. When I look at my own career, I realize that from a professional, hierarchical point of view I am the bottom of the ladder. Despite a doctorate from Columbia and all sorts of certification, I'm still a classroom teacher instead of an educational dropout.

Educational dropout?

Administrator. The money is in administration, not the classroom, and whatever prestige is involved in education is in administration.

In fact, because I'm introduced as Dr. Applebaum and am approaching 60, when I meet people, they just assume I am either the district superintendent or the building principal. When I say I am a classroom teacher, I feel almost apologetic. I'm letting them down, and they're disappointed–although they cover it very well. The classroom teacher is no one unless there is a crisis–local, national, global–and then he is important for a short while.

Are you unhappy here?

Not at all. I find the classroom very pleasant. Certainly it's unstressful. I joke with the people here that when it is time for me to leave, I should auction off my job. This is despite my reservations about administration, the school board, and parents–who rarely get to know teachers very well. You know, people ask, what is going on in the schools? It's a good question. I don't know what's going on in those other classrooms.

Should parents be more involved?

That's a hard question. Years ago I would have said yes. But today they cannot be. The don't have the time or energy. If they have too much time, they are going to be negative interferers. What is the best way for parents to be involved without being nags, interferers, pains in the neck? I don't have any answer there. They are concerned, but how are they concerned? For all the rhetoric about parent-teacher contact, the truth is that no one sector wants to be that intimate.

There used to be much greater intimacy. I know that when I started out, I became very involved with visits to homes that had problems.

Home visits! Just like the family doctor 30 years ago.

A different world. But those home visits were like the sensitivity groups we used to have 15 years ago: there were plusses and minuses to them. Once you extend your range of contact, it isn't easy to stand back. The question is, Who is ultimately responsible for the life of somebody else? If you are a teacher, how deeply do you get involved with the lives of your students' families? Minister, rabbi, priest, counselor, psychologist–what are you?

In the forties, schools recommended that the teacher get to know the families. But you can become too involved, psychologically and financially. And is everybody working with the same game plan and rules? What are the safeguards?

Now if youngsters wish to approach me, I'll do the best I can. But I make no extended overtures to visit their homes, have lunch, and so on.

Have the students changed much during your time here?

I find the children today far easier to work with than when I began here in 1955. I find them much more cooperative and far less aggressive than they once were. Parents may be a little more aggressive about their desire to make sure their children have all the skills necessary to meet the demands of the outside world.

I have not heard this view very often. If anything, I hear how kids are more difficult, undisciplined, and so on.

It's possible that the kids have more personal problems now, but I still say they are far easier to work with than in the past. Maybe it has to do with my age or position in the school; I have a reputation as a semityrant, a hard taskmaster. But I tell students that I treat school as a serious business; I expect them to take it seriously. There's a pattern: they come as pilgrims; then they're pupils; later on full-fledged students; and finally, scholars who will teach their former teachers. For me their time in school is as serious as their parents working for an income.

You know, talk about kids is like the discussion about permissiveness. We had more rules 30 years ago, but they were just as easily broken.

In fact, the only problem the children have in cooperating with me is that their schedules are far more demanding than in the past.

Their school schedules?

School and social calendar. When I first came here 34 years ago, social studies was taught in 2-hour blocks of time. The content included everything from physiology, health, and nutrition to a little bit of history and language arts. It was what we used to call a "core curriculum." Now I have 40 minutes. It would be better if we met for fewer sessions and had larger blocks of time.

There are fads in curriculum. During the Soviet Sputnik explosion we moved away from health and nutrition issues and into world geography. This school piloted and was in the vanguard of a tremendous new program in world geography. It drew a lot of attention and expanded into something very unique. But because of changes in curriculum over the years, that program—like many others—has been disbanded. [When I observed his class, he was working on maps with the students—something he tells me he added to the curriculum because geography is out of vogue now.]

The state mandates your curriculum?

Yes and no. One does what one *thinks* the state mandates; and if no one comes in to check on you, there's room to do a lot of things. I continue to do what I think is important. I could be criticized, but the question is, Who does the evaluation? Who knows better than I?

Who does?

I'm critical of the new state curriculum because anytime you put things down on paper, it becomes something like the Ten Commandments. Folks think that they ought to obey what they think the law says, and pretty soon you have what many of us, a generation ago, smilingly referred to as the "French syndrome."

What's that?

When a French superintendent from Paris walked into a village school in La Rochelle, which is five hours' train ride away, at 9:45 in the morning on a Thursday, he would expect to hear and see a teacher doing what any other teacher from Lyons to Marseilles was doing at that same moment all over France.

Of course, if you gave academic freedom to every teacher and put nothing on paper, it would be very difficult for any centralized body to know what was going on. But how centralized do we want our education to be? We are taught that education is a local thing, and then we put all sorts of restraints on the community. On the other side of the coin, what if the local community does not have the wisdom to decide the curriculum? [By now he is gleeful about how many times he can turn the coin over, a trait that I think many teachers possess.]

Do parents come in with objections or suggestions about the curriculum?

I have never had a parent ask for a different curriculum. But most parents are more comfortable with a curriculum that is like the one that they had. Change is always a difficult thing to accept.

You are an expert in curriculum?

That is the subject of my doctorate, but I'm not sure I believe in experts. For the years I have left after I leave here, I would love to be invited to set up a teacher-training program—new staff, new curriculum, new students. And it will never happen; we are still training teachers the same way we did 40 years ago.

Isn't it time for a change?

Postscript

Who Is in Charge?

Passing the buck may be our true national pastime. It is certainly part of what happens when teachers and administrators talk about each other. Nonetheless, I think that teachers resent administrators and the world of administration with good reason.

For teachers, administrators are not education's CEOs. They are dropouts, the people who did not like to teach, took some mumbo-jumbo courses, and became administrators. And if, as I have heard many administrators say, they got out in order to have a greater impact, then teachers want to know why those in power don't consult those in the classroom.

Not being involved in the critical decisions that affect their schools—indeed, standing by while they see genuine educational needs take second place to public relations—is a major frustration for teachers.

It doesn't help that administrators—perceived as having the easier jobs—earn far more and garner whatever prestige is still associated with education. Nor is it a comfortable situation when the person you should be able to consult when you think your classroom is in trouble is also the one who evaluates you.

206

Beyond the teacher's own school, moreover, is the larger administrative structure—a monstrous bureaucracy. When in New York City the new superintendent of schools wanted to know how many people worked at the central board of education, no one was able to tell him. Finally, he assigned someone to find out, and his deputy chancellor for financial affairs actually did a head count—6,447 employees in New York's central office (and our other large cities' figures are similar). No one was clear about what all these people did. (They are *not*, I know, answering their phones.)

Whatever these bureaucrats do, teachers feel it is not as important as putting more teachers in our classrooms. Teachers are in favor of cutting the number of bureaucrats at every level. And they want to join with administration in the running of their individual schools.

But what worker does not grouse about management, and what bureaucracy wants to self-destruct? Isn't the point of bureaucracy to expand? Schools, as you might expect, work pretty much like everything else.

But that, I think, is one of the big problems: the model for our present schools took shape in the late nineteenth century and was based on the brave new factories of smoke-stack America, themselves now obsolete. Under this model strong principals are the equivalent of factory foremen. They wield the authority while teachers—akin to blue-collar workers, who are more or less interchangeable—do the work and take orders.

This structure, known in management circles as a "top-down hierarchical structure," may have been an excellent way to organize factory life; but it seems to be a poor way to run a school or, for that matter, to educate. It is, after all, the children who become the products along the assembly line.

It makes far more sense to involve teachers in making the decisions that affect their work in the classroom: not only is their input needed, but it would also make them *more* accountable for what happens in their schools. As it stands now, the division of teachers and administrators into labor and management creates an "us" and "them" mentality. But seeing both on the same side would cast teachers in a role that allows them to be part of the solution instead of being seen as part of the problem.

Shared decision making has invaded industry, however, and there are signs that schools, which have always aped the industrial sector, will follow suit. For example, the school boards in Rochester and Miami have made some innovations in their school systems. In both cities some schools are now being run by management teams of teachers and administrators. And in Boston, corporate leaders have made this kind of power sharing with teachers a condition of their pledge to hire more high school graduates.

Support for the idea is widespread, even if action has not yet followed on a major scale. The opposition comes from middle management, which stands to lose some power. And some people are skeptical because related programs, such as New York City's decentralization of its schools (aimed at increasing neighborhood control), have been far from successful.

Admittedly, there would be problems. I wonder how teachers could fit in any more demands on their time and what would they be able to drop from their schedules. Still, it appears that what people now call the "factory-floor model" was a mistake from the start.

To recruit talented new teachers, schools must be able to call teaching a "profession" and mean it. Shared decision making would help make the word ring true.

> "Even though it has changed, they need us
> more than they ever did. We teachers think
> the way the police think: if not for us, the
> deluge."
>
> ASHER ROSEN
> high school English teacher
> *Los Angeles, California*

I Stand Proud

In 26 years Asher Rosen has known all kinds of schools, and like Manuel Montalvo, he too has seen a decline in public education. Nonetheless, Rosen is able to say, "I stand proud."

Schools are havens for him, places where children are safe and free from real danger. "We teachers are soldiers," he said. "If the kids were not with us, I shudder to think what they would be doing. I remind the kids all the time that they are safe here. In the school they have a place that is decently quiet, safe, and secure; and there are people here who love and care for them."

In effect, that will have to do until more students care about schools as places to learn. As far as Asher Rosen is concerned, teaching "is a useful profession, a noble profession. We're a little frayed around the edges, but we are still out there."

I told him he did not sound like a burned-out teacher, and that is where we began:

I'm not really. I've been in every kind of school situation and was hired here at John Marshall High [a suburban school] in an instant.

I've had a full life of teaching. It may not be the last thing I do, but I've got to stay with it 10, 15 more years. I've got a mortgage, and my children are young. I want my kids to see me as a teacher, not as someone just working for money. That's real important for me and for them.

How good a job is your school doing?

It's uneven, but in the main we are doing a fine job. How we do has to be looked at in relation to state and national priorities, and our commitment to education has always been cyclical: Sputnik, why Johnny can't read, and so on. We are about due for a general national commitment.

Right now California has an initiative [proposed legislation—to be put to public vote] to earmark a certain percentage of the state budget for education. That's terrific. It's like getting married, as opposed to having an affair. You say, "This is it," and you set the money aside and make a commitment to education—to teachers, to salaries, and to new schools.

I see all sorts of office buildings and condos going up, all sorts of luxury next to poverty, and I think that things in the public sector have to work in parallel fashion. We've neglected our schools for decades.

Schools have to be so damned attractive that the kids will love to come there, and they will think that the teachers have to be safe, the students have to be safe. There have to be materials there, and, above all, there have to be qualified teachers. Teachers can turn a school around *provided* there is some support on the state and national levels.

Look, if the block where they live is safe, I can talk decency to my students, and they will be decent kids. But if the block is not safe, I can preach all I want, and my students will come home, look around, and decide that being decent is crazy. They'd be fools to be good citizens on a dangerous street. The same analogy holds true for teaching. Kids see that even with a good school, good teachers, and good administrators, the neighborhood is rotten. Things don't work so well, and the kid who was supposed to go to Cal [State] or Yale, maybe he got shot in the alley.

Can you say anything about how kids have changed since you started teaching?

All of us were so naive in the sixties. I think youngsters are less patient now. Remember what we have gone through–a president who in essence quit and a vice-president who got booted out, Vietnam, a staggering debt. These things add up, and schools are caught up in the backwash.

At Marshall, a good school, people in the drug program are talking about 25 percent of the students being chemically dependent. That is insane. In a class of 35, I'm looking at 8 kids who are on drugs, when they are all there. Mondays and Fridays are a little iffy. Kids take long weekends now, blatantly, and they don't return books. It's a snowball effect.

My wife went to Marshall in the mid-sixties. She remembers a few kids doing dope in the bathroom, but they pretty much had things under control. Now you get a questionnaire from the anti-drug people every few weeks: So-and-so has been referred. Is this person sluggish? Is his attendance record poor? And so on.

But kids still like a good poem or story, a teacher with energy–the basics, good stand-up teaching. You don't need complicated instruments. You need good people with the classroom decently quiet and kids ready to go. Basically, in the heart of the week (Mondays and Fridays are a little bit marginal, and we just schedule activities accordingly) they still need human contact–a good, straight person, maybe even an out-of-touch person. They often tell me that I'm a fuddy-duddy, but I point out that I'm older and that I can resist a lot of the things that influence them.

Do you assign reading to do at home?

I do, but that is not successful. Youngsters spend more time avoiding homework than doing it. And I don't know how to manipulate them to get their parents in on open-school night. Some teachers give the students extra credit, and the school used to give them a ticket to a movie in the auditorium if they could get their parents to attend.

I encourage the kids to bring their parents in *anytime*. If I'm having trouble, they can help me out with their kid. If they want to read or give a lecture, I'll sit back. I do not take the view that the classroom is my little fiefdom.

How do you react to teachers who say "I can't teach these kids. They are not motivated"?

It's nonsense, nonsense. Sincerity and consistency are important. Kids want predictability.

**But the fact that they don't do homework, don't show up on
a Monday or a Friday—**

[Interrupts] My wife is frustrated when she looks at my roll book
and sees so many absences and tardies. She can't believe the number of *Ds* in my grade book. She remembers Marshall from the sixties, when this school was the crème de la crème, every kid pol-
ished and perfect. Now they get out of bed and put on a T-shirt.

All this appalls my wife. Me, I appreciate the difference in 20
years. I don't know if it is callousness or just reality adjustment. I
am appalled by how many youngsters are resigned to just passing,
but I tell myself this doesn't have to be forever; it is now. They have
other things going, and the economic pressure is key. They've got
jobs at the Galleria [a large mall], a shoe store, the ice cream stand.
It's either dope or jobs or family problems or a combination. There
are reasons in this society why my students are absent. So I adjust
myself to a smaller class size on Mondays and Fridays, and the kids
who miss the points, miss the points. Maybe they'll be happy just
to get through.

It's true that their low expectation level frustrates and disap-
points me. But then I say, "Wait a minute; we've got a president
who doesn't want to be awakened when Libyan planes are bomb-
ing our men. He's asleep too." Look at all the infrastructure work
that needs redoing—hospitals, parks, bridges—all basically on projects that were built during the New Deal (though Eisenhower did
work on some highways). We need a commitment to the public sector and to education. Then maybe kids will understand that it is
important.

In the old days I had a friend who taught in Chinatown, and one
day, just before lunch, he threw his notes into the wastebasket. And
you know what happened? The bell rang, and all 35 kids just con-
verged on the wastebasket to get the notes. Teacher's notes! Outrageous...imagine. That was in the late forties, early fifties.

**It's not easy to imagine anymore. Earlier you said, "We are the soldiers."
I keep wondering whom you are fighting.**

Ignorance and self-hate.

In the old days schools were for school. That's an idyllic Hollywood picture, but it's true. Now schools are for social training, for
lunches, for baby-sitting. Schools are the catchall, and it makes
things tense and high pressure. We're the recipient, and it makes it
all a battle.

My high school teacher would get up at the blackboard, and we'd all pay attention. There was no lunch program, no drug program, no teacher aide, no complicated scheduling, no adviser center. You want to go to Harvard? Then study hard and apply. Now we have to do everything for them.

Then how do you keep up your enthusiasm?

I have a mental trick. Sunday evening is a bluesy time for everyone. I have to prepare myself for the five-day cycle—the quiet Monday—and I have to remember that I don't have to be on stage all the time. I can be in the background on Monday and function as a reference center.

I also have to remind myself that I go in for the academics, not the kids. I want to read this paragraph again, and maybe I'll learn something new. Then if the kids are in a bad mood, I am not disappointed.

That's my psych-out. I ask myself what are the pluses and minuses: if I were selling real estate, I'd have to take this clunk out who wouldn't buy the house anyway. Don't think I haven't thought about it, but teaching still comes out the best. The kids need someone who is contagiously intellectual, and most of the time I am.

What do you think of teachers coming into the schools now?
Many say they are not the same quality as your generation.

That has to be true, but not because the *Los Angeles Times* writes a piece about how some teacher can't spell. I remember how I thought in my university days, and I see how people who are in teacher-training programs now think. They haven't any intellectual life. They are thinking about career, and they mumble about safety valves—what they can do if they don't teach.

Now there's a high turnover rate. When I started teaching, we had one or two silver-haired retirements per year. These days people get out in five, six years.

You've been in many different schools. Can you briefly describe what the ghetto schools were like?

Depends on the time. In 1964 I was in an all-black school, and those first three years were my best years of teaching. I've figured it out since. The school had just changed from an all-white school to an all-black school. There was an economic range—from an underclass to lower class and a struggling middle class. Because kids from the underclass saw other black kids from the community who were achieving, many of those kids made it. Also, teachers were still in the driver's seat, inspired enough to really charge at the kids and get the maximum from them.

The situation in those schools now is horrible. I've subbed there and can see the change in schools where I used to be pleasantly received. There is more bitterness, more resentment, deeper poverty. Black kids who got up early enough in the morning and got their parents' permission were bussed out. In one sense the ghetto student bodies were drained of the black kids who would have been the models.

The Watts riots took place in 1965, and certainly the racism was there. But integration did not work, because it was not supported at all levels. It was a numbers thing in which we moved kids around—an overlay to what should have been a deep vertical program. We're wiser now, and we still need to integrate. When we have full support from state and national authorities, it will work.

Was being a white teacher in a black school a problem?

I remember in one school a black kid defended a teacher by saying, "She ain't white, she's Jewish." [Laughs] But seriously, there is always a testing, and you've got to pose tough in the ghetto. If you are white, you have got to know what you are doing, what you're all about.

It makes sense. You are the person in their house. You have to get through a baptism by fire, and then everything is okay. You've got to know what sounds there are, what habits there are, what's cooking in the kitchen; you've got to know all that. That's true whether it's a black house or a Japanese house—you have to know where you are and what to do.

Teaching in ghetto schools was good, but it was draining. It was high pressure. There was someone who said that we have to get young teachers with strong voices to work in the ghetto. The noise level is high there. For the kids, it's high at home, it's high at school.

[We now talk about some of the other schools in which he taught.]

In the mid-seventies I became frustrated with my classes at the "opportunity schools." I switched to elementary school for three years. That was *tough:* a big school, split session, year-round. Noisy, a big factory.

Opportunity schools?

The euphemism for where we place troublemakers. These are the "bad" kids–wayward boys and girls–and they are rough. I was tense there. The best policy was to keep your eyes and ears open. I was like a mountain lion–wary. You had to stay awake, watch very carefully. One kid showed me a knife, and I said, "You should not have done that. That was dumb." He said, "I thought I could trust you." I said, "That's not trust." I asked him for the knife, he refused, and the office took care of it. He got kicked out.

Kicked out of a school for wayward boys?

We expelled kids. There's a sequence–you go from regular school to a "social adjustment" transfer, and then you go to an opportunity school. After that, it's "Tri-C," which I think the department of corrections handles. Tri-C is a storefront setting, and kids are put on contract. They agree to go to school some part of the time, and their corrections officer sees to that. They come and peck away at their diplomas.

It's crazy. Instead of getting them a job cutting trees in a national park–as Roosevelt did with the Civilian Conservation Corps–we bounce them from school to school. But we should get them out of the city. The city is sick. They destroy themselves and others.

Obviously there's pathology here. We need to get them into a better environment.

Where I am now is mixed–ethnically, racially, and economically. The kids are nearly 50 percent Hispanic, 20 percent Anglo, and almost 30 percent Asian. There are few blacks. A mixed school is basic insurance for the least amount of problems because one group kind of offsets another.

There is a cliché about what high achievers Asian children are. That's not always so. I've had kids–third generation Japanese Americans, for example–who are just trouble all over the place. They don't attend, they don't pay attention, and they don't turn in their work.

But it has been my experience that Asian people–Japanese, Korean, Chinese–tend to renovate the community and to stay put. Their culture is so old and secure; they know who they are, and this comes through in the classroom. The kids may not be as smart as their reputation indicates, but they're there. And guess what? They hand in their assignments, and they stay in school.

Their culture and conditions make the difference, not any innate superiority. The key is when you have students who constantly question. Asian kids, any kids, are teachable under certain conditions.

Certain conditions?

If kids are too tired, or their mother is beating them, or their father is away, they don't ask questions. They're not ready to learn.

You know, even without a troubled home life, it's difficult. Their whole society just bombards them. There's no coherence, no order, no purpose. They have trouble recounting a plot line. They are a mass of sense impressions.

But they know they need a mature person to lead them, to put it all together, and I stand proud. They still need us, and that is good.

In the Second Grade

Most teachers are anxious to talk about their work but are not that quick to invite you into the classroom. On one occasion, when I asked permission to observe second-grade classrooms in a New York suburban school, the teachers asked to meet with me first. We sat around on those child-size seats at a low table, and they in effect interviewed me. Why did I want to observe their classes? What did I think one day can reveal? Why this book? What questions do I ask? Have there been any surprises?

I was there for an hour. By the close all but one agreed to my visit. Why she refused wasn't clear. But she was livid about her need to work extra jobs in order to send her own children to private colleges. She talked of nothing else.

The others talked about how the community sees them, and all their reports were negative. One teacher mentioned how a workman, who did not know her profession, complained about how "we" pay for "their" teeth. A second said that people resented teachers' long vacations, and a third complained that people thought they didn't work very hard.

"But," went the chorus, "we all work very hard, far harder than middle- and upper-school [high school] teachers. We are totally

responsible for thirty children, Monday through Friday, eight to three, and we cannot even go to the bathroom. It is very demanding work."

This all happened on a Monday. The teachers agreed that I would return on Thursday and observe their classes. We'd meet as a group during lunch and talk again.

What follows is our second lunchtime conversation. Again, we sat in a second-grade classroom. (It was a little chilly because the thermostats have been encased in plastic in order to prevent teachers from making individual adjustments in room temperature. What some do is to wrap the thermostat in a cold wet cloth–a trick they picked up in city schools– and thus lower the thermostat reading, causing more heat to be pumped into their rooms.) The walls were lined with student work, a colorful oversize alphabet, and a "Writer's Checklist" that asked, in part, "Did I...Start with a capital? End with a . or a ? Use interesting words? Write neatly?"

Four teachers took part–identified here as Ann, Polly, Joan, and Louise. All but one had worked in the inner city before moving to a suburban school. Joan, the group veteran, has taught for twenty-nine years, and Polly, the least experienced, for seven; Louise and Ann have each taught for about a dozen years.

Remembering how suspicious they had all been a few days earlier, I began by asking a question that left the field wide open.

What are the biggest rewards and/or frustrations in your job?

Louise: I think the biggest reward is watching the light bulb turn on in somebody's head. You try five or six approaches to get an idea across, and all of a sudden the child says, "Oh, you mean... and you say, "Thank you, God. Yes, that is what I mean."

Ann: I agree. Also to watch them grow and see the people they have become by June. What has been achieved is very measurable at this age.

Louise: The frustration is time. There isn't the time for all the things we want to do. Some days I feel that I am on a treadmill; I keep moving and moving, but I'm not getting anywhere.

Ann: We add to the curriculum–this year we are going to add an AIDS curriculum–but we do not remove anything. [How an AIDS curriculum works in the second grade is not clear. The program is still in the planning stage as we speak.] It's tough to squeeze it all in, and there's no room for extras.

As for frustrations: parents! The ones who haven't the time or wouldn't make the time or apparently don't care. That's a frustration because you can give so much here, and then it ends. We only have the kids five or six hours a day, and then they go home.

Joan: Seven hours a day!

Is lack of parent support a major problem?

Ann: Not the way it is in the city. But because most children are, if anything, overindulged, those few who are really emotionally needy stand out very strongly.

Are there services for the emotionally disturbed kids?

Ann and Louise [both answer]: There is a system, and we do try our best. But there are a lot of children–even in this kind of area–who need support. When you find a child who you know needs some kind of help and he is 13th on the list so that he won't get tested until April, it's a frustration.

That is happening?

Louise: It may not be the same kind of numbers you see in a city school. But when it is *your* kid, and 12 are in front of him, well, gee whiz, this kid still needs help too.

Why should it take so long?

Ann: The budget. We spread the psychologist thinner and thinner when there is more and more for him to do. We used to have one in the building, but now he spends part of the week doing reevaluations at the high school.

Parents are told that we have made budget cuts but that they don't hurt the child's program. That is the public relations, and it isn't apparent to parents that children are losing out. "It doesn't hurt your child's program," they're told, but of course it does. When it hurts one child, there's a ripple effect, and the other children are hurt too.

Joan: We used to see the necessity for social workers and counselors only in the high school. Now there's a move to get them into the middle school. But the truth is that with all the problems in society, we also need them in the elementary school.

Our psychologist used to offer a therapy group. There is no way he can do that now; all he can do is test them all and indicate what the problems may be.

Ann: The children need more support. There should be a counselor on the staff. We have certainly never seen it like it is now. Services are more and more fragmented, and children need more and more support.

Last year, on the third day of school one of my kid's fathers walked out. That child needed support, but since she wasn't a basket case, there was no one, except me, available for her to see.

Polly: The budget crunch is only part of it. There's a belief that help is more needed and more effective in the higher grades. In the lower grades the children's need is not as apparent because the discrepancy between their age and their achievement level has not gone that far yet.

If in second grade you are reading at a first-grade level, you are only a year below. But when you are in the ninth grade and functioning at a third-grade level, that discrepancy is so much more apparent, and you get more attention. They are just as needy at our level, but attention is not given to them.

We can recognize who needs help. I'd bet that everybody in this room can look down a list of students and be absolutely correct about which ones are going to be in need down the road. It's not addressed now because it's not as glaring.

No matter what question I ask, we soon go beyond the classroom. It sounds as though you are picking up the pieces for our society.

[A chorus of agreement]

Joan: Absolutely. We've learned a great deal about how to teach. Teaching methods are wonderful, and they are being improved all the time. But the great frustration is how to teach all the children *and* cope with all the problems that changes in society have raised.

Louise: This year my class is abnormal. Twenty-five intact families!

Ann: You don't expect family breakdown in the suburbs. I've got nineteen intact out of twenty-six.

[Each gives the marital scoreboard for her class. They also talk about kids who are shuffled from house to house and can't remember with which parent they left their workbooks.]

Louise: Now everybody works. The kids are with baby-sitters or at the school till six each night. They never have a friend over or go to a friend's house. When my kids were young, they played with other children a couple of times a week.

Polly: Kids are never home. No one is home. At least in the more-affluent communities, where there is live-in help, children can have play dates.

Joan: The number of working mothers has had a great impact on schools. It may be a great step forward for women, but it impacts on the children. It's hard getting them out in the morning, and they come to school without their lunch. One child said, "I'm buying, but I don't have any money."

Louise: They buy peanut-butter-and-jelly sandwiches. Why don't parents keep a jar of peanut butter at home?

But aren't all of you working mothers?

Polly: Yes, and we know the strain of getting children ready for school when we also have to go to work.

I think sometimes parents forget what our job is like. We need to remind parents more of our constraints and our responsibilities. That way, if we mark a paper incorrectly or do not provide a costume for the kid who doesn't have one or don't provide a snack for the child who has forgotten his, they'll know why.

Don't shoot me for saying this everybody, but I think we need to get more parents—not in the classroom—but—

Louise [interrupts]: Involved! Parents think their responsibility ends when they send their child to school. For those six or seven hours they expect us to provide everything! Half the time they expect me to feed them.

Here's a good example of the way mothers think: school supplies! Because the lines are terrible when school opens, I always give the children three or four days to bring in their supplies. Then they come in and tell me, "Mom didn't have time." Guess what? This mom did, and I stood on those lines. The attitude is, "Don't worry. The teacher will provide the pencils and the notebooks."

Ann: Except that we don't have them.

Joan: We used to order pencils, paper, crayons, scissors. Now we ask the children to supply them. Right now the school appropriates $25 per year per child, and that is supposed to cover textbooks.

Priorities are backward. The district spent $15,000 for a trophy case at the high school, and we don't have enough readers, let alone supplemental books, to support our program.

People who run corporations get up at school-board meetings and think they can "shape things up." But schools are not for profit. The bottom line here is the children.

[Everybody contributes a story about lopsided priorities. They think the schools support what the public can see: sports have a glamour, and it's a way for "dads to relive their youth." The budget, which is scrutinized line by line, comes under heavy fire because it is visible. It is one of the few places where the public feels it "can have some control."]

You are short on supplies but not on kids. The classes seem too large.

Louise: The classes are enormous. In kindergarten there is not enough room at the tables for them to draw.

How about using parents as classroom aides?

Four voices: We have them. [Each explains why parent volunteers are a mixed blessing.]

Ann: It's no good if parents volunteer for the same grade as their child is in. They are competitive. "Why aren't you doing what I saw in so-and-so's class?"

Louise: I have 25 children in my class, and I don't have the time to train a volunteer—no matter how wonderful she may be. There are also many jobs that only I can do. I have to know where my kids are.

Polly: I had a problem because after only one week the volunteers began to call and say they could not keep their appointments.

Joan: Volunteers are a help, but they are not the answer. We need smaller classes. When we had 20 in the classroom, it felt like heaven. It allowed for a different teaching style.

We do not have enough time for any of our kids, and for very bright ones we have no program at all. We've cut the gifted-and-talented program out in the lower grades. The school would not dare cut the remedial program, but it's also very difficult for the gifted child to function in an ordinary classroom. People don't know this, even though the state recognizes gifted as a "handicapped" condition. The school thinks that the parents of these kids are overdoing it. The attitude is, "Stop bragging."

I noticed that many of your kids are just starting to read. What do you do with the one kid in 25 who is a fabulous reader?

Joan: As best we can. We try to hook him up with a third grader or get him out into a science project. It's difficult because young children cannot work independently very well, and they don't want to be isolated from the group.

Ann: If we had just one group for the advanced readers in each grade level, it would be okay. But it is the budget again. People will not pay for it.

[We run out of time, and Polly, who had begun to clear the table of sandwich wrappers and coffee cups, looks uncomfortable. Then she speaks out]

Polly: You've heard a lot of complaints, but let's not forget that we love the kids. We would not be here if we didn't.

[A chorus] Hear! Hear!

"I have to try to find a way into that small world so that I can help expand it a bit. I can't do it from the outside in. I have to do it from the inside; I have to get in there."

CYNTHIA FREMONT
high school English teacher
Westchester County, New York

From the Inside Out

Cynthia Fremont works very hard at teaching "from the inside." As an English teacher she finds it pays off. But to know her students well enough to figure out how to approach each and every one of them takes boundless energy—the kind of energy that is in short supply after a teacher has faced 150 youngsters each day and graded 150 papers every few weeks.

Nonetheless, some teachers—Cynthia Fremont is one—have that kind of energy. It's apparent in her classes: she listens intently, makes a comment, asks a question, goes over a paper, and never loses sight of her students. As she put it, "What I teach is not always what they learn, and I am more interested in their learning than I am in my teaching."

She has an open-door policy in her classes, and I was able to observe a number of them. When I observed her advanced-placement English class, the students sat around in small groups and talked about the papers they had drafted on Oedipus Rex. The usual approach to written work—how can I fill three pages with what "she" wants—was nowhere in sight. Students were really working on those papers and actually thinking—in 1988—about Oedipus Rex.

A second English class I observed in that same high school later in the day was different. In this class a group of very bored and noisy teenagers were given vocabulary work sheets and asked to fill them out. This involved looking up 10 words in their dictionaries, filling in the definitions, and then using each of the words in a sentence. Minutes before the class ended, 10 students were asked to put their answers on the blackboard.

No time was left to go over the words, and 10 more words were threatened for the next day. People in the teaching business, I later learned, call this kind of English class the work of a "ditto teacher." Ditto teachers hand out busywork. They are very much like the "can do" teachers, who scrawl work on the blackboard that the students "can do" during the 40-minute classroom period. Both have found ways to "manage," if not "teach," their students.

Such classes, as terrible as they are understandable, are not uncommon. They represent some of the compromises and shortcuts English teachers make after they have handled too many students—and too many papers—in the course of their career.

This kind of class also showed me how special Cynthia Fremont's classes had been. She has taught for 23 years and is still excited by what she does and inspired by her subject.

Fremont started teaching when the need for "mental stimulation" drove her out of the house. "I was the suburban wife and mother, very much involved in my home and community—PTA, Junior League, church affairs. Good Housekeeping told me that my life should be truly wonderful. But I was tired of all these activities and worried about what would happen to me when my children were in school all day. What would I do that would be stimulating and interesting to me and also be of service to people?"

Teaching was her answer. She conceded that she is "sometimes frustrated" and asks herself why she is there. At those times she does not think she is influencing the lives of children. But most of the time, she said, "I feel that the work I do is important. It's important to me and to the young lives I touch. The ability to read and to write and to deal with ideas is critical in our society."

Also critical is an English teacher who believes those words enough to make them a reality—year after year, with no burnout. How has she done it? A few times in the interview I returned to what really baffled me:

How have you kept teaching alive?

I'm sure there are lots of things we can do, and I've done a good many of them. I've gone to school, I've taken courses, and I study regularly; I'm involved in many professional organizations and have been an officer in a couple of them.

I also found that I have skills and abilities that I can share with other teachers. For years I have found and been offered chances to do teacher training for New York State.

Right now I teach a class with one of my colleagues that involves working with teachers from all over this area. This class is a challenge, and it constantly makes new demands on me. I am always having to rethink what I know and make sure I keep up. I read journals, I go to conferences, I follow the new work that's being done.

Are you unusual?

I've met many teachers like me. This summer I was privileged to attend two colloquials sponsored by the New York State Bureau of English and Reading. Being with colleagues from other schools who have the same interests and dedication and enthusiasm stimulated me. These words—*dedication, motivation, enthusiasm*—I know they are used all the time, but they are real qualities, and they are necessary to be effective in a classroom.

They are words I don't hear too often.

I think it's important to live them. I'm not a passive person. Attending seminars, attending colloquials, teaching classes, being active in the New York State English Council, doing workshops for other teachers, these are ways of not only motivating and stretching myself, but of meeting colleagues from other schools and areas who share my interests.

It's very easy to go into a classroom, close the door, and be all alone. Maybe you know a few who share your interests and a few of the other ones—the burnouts. But I believe the burned-out people should be avoided. I don't think that's true just in teaching. It's probably true in life too.

Why don't they get out?

Money, I guess, or habit. Teaching requires an enormous amount of energy. I was asked at one time, What are the qualities required to be a good teacher? You have to know how to learn because you'll never know enough, and things are always going to change. You have to be a lifetime learner and be turned on by learning. You have to know your subject, maintain your enthusiasm for it, and be interested in young people.

Just to get through the day requires a great deal of energy. If you don't have that, no matter how well you know your subject, I think you will have difficulty in getting the students interested in what you want them to learn.

The classes I observed you teaching were motivated and interested. Is that true of all your classes?

No, and it's not always true of the advanced-placement students. While A.P. students are often motivated, sometimes they are there because it is going to look good on their records or because their friends are there. They are the ones with whom I have the greatest difficulty because they have the skill, but no real interest.

I've also had students who are so afraid of making a mistake that I cannot get them to take intellectual risks. They have difficulty in advanced placement because by the very nature of the kinds of assignments I create, they have to take these risks.

Isn't there something about the whole school structure that may contribute to young people being afraid to take risks?

Especially for the most capable students. So much depends on standardized test scores and on class averages that they sometimes forget that there is joy in learning. They'll take the easy route. That's human nature.

This is where the teacher makes a difference. Help the student feel confident enough to take the risks, give him the skills to encourage that confidence, and invest yourself in him as a person to make him believe he can take the risk. We're back to energy, right?

Do you see any marked difference between your students now and the ones you taught fifteen years ago?

Yes, I do. Fifteen years ago the social environment encouraged kids to take political stands. Whether they really understood what they were doing or not, social activism was encouraged.

Now students want to get high scores and good grades so that they can get into a good college, work hard, get a good job, make a lot of money, and retire. We've got them programmed for the formula of money equals success. Youngsters are much more consciously pursuing the American dream.

I've read, however, that the stock market crash [October 1987] has made some students reconsider the careers they want to pursue. Maybe some of them will decide on more altruistic, and less material goals, and it will turn around.

Do you see a change in student academic performance?

I think there are some changes in the general population. I see more and more homes where there has been divorce and more and more homes where the mother and father both work; so the children get less stimulation at home.

I've heard other teachers all over the country make the same point. I don't pretend to be a sociologist, but I know this much: I believe I work harder now—in all classes, A.P. or remedial ones—to help students see what I present as relevant to their own lives.

I still believe that children want to learn. But if they are not involved personally, whatever I have to offer them is not going to mean much. The motivated youngster will try to learn it anyway because he wants the grades that will look good on his records. But I'm not sure that's real learning. That's going through the motions, that's schooling. When any of us learn, we retain what we internalize, and we internalize what has some relevance.

Do you have to work harder than you did 20 years ago at making the students see that books are related to their lives?

Yes, they know less and are far less sophisticated. Their worlds are smaller, and I have to try to find a way into that small world so that I can help expand it a bit.

Are you getting any help from parents?

I've had success with parents, and I think most parents want their children to do well. But the parents of high school teenagers don't know what to do. They get frustrated. We should probably all take classes in parenting.

I believe most parents will be my colleagues to the extent that they can, but the responsibility is on me. I'm the person who should work to find a way to help my students learn. My specialty is writing. I am a writer. I enjoy writing, painful as it may be, and I do it in order to find out what I know. As E. M. Forester said, "I don't know what I think until I see what it says."

So learning how to write is really learning how to think?

Absolutely. I found early on that you can learn how to write, but not from making up forced writing topics or looking for topics in text-books. To teach people of any age to write takes time. It's a process: we brainstorm, we draft, we revise, we edit, and we correct. You don't know what anyone thinks until he either says it or writes it. Perhaps he learns best when he can write it and look at it—that's the learning made visible.

I create model compositions for my students and show them how to write, but I think I am doing something more basic. I'm teaching them how to think and how to translate that thinking into the most powerful form I know of, and that's the written word. This gives them something they can hold on to like an extension of themselves. This is power.

I know I deviated from your original question, but being able to facilitate that kind of learning and to enable students to feel that kind of power is enormously rewarding. It's a natural high, and it keeps me in the classroom.

What do you mean by *power*?

Perhaps I can best define it by an example. I had a student who came to me last year in the remedial-writing lab. He didn't want to be there. He was very angry about being there, and he said, "I don't write, and I hate English, and I hate being here." Those are power-ful feelings, and I asked him about them.

He told me he was a tech. student [a student enrolled in a voca-tional, as opposed to academic, program] and that's where he be-longed. He described his tech. studies, particularly what he does in carpentry class, and at that time he was learning how to use power tools. I said, "I've never heard of those tools, tell me about them." So he started to talk about them. Then I said, "Would you mind if I jotted down the names of these tools and just a little bit about what you've been telling me?"

He became less angry and told me that I had a lot to learn. I took notes while he talked to me. That was one period, one whole period. The next day I showed him this list I had made. I said, "You know, I would like to know more than what you told me, and I'll bet other people would like to know this too. Could you take this list—I probably have it all in the wrong order—and expand on it a little bit and write more about how these tools are used and give me some examples of where you would use this tool and that tool?"

So he started to work on it. He said, "I have to do a report for Mr. So-and-so, my tech. teacher. Do you think I can use this?" We worked on that report for about four weeks altogether. We went through the entire writing process. I introduced him to the computer so that he could use word processing. He ended up with a 2½ page report with an introduction, a body, and a conclusion on three specific kinds of power tools. His conclusion was wonderful. I was so proud of him.

I cannot tell you how many drafts we went through and how many times we revised before we ever began looking at the mechanical problems; we saved that for the last. He said, "You are an English teacher, and you don't care about these mechanical errors?" I said, "I don't care now; we are going to care later." When we were finished, he said, "You know, I never wrote anything before." After that he was mine, he was mine. I could get him to write anything. He passed the Regents competency exam in writing. That gave me such a feeling of power because I had enabled him to use language in a real and meaningful way. And he felt good about himself; he felt good about learning. He was no longer so terrified of the blank page. So many youngsters are tyrannized by that blank page.

Remember what I said before about working from the inside out? I couldn't hand him the Regents competency exam and expect him to work on it. He wouldn't have done it. I had to find out where he was. I had to let him ventilate. I had to let him tell me enough about himself any way he wanted to until I could find something within him. Can I always do that? No, I wish I could say that I've always had that success. I have my failures, but I don't dwell on the failures except to learn from them. How could I have done better? Sometimes I couldn't have done better because what came between some youngster and me was cocaine or alcohol. Youngsters whose minds are controlled by drugs and alcohol don't let me in. I can't deal with that.

Have you seen a lot of that?

I've seen enough of it.

You know, I felt far more successful with that boy who wrote about power tools than I do with many of my advanced-placement students. I don't have to do as much teaching and facilitating for the A.P. kids as I did with this boy in the remedial class.

Working with him on a one-on-one basis was critical. Remedial-writing classes are deliberately kept very small. Without small classes the chances of helping many of these children are nil. Is that expensive? Yes, that's expensive help. I'm costly. But in the long run aren't we going to spend more as a society if we have adults who can't use the language effectively enough to get jobs that will support them and their families? Language is the key! See, I believe that. So if I help them with the language, then I can convince myself that I'm doing more than just helping them. I'm contributing a little something to a better future.

Can we look at the future in more general terms. What are some of the issues facing education now?

A big question.

I'd start with all the responsibilities society has imposed on schools: we've become a socializing agency, a civilizing agency, an educational agency, and even a religious agency in a broad sense. I don't know how we can do it all. I don't think we can!

Now, for example, we have AIDS education in the school. I'm not saying this isn't critically important for us to have. But how many hours a day do we have with these children? How much can we take on? As we take on more and more, I'm very much concerned with our ability to do any of it well.

I don't see an end to it either. The responsibilities imposed on schools seem to increase all the time.

How so?

There are very frightening statistics about the number of children being born to very young and drug-addicted mothers. These children are damaged at birth. They are going to become our students. We are going to have to invest enormous amounts of time and money in trying to cope with them. I'm worried about that.

Also, demographics for the country look very bad. The situation with divorced, single-parent homes leaves a great number of children without any stability in their lives.

And more than ever in need of good teachers?

Exactly. But I also worry about who will become teachers. It's true that better salaries are now attracting young people. But generally, our best and our brightest have not gone into education. Look at the data. Those youngsters who have the C average, the C average, those are the people who have been majoring in education. Not that I think there should be education majors. I believe in getting subject-matter training, and then you take the courses in how to teach it.

Have you had much contact with new teachers?

I've seen quite a few student teachers, and I've talked to colleagues who teach in the colleges and universities throughout the country. The candidates for teaching are not our best. They don't know their subject matter, only "how" to teach it. We had a student teacher here not too long ago who came in very happy about something she had done one day with her master teacher. She came into the English office and said, "Uh, me and Miss So-and-so..." Pretty basic grammatical errors. For the most part, teachers are models. I am careful about the way I speak, and I am careful about the way I dress.

I noticed that incidentally. [Fremont is very well dressed and looks more like a corporate executive than a high school teacher.]

I believe we set tone in a classroom, a serious tone. Not that it can't be fun, but this is serious business, this is real business. We are also models for striving toward excellence.

Do you think allowing female teachers to wear pants might have been a mistake?

Pant suits can be very smart. It's the attitude toward dress and appearance that's important. Also, the attitude toward language. This young student teacher didn't even know the language well enough to hear herself make pretty basic grammatical errors. She's not alone. Teachers who have been teaching for a long time—in various subjects—make simple, basic grammatical errors. Sometimes very amusing things come out.

Amusing and appalling?

I think it is. Sometimes people laugh at me and say, "You make such a big deal out of it." But we are trying to teach our children how to use the language. If our teachers don't try to set the very best examples, using the language as educated people—not as English teachers, but as educated people—in whatever the subject, how can we expect correct or even standard use of the language from our students?

[An impassioned monologue on the need to create a "literate environment" in which "all teachers are teachers of reading and writing" follows. I then described the other English class I had seen, in which students filled out vocabulary lists.]

The drill-and-kill approach. That's just shameful and a waste of everybody's time. I feel badly for the kids. I wish teachers who do that knew better ways. But you have to understand that it's much easier to hand out work sheets.

I do. Frankly I thought, This is a man who doesn't want to work.

Handing out work sheets, having the kids fill in the blanks, is easy.

But if the faculty was more cohesive and teachers talked to each other more, wouldn't there be a lot of subtle ways to convince this teacher to change?

I have been in too many schools, especially schools where there are many veteran teachers, to be sure of that. Teachers sit in workshops and tell us they have more than 125 students. They say that they are not going to change how they teach until their class size is reduced. Even when they recognize that taking the time to devise lessons appropriate to each class and assigning many papers are what should be done, they say they'll consider it *after* their classes are reduced in size. Maybe they will, maybe they won't.

It sounds like a fairly reasonable argument.

It is a reasonable argument. Schools that put large numbers of students in English classes are completely reprehensible. I think those administrators either don't understand or don't care about what they are doing to impede learning.

How big are your classes?

My classes vary in size. I have one class that is much too large–29. But my other classes are small, partly because of the nature of the courses I teach. Teachers who have large classes can't handle the exigencies of the kind of teaching you saw me doing today. There are just too many kids. There's not enough time in the week to sit down and go through their papers carefully and teach them how to revise. I can read this stuff and put a grade on it like a speeding bullet, but that's not helping the youngster learn. To go through, to show him, to work with him—that's what we need time to do.

Do you do that with every student?

I try to do it with every student. We are back to energy. Teachers who know that there are other and better ways to teach may choose not to try them because of the amount of work and time that has to go into it. They may have been teaching for a long, long time, and they are not about to throw out everything they've done. There are also many teachers who are insecure. The insecure teacher is not going to be willing to take the risk of engaging youngsters in important kinds of discussions.

Or engaging them, period. I must say I've begun to see some teaching that looks like a charade.

You mean when we ask questions that almost answer themselves so that students can feed back what we want to hear? That does happen. It's justified if you want to find out if the youngster has read the materials.

But our real task is to engage their minds. We have to ask them questions that will allow them, or force them, to think. Again, I'm talking about getting inside the student's head and helping him find ways to direct himself.

It's a risky business and demands a great deal on the part of teachers. I have been teaching for 23 years, and I still plan my lessons. Teachers who don't plan, don't teach well. Every class is different, and each year is different. What happened today in one class is forcing me to change tomorrow's lessons.

I wish you had come into my second-period class. It's a mixed class and needs a lot of encouragement. With them, I deliberately create many group situations—it's called "jigsawing," and each person does part of the puzzle. The more-able student works with the less able, and they have learned to share. That's an important kind of learning also.

How many hours a day do you spend at school-related work?

My husband would say 24; but I don't. I have a pretty active social life, and I am a reader. I love music. We go to concerts regularly, and I've been known to take a portfolio of papers along. We've had a subscription to Carnegie Hall for a good number of years now, and the man in the box next to us is a math teacher. Sometimes he has papers to grade too.

I try not to do that too much, because if I'm teaching school all the time, I don't think I'm a very interesting person. I listen to PBS [public television] so I can get a little broader view of what's going on. I read *Newsweek,* the *Wall Street Journal,* and the *New York Times.* I need that. I need it for me as a person; I need that for my classes. I need to play, I love to cook. I like to have dinner parties. I like to go to the theater.

Many people see teaching as a nine-to-three job.

Not at all. I have three close friends who are doctors. They take vacations, but they're on duty even when they're not officially on call. Medicine is not only their profession, it is their calling in that literal sense of vocation. I feel that way about teaching. I love it. Someday I'll retire. But I'll still be involved in writing educational materials and in teacher training. I can't imagine myself withdrawing from teaching, but I can see myself withdrawing from the classroom because the energy will begin to diminish. That's just part of the natural aging process.

"It used to be a 50-50 arrangement. But now I get the impression that if I ever stop talking in the classroom, everybody will go to sleep."

FRANK HALLORAN
high school math teacher
Westchester County, New York

It Used to Be a 50-50 Arrangement

Frank Halloran has taught in the same school for 32 years, and he is very definite about what has changed: he believes the shared enterprise that teaching once was has disappeared, largely because his students lack motivation. "I tend to think the horsepower is still there," he said, "but they don't have their foot on the gas any more."

He sees a lot of kids who don't have their foot on the gas, and that's in a high school whose standards have declined.

This interview took place in his office—an ingeniously transformed closet lined with bookshelves and outfitted with a desk, toaster oven, computer, coffee pot, and bulletin board—and in a hallway where Halloran engaged in what he called "hallroom duty."

There was no such thing as hallroom duty when he started out in the fifties. Teachers spent less time monitoring students, and a teacher's work was considered to be important. "We had an essential rating that was probably just below that of nuclear physicists," he said. Teachers received support and there were plenty of resources. "If I had requisitioned a big whale, they probably would have brought it in. Now getting a piece of paper is difficult."

He also explained how his students and the math curriculum were different:

When I started teaching, I paid almost no attention at all to the New York State math Regents. I used to go through the year the way I felt it should go, and then at the end I would say, "By the way, we are going to take this exam at the end, maybe you'd like to look at a copy of it." But as performance levels went down, I soon discovered that we would have to devote more and more time to the Regents in order for kids to pass it.

Now in order for kids to pass the Regents, we have to spend almost all our time preparing for it. We need to cover all of its topics and leave time for a very extensive review. An awful lot of students don't switch on until the review, when panic sets in. The sad part about it is that the Regents is a minimum exam. It was meant to test minimum abilities—the standard we shouldn't fall below. It wasn't supposed to be a goal!

What happened?

Every teacher wishes he could look at a student and tell for sure whether the kid didn't have the horsepower, or he just didn't have his foot on the gas. If he could do that, a teacher would really have a wonderful ability because he'd be able to tailor his approach to each individual kid. I tend to think that the horsepower is probably still there, but the kids don't have their foot on the gas any more.

Why not?

The usual explanation is that our school population has changed and that may be part of it. Also, people like to blame television. Kids put in an awful lot of time at the television set, but they don't see homework as something that you go home and do to the best of your ability. If they are out for a day, they miss the work and the homework review. Why take a one-day absence and turn it into a two-day absence? Why are our kids wiped out by our Asian students?

I don't know. Why?

I don't know why. But I do know that most of our Asian students see homework and school as their job.

I tell students, "This is your job. Mom and Dad are out working to provide an environment in which you can come to school and work. If Dad came home and said, 'Gee, I'm really sorry there is no food tonight because I didn't really feel like working,' you would be highly critical. But that's how you treat your homework."

Homework is a hit-and-run thing. It's either copied or left half blank. You hear, "I looked at it, and it looked really hard," or "I can't do it."

I don't expect it to look like a thing of beauty. As a matter of fact, I had a girl last year whose work looked like she had perspired all over it. You could just see that…I loved it.

Apart from this girl, it sounds frustrating. Yet you seem very calm.

Getting mad or upset will not achieve much. Some people say the community gets the school it deserves. But if the school doesn't do the job, who will? I believe that we should try, as best we can, to bring our students to the point where they have a better sense of priorities and of responsibilities.

Last year when everybody passed the Regents, I was told, "Well, you are an SOB, but you get them by."

Insisting they do homework and pass the Regents makes you an SOB?

[Laughs] It's ironic, but I'll take the heat in order to do what I think is appropriate. You have to be tough–I just believe that right now school is their job. For most of our Asian kids, who (it's true) come from achiever families–executives with Hitachi and so on–school is their job number one. They are not nearly as distracted by all of the other things as our native kids.

Do your boys do better in math than the girls?

I've had an equal number of top math students who were female as I've had who were male.

Do you have much contact with parents?

Not a whole lot. We see more parents from the accelerated classes, but by and large my experience has been that parents are more likely to want to blame the school. A good 60 percent of them start out in an adversarial position.

Blame the school for what?

For the fact that their child is failing. But I've looked around, and

I think the teaching here is pretty good. I can't talk about new teachers—we have so few of them and enrollment is going down.

What has kept you relatively alive? How have you fought the burnout question?

Because you always think you can do it better. If I didn't think I could do it better each year, I would quit. You always think you can improve. One of the things that is happening is that the teacher is now doing more and more of what's going on in the classroom. He is providing more and more of the energy and work in order to get anything done. It isn't healthy. Students proclaim a great desire to do well, but they don't back it up with work.

I've heard that many kids think the mere fact that they have said they are trying should be enough to pass them.

They try to float that balloon in here. I had a parent in yesterday who claimed that since the daughter tried so hard, she should pass. I felt like telling her we don't grade effort, we grade performance.

Was the daughter trying that hard? Well, people think they've studied for three hours when they were sitting and looking at the book. In summer school, kids believe that they should pass because they've shown up. They've served their sentence.

Our culture seems to allow this cockeyed attitude.

We no longer ask if a thing is morally correct. It isn't a question of right or wrong, but Did you or didn't you get caught? But when something is right, it's right whether anyone is watching or not. If we lose that, we've lost it all.

Have we lost it?

I think we've come perilously close. About 15 years ago, I had a student, a nice kid, who told me that "of course, we cheat." When I asked why, he said, "It's all right. We are supposed to cheat, and you are supposed to catch us."

I said, "Do you see this as a war zone, and we are adversaries? Is that how you see the classroom?" He never saw that. He did not understand my point. Yet he was a good kid that I knew well, and he really shocked me.

I still remember how he said that somehow cheating was the right of the student, and it was up to the teacher to prevent it. If I catch a student who is cheating, then I will fail him.

Will the administration back you up if you fail him?

I don't really know. We're judged by how good the school looks, and the standard by which success, or tranquility, is measured is getting the greatest number of kids through the Regents.

Whose tranquility?

The tranquility of the school and the community. I've often said that I thought we should dig in our heels and quit playing games—fail all these people who really deserve to fail. For six months it would be pure hell. Then we can start building on a firm foundation.

Would the other math teachers back you up?

Maybe. But you would have to be very sure that you would be backed up by all subject disciplines. If students are weak in math, then they are probably weak in other subjects as well—though maybe these subjects are easier.

It is easier to pass an average English class than a calculus class?

Yes, because math is either right or wrong—which has its advantages. I tell the kids that math is a 100 subject. Nobody can take your 100 away.

Are grades inflated?

I think games are being played. The past few years it's been suggested that since kids do pretty well on the Regents, but not during the year, we ought to calculate the yearly work differently. But if we have a valid test instrument and they are not doing well, we have to discover their weakness—not just paper it over.

I try to make the math as clear as possible, and I enjoy trying to reach them—to give them the satisfaction of learning a thing as thoroughly as possible. But the rest, all the Mickey Mouse stuff... the teacher across the hall always reminds me of what I said years ago. I dislike everything about teaching except teaching.

If you were starting out now, would you become a teacher?

I don't know. I like my time. I had seen the business world; I had seen what it did to my father, and I decided that I wanted more out of life than just making money. But in the old days the compensation was that, although teachers didn't have a lot of money, people felt that they were doing a tremendous job. Society felt that teachers were making a major and very important contribution.

But that's gone now, and we have become such a money-oriented society that I'd probably have to reevaluate whether or not I wanted to enter into adult life this far down on the social ladder.

In my personal life the reevaluation started a while back. We were doing fine until my own kids became teenagers. I didn't make as much money as people I had graduated with, but it wasn't that disparate. But suddenly the kids were teenagers, and nothing can consume money like a teenager. The people I had graduated with are making at least six-figure salaries, and I'm back in this district making, at the time, $35,000 or $40,000. Then I began to question what teaching had cost me.

I suppose it was slowly beginning to dawn on me that somehow or other if you were a teacher, then you were not a full-grown adult. The message was that a full-grown adult would have a real job, and that's how we were treated.

I'm not sure I follow.

The message was that somehow this wasn't really a full-fledged job, and you weren't a full-fledged adult. If you were, you would be out making money and achieving, and you wouldn't be content to be doing this piddly little thing. Well, from the inside it doesn't look piddly—it looks pretty important. But from the outside…

As a faculty member you are treated like a child. There is very little indication that you are regarded as a professional. Rather you are treated like an itinerant day laborer who is really quite eager to get away with everything he can. That's the impression I get as a faculty member here.

Is that the impression you have had for 32 years?

[Laughs] I've changed, just as my school has changed. When I first came here, the principal was a fellow by the name of McDonald. I can remember being in Mike's office one day when a woman came in to see him dressed in slacks, and he sent her home. He said, "When you are properly dressed, I will talk to you." He was probably wrong, but it suggests how far we've come. Now the kids come to school dressed for a beach party. But then, so do teachers.

Schools are no longer special places?

I come from a private-school background, where the teacher is an important person and has an impact on one's life. Perhaps I saw more in teaching than there is.

You went to private school?

I went to a private prep school, and then I went on to college in the liberal arts. After that, I got a master's in mathematics; I was fortunate to be educated before I was trained.

Trained?

Before I took the education courses. I remember at one point I was eight critiques behind in a course, and the instructor called me in to chew me out. But I was very tired and said, "How can I write critiques about nothing?" [He looks at his watch.] I have to go to my station—hall duty this week.

[We move ourselves and the tape recorder to the hallway. It's very noisy out there and feels a little bit like a stampede. The kids are sloppy, their hair is feathered—in other words, your typical high school bimbos. He watches them also.]

The kids are nice kids, and they're a lot of fun. But have standards of courtesy and what we might call "class" diminished? Oh, absolutely. All you have to do is walk down the hall and listen to the language of these lovely ladies, and you know that they have diminished.

I noticed the lovely ladies—

[Interrupts] But did you happen to notice the sign in the back of my room that said, "No gum." They will put more energy into the gum than they will into the work. There is a four-letter word I simply will not tolerate, but how much can I influence community standards or those of the home? When parents come in and use those same four-letter words in my presence, I've walked out.

You walked out?

I've walked out and have been labeled as arrogant, out of touch.

Do your own kids think you are out of touch?

They know I think the public-school environment is rude and crude—that is one reason I sent them to private school.

You teach in a public school and sent your kids to private school?

I have no problem with that at all. I was hoping that by sending them to private school, they'd be with classmates who came from homes that had pretty much the same values that we had. I didn't want to be saying no all the time. It's very hard when kids get to be a certain age to be saying no all the time.

I still have a letter that my oldest daughter wrote to a friend and never mailed. She said, "I am being sent away to school in a far-off place called Greenwich." We live only a few miles from Greenwich, and she had chosen the school—it's an environment whose values we share.

Also, the crudeness of public schools offends me. I was hoping to avoid that. If your next question is, Did sending them to a private school solve the problem?, the answer is, I don't know whether it did or not. If you ask me about academics, well, anybody who sends their kids to private school puts academics in second place.

You mean the private school was not a better school than your local public high school?

I don't believe that a private high school is academically better than a public high school. Why would it be? It doesn't have the budget, and it doesn't have the staff. How are you going to run a better school with less money and more poorly paid teachers? A teacher who can teach in a private school wouldn't be qualified to teach in a public school.

You sent your children to private schools for reasons of class?

Class considerations—not money but courtesy and refinement—motivate parents who send their kids to private schools. People say, "We have to do a better job of teaching because we are losing 27 percent of our students to private schools." But it has nothing to do with teaching. The teaching in public schools is excellent. It's the rest of it parents want to avoid.

"Some of my kids are here to learn, but some
are here for exercise or to keep warm—when
the heat works! You've read the reports. Is
Paul Revere a rock star? Who fought in the
American Civil War?"

ROY MARSHALTON
high school social studies teacher
Westchester County, New York

Is Paul Revere a Rock Star?

*Roy Marshalton is Frank Halloran's colleague. He agrees that kids "back
then were in better academic shape than they are now." But he thinks it is
only the home, not the school, that has changed its standards.*

*These standards are narrow and materialistic—largely untouched by
the wider concerns of New York City, some 20 miles to the south. Very few
of Marshalton's students venture beyond their hometown or show much
interest in what happens beyond their own doorsteps. When they leave
school, Marshalton fears they will probably "duplicate their parents' attitudes, and that will be the end of them."*

*Still, he tries to break through his students' white-ghetto mentality.
The day I visited one of his classes the subject was "evil in southeastern
Nigeria." His students seemed to find each anecdote he told about Niger-
ian customs more preposterous than the last. Some guffawed, slapped
their desks, and made the all-inclusive teenage comment—"Gross."*

*Few seemed to treat the subject, or the teacher, as more than a joke.
Yet Marshalton took it all in stride: he ignored the snickers, the din of side
conversations, and the subdued pandemonium.*

*When he was free, and we sat in his chilly classroom to talk about his
23 years at the school, I asked, "Doesn't it bother you if a student is blow-*

244

ing bubble gum, looking up at the ceiling, or drumming on his desk?"

If you had been in more of my classes, you would have found that I am not a regimented person. I discipline with my eyes, not my mouth, and you'll notice that the kids address me as Marsh, not Mr. Marshalton. It's a sign of affection, and even their parents call me Marsh. I don't mind at all because I feel I can obtain more with a look and soft voice than I can with yelling. When I do yell, the response is immediate and usually thorough. Others yell all the time and get nowhere.

I do allow them to chew gum, but of course I always tell them, "Make sure you look at yourself in the mirror when you chew gum. See how ridiculous you look, and if that is the way you want to look, then it's fine with me."

In the beginning of the year I terrorize the girls. I pick on the girls, and I will continue to do so all year. It is one way to teach the elements of propaganda and of prejudice. They are shocked at first, but they eventually understand.

You're teaching the girls the elements of propaganda by teasing them?

Here's an example. In my class, if something is wrong, then it's always the girls' fault. Regardless of what it is, it's the girls' fault. I say that and refer to the Bible and Eve, who made the first mistake. I tell them, "You're all like Eve." So I am teaching them about generalizations and about getting on bandwagons.

Then, of course, there is also prejudice. One day somebody said, "I'm hungry." I went and got a big box of candy, which I offered to the boys. The girls stood there just totally dumbfounded that I would give it to the boys and not to them. After class I said, "Would you girls like some?" Hopefully they'll learn in a very safe setting what prejudice is like.

Is there a bit of women's liberation thrown in here?

To be truthful, women's liberation doesn't exist for them. But I have assaulted their little cocoon. I'm safe, but what I've done is strange.

Cocoon?

They live in a white ghetto and are always in a little huddle. To go to White Plains [a city located 10 minutes away] is an experience. They go to Florida, but with one another, or to visit a grandmother. The sameness is unbelievable, and their exposure has been so limited.

Do you think you get through to them?

They remember the strange things that I do. For example, later this year I will put on a beard and wear different glasses and different clothes and come in as a person from the Soviet Union. I will tell them I am here as a guest. I'll also get a number of them to sign a blank petition. Once I've filled the petition in with outrageous propaganda—for example, how all students from the east side of town must remain in school for an additional fifth year—I mail it to their parents who confront them with this thing they have signed. That's usually pretty effective.

You don't teach out of textbooks?

My teaching is a compilation of a lot of things. They do have to do some reading, no doubt about it. But one of the things that is not done around here is reading. They just don't read. They read upside down.

Do they do their homework?

About two-thirds of the class do the homework. They are allowed to hand it in with a ten-point penalty up to three days after it is due. But I notice that even with the offer of the three extra days to do it, they still won't do it, and they don't.

I tell them from the start that there are no free lunches. You don't do it, you don't get the grade. But they are just not passing with the scores they once had. Now we are talking about a heavy concentration in the high 60s and low 70s. There are very few in the 80s and nobody in the 90s.

Do you have any sense why that's so?

Yes, I do. First of all the amount of money that kids have access to in this area is not healthy. It insulates them and makes them look for instant gratification—nothing more.

Life is really quite easy for them. They're not really exposed to any of our society's major problems and are probably too comfortable to care about them. Even those who don't have an unlimited charge account work only as target laborers. They work for a car or some other material object, and education seems to take a backseat.

Then, of course, there is television—soap operas and quiz shows. Given the trend to hide any intellectual interests, public television probably goes untouched for weeks in some of their homes.

There's this attitude on the part of some of the kids in the school that to achieve good marks is just not cool. It's not being in the right place at the right time, and unfortunately, the more susceptible, or gullible, students seem to fall under that spell. I've seen some very good minds just slide right down the tubes because of friends who say that being smart is dull.

Even some parents think that! Or at least they don't support what we do.

Is this lack of support from parents a major frustration?

It is a big frustration. By the time the kids get here, they have been sold on material values. While they may recognize that they are behind the eight ball and are not going anywhere, they have enough support around here from their peers and from mothers to just spin their wheels.

Do you fail a lot of kids?

I have roughly 100 students. There will probably be six to eight failures. I have no compulsion about failing anyone who fails to perform as required.

Even faced with students who aren't interested, how do you keep your excitement for what you're doing?

I am probably one of the few people I know who always wanted to be a teacher. From the time I was small until the present, I've always wanted to be a teacher. I enjoy it thoroughly, and I always have.

There's always the challenge to find another way to reach whatever is sitting inside the old head and perhaps get a spark of life out of that one individual. Right now I have a track-three class—very slow learners. I've never taught them before, and I find it both frustrating and rewarding. I can see progress, but it isn't progress by the old standards.

Sometimes, of course, I feel stuck, but I don't think it's serious.

I'd like to try something else, but it would have to be something associated with people.

When you feel stuck, what do you do?

I remind myself that I am like a utility infielder. Do you know who he is?

No.

Utility infielders play any infield position. When we make up the schedule and there's an oddball pass, it goes to me. I'm now teaching economics—a first for me—and before I began, I took a university economics course. I really enjoy teaching and like to teach new things. Oddly, I have never taught American history and I have a master's degree in it. Through the army, I also have a good European studies background, and I've taught European history twice. Strange, isn't it?

It doesn't sound like great planning.

It's like the army. We called it the "puzzle palace," a good name for this administration too. We have no leadership in the front office and to that extent are semibankrupt.

Why not go to another district?

For an over-the-hill guy like me, no one is going to pay me for my 23 years of experience, no matter how good I am. This must be one of the few professions where you lose money if you change companies.

You feel underpaid here?

Money and benefits are of course not what they should be after the investment I've made in my education. But I'm more disturbed about the lack of money for programs and for staffing. At one time we had an unparalleled series of electives available to the kids in the school. But now we are at the point where there are two sociology classes held each school year, and that's it.

Young people who do get in here are driven out because they're offered so little and given no support. Then there's this building. This is probably the third time in 23 years that you can come in and find heat. Our windows don't open, and they fall out. The janitorial staff is nil; I fix things myself.

But don't get me wrong. We have an uphill battle to meet high academic standards, but we are trying. If the community saw us as more than tax headaches, maybe we would succeed.

Out of the Trenches

"About eight years ago I attended a big workshop for women in Long Beach. It was about career change and not specifically aimed at teachers—though they had sent out hundreds of flyers to the schools. About 90 percent of the women who attended were teachers dying to get out!

It's big business: all these books, conventions, and workshops for teachers who want to find a way out."

MARGO SILVER
ex-elementary school teacher
Long Beach, California

Out of the Trenches:
EX-TEACHERS HAVE THEIR SAY

This chapter is about some of those who did get out. Some taught for only a few years and others for as many as 10 years. Most went into business and are now paid far more for their work.

They had few regrets about the move, but most felt teaching was the toughest—not necessarily the most challenging—work they had ever done.

Ex-teachers are the kind of people who tip well because they remember what it was like to wait on tables. They give teachers a lot of credit because they've been there and found, especially in the inner city, that they could take only so much.

One ex-teacher, now the vice-president of a major real-estate development company, said, "You know, I woke up one morning and looked in the mirror and realized I was not Albert Schweitzer. If I didn't have a total commitment (comparable to Schweitzer's), then I was in the wrong place, and I was the wrong person.

"That's why I give the greatest amount of credit to people—and I don't know many—who can make a profession out of teaching in the ghetto and who are able to successfully conduct their personal lives while doing an effective job. They are providing an absolutely invaluable service that I respect and am thankful for. It is a real service to society."

This man taught for eight years. Like other inner-city teachers, he often felt he worked against "insurmountable odds" and could have little or no impact on the lives of children. His low salary—emasculating in a society that measures success in dollars—was also a major reason to leave.

Many teachers, especially women, left not so much for money, but because they were tired of living in a juvenile fishbowl. They needed more adult contact and stimulation.

If not the initial motive, then lack of social cachet or esteem was very often the last straw. Why struggle with a very difficult setup and get no recognition? Many answered this question by getting out.

Yet when you listen to ex-teachers, there is a strong sense that teaching is still a part of many of them. They've seen a lot, remember it vividly, and are probably the strongest fans that teachers who are still in the classroom have right now.

NINA LESSING: THREE YEARS IN A CLASSROOM
(YONKERS, NEW YORK)

Nina Lessing is a writer and editor. She taught elementary school in Yonkers for only three years and then moved to Hollywood, California, where she is senior editor in a Los Angeles publishing house. She will probably never teach again. Her reasons were powerful ones:

I went to Columbia [University] Teacher's College for a master's degree, largely because I didn't know what to do. It was absolutely the most ridiculous educational experience of my life. Any day in high school was harder than any day in Teacher's College. I didn't have to think. I didn't have to work. I became a star without any effort whatsoever. The other students were hopelessly mediocre, worse than mediocre, just the dumbest, most boring people I have ever met. But on the other hand, they wanted to become teachers. Their motivation was real, and for all I know, they may have become perfectly good teachers.

It is such a low-status job that the people you meet are not very stimulating—not that you spend any time with adults anyhow. As an elementary school teacher you are totally trapped in your classroom. You can't have a cigarette or go to the bathroom. If you have not taught, you cannot possibly realize what it is like to never leave that space. The responsibility is constant and complete.

When I went to parties—I was married so it wasn't as if I was running around trying to meet boys—people would ask what I did. When I said, "I'm a teacher," their faces would go blank, and they'd be gone. I thought what I was doing was fascinating, but nobody wanted to hear about it.

It wasn't just the prestige I missed. There was no prestige, no intellect, no glamour. There was nothing.

In the second job I had, where I worked very hard and was well regarded by the principal, I just felt this overwhelming hopelessness. I would come home at night and dream about these children. I was obsessed. I was so tired at the end of every day.

Look, my job now is extremely demanding. The hours are long, and there is a lot of pressure. But it can't approach the tiredness I felt at the end of a day of teaching these kids.

I felt—and maybe it was wrong of me to feel this way—that no matter what I did, I could see where some kids were going to end up, and it was not pretty. In kindergarten they were the brightest-faced, most beautiful children, all eager and bright. Then at three o'clock their older siblings, who probably also looked bright and eager when they were five, picked them up from school. They were rough kids, kids who had knives in their back pockets, who were always in trouble. I just felt that I couldn't make enough of an impact. There was no reward, no status, no adult stimulation.

Then I got laid off. This was the early seventies, and Yonkers was going bankrupt. When I was offered another teaching job five months later, I was already working as a free-lance editor. I liked publishing, and teaching had no future.

What does happen to those bright faces? What goes wrong?

I think it's pretty obvious what goes wrong. The world just goes wrong. The older they get, the less protected they are from their environment. They are not cute little buttons anymore in their families, and the families start expecting more and more of them. The school system fails them because their cultural deprivation is so great from the start, and there isn't enough done to compensate. They just get sucked into the ugliness that surrounds them.

The kids were mostly black. There was a small group of parents who were doing whatever they could against ridiculous odds. Virtually every kid in the school was on free breakfast and free lunch. There was one kid I adored. She was very cute and sweet, and her name was a lot like mine, and I guess I felt connected to her that way. In one year they changed her last name five times for each new "uncle" that moved in.

You also taught in a private school?

Yes, I started out in a lab school that trains new teachers, and it gave me a lot more adult stimulation. But most people I taught with there are no longer teachers. For whatever reason, they went on to bigger careers.

It's hard to compare the private school with my experience at Yonkers. I had moments in the private school that were incredibly rewarding, but I would never have made much more than $20,000 a year there. My only reward would have been the great love of teaching.

If teaching paid and society—

[Interrupts] I would do it. But respect for teachers is not just a prestige issue. I still bristle when I read the papers and see another article on the way schools are going to solve our social ills. Schools cannot be the only institution that is going to cure society's problems. We move from one solution to the next—magnet schools, year-round schools—and the money keeps being cut.

It's all so backward. I'm totally for integration, and yet I can't help being sympathetic with teachers who are upset by how it is handled. Yonkers is a perfect example. It integrated its schools a while back, but are the schools any better? Did the money that was spent help any one of those bright-eyed children that I did not want to see grow up?

The problem is that the money goes for the implementation of an integration plan and not, dollar for dollar, into 10 kids, some books, and *more* teachers. It's like the money now being spent to integrate Yonkers housing. If they stopped paying legal fees and gave the money to the poor people directly, some would be able to move out of the slums.

You're always reading articles about how we are going to make the schools better, but you never read an article about doing the one thing that I think every teacher agrees would make a real difference: cut class size. There are just too many children in those rooms. Give me 20-year-old math books, that's fine. Math has not changed. But cut class size. You don't need more books; you need fewer children in the classroom.

What do you remember most about teaching?

I guess I remember how tired I was.

What advice would you give a 20-year-old who was about to start teaching?

Sometimes I think 20 is too young to begin teaching. Maybe I would feel differently if I had started later. I'd say to spend as much time as you can in the classroom with people who teach, and learn how it is done.

MARGO SILVER: TEN YEARS IN THE CLASSROOM (LOS ANGELES SUBURBS)

It was Margo Silver who told me about the workshops for teachers who want to change careers. She taught elementary school for a decade and then left to become an editor and writer of children's books. I've read some of them—they're funny, show a feel for kids, and have a scrappy intelligence.

But the books do not pay her all that much, and in 1986 Silver returned to the classroom for a year. Her motivation was mainly financial, just as it had been when she originally went into teaching. She said that she had a bachelor of arts degree, and teaching was "better than being a checker in a supermarket." She was most emphatically "never one of those stereotypical superdedicated teachers who would teach, even if unpaid."

For someone who was, admittedly, in it for the money and who saw teaching as "the job I had," she still worked at it. "It was a job, and I did it very well because I like kids and because you cannot get into a job unless you really do it."

You can't know, listening to someone, whether or not she did in fact "do it well." But Margo Silver is a born entertainer, a wisecracker, and quick on her feet. She has strong opinions, and I expect she voiced them often.

First, I taught in the Saugus Union School District in the Santa Clarita Valley. In 1969 that area was very rural and largely white—an old-fashioned place. Most of the mothers did not work. Macho man was supposed to be the breadwinner, and that was okay because you could buy a house for $20,000, $25,000. (You know, they put them up by the hundreds, and they are all falling apart now.)

The mothers did get involved, and they were wonderful. We had school picnics where everyone brought homemade bread, jams, and cream; and parents invited us to their ranches. Great times!

Of course, there were the Mexican kids, who were shortchanged in every way and lived in garages without any water. Their parents worked in either the glass factory or in the carrot fields. The kids came to school just filthy, stinking like you would not believe. How could I possibly help them to assimilate when no youngster would go near them because they were so dirty and smelled so bad?

What did I do? One little girl not only reeked and wore filthy clothes, but she had no shoes and was very nervous. I called her doctor and asked him to talk to her mother. He told me I was a racist. Can you imagine?

Nothing was done?

It was terrible. I had to take time away from the other kids in order to wash this kid at our school sink. [Silver is incredulous as she tells this.] I taught her about soap and how to wash. She had never learned. There was no reinforcement when she got home.

Or no sink?

It's possible.

Not that I think it is only the poor who neglect their kids. I live and have taught in the Palos Verdes Peninsula District. It is the Rolls-Royce of school districts, and this is what is going on: parents have so much money that they often hire non-English-speaking help to stay with their kids after school. The kids are not getting so-called quality time—or any kind of help—from their parents. The parents are taking fabulous trips, and they leave the kids, sometimes for weeks, with this woman who doesn't speak any English.

You have taught in two schools?

I spent ten years in the two districts and left in 1979. I knew it was time to get out when I found I could not talk. It was psychosomatic and vanished when I left. But in 1986 I returned to Palos Verdes for one year.

Had it changed?

Yes. When I began teaching, the boys still wanted to be firefighters and policemen, and the girls wanted to be teachers, or they wanted to be homemakers and secretaries. Some boys wanted to be doctors and the girls, nurses in order to "help people." By 1986 they all wanted to be investment bankers. They knew that term. Or they wanted to be doctors so that they could make "lots of money."

They voiced this very clearly. "I want a lot of money." "I don't

want to help people anymore." "I don't want to have fun anymore"—
you know, at least the firefighters go down the pole, and that's fun.
But they said, "I want a lot of money." I found that quite chilling.

What about their skills?

Fantastic. Head Start and private nursery schools have both made
a difference, but minority kids are still behind. The parents of the
white students and to some degree the Oriental students understand that you have to be involved with the schools. That is absolutely essential.

You know, teachers are human. A teacher who sees that a parent is there and cares is going to spend more time with that parent's kid. She'll work with that youngster because she is not alone.
You have to have support from the family.

Also, I think we must teach all our classes in English. At Saugus
we didn't have a bilingual program, and when the kids were im-
mersed in English, they learned to speak it within a year.

Hispanics are the only students who are taught in their own
language. The others—Persians, Chinese, Koreans—all learn
English. If I were Hispanic and had any brains, I would resent
bilingualism. It shortchanges Hispanic kids. Look, you came here,
you learn English.

I understood the program to be transitional.

It lasts for years, and those kids—already disadvantaged—are kept
down.

What can we do about it? The only solution I see is economic.
Inner-city school districts are falling apart while in my affluent
district there are empty schools—empty beautiful schools with
ocean views. But do we want these disadvantaged kids out there?
Absolutely not. Would it help alleviate the overcrowding in inner-
city schools? Of course.

I'm a teacher. I care about kids. But I do not want poor ones in
my community. My community is called an enclave of the rich. I'm
not rich; a lot of people who live there are not rich. We are generally
people who have worked very hard to make it a quiet, tranquil
community.

We have nothing against black or Hispanic children, but we
don't want what accompanies them—the trashing of the neighborhood and the graffiti. That's what everybody is afraid of, and I
don't want that to happen either.

Downtown they need to build new schools very badly. I don't mind paying taxes for new schools.

Who is going to teach in them?

If teachers are paid $50,000 or $60,000 combat pay, I think they will teach. I probably would for that kind of money. With certain conditions: regulated class size, removal of disruptive students, guards in the parking lot so that teachers don't have their tires slashed or are not raped on the way to their cars.

A friend of mine got a job in the ghetto. She's a tall, blond, white, Jewish teacher. Her first week there she got beaten to a pulp by sixth-grade girls. These girls were fighting each other, and she tried to break it up. She was very stupid. She was doing her job.

Let's face it. There are good teachers in the ghetto, but you can bust your butt in the classroom for the child all day, and when he goes home, everything is destroyed.

What makes a good teacher?

A good teacher follows the curriculum but not slavishly; she controls the class but also whets their curiosity. You have to be structured but flexible. If you've got a hot discussion going on about evolution, you don't look at your watch and say, "Okay, time to take out your math books."

It interests me that you don't claim that a teacher needs to be dedicated.

It's a job. I believe that whatever job you take on should be done well. I may teach again. I need the money.

Do you think the best and brightest get out?

That is often true. While I have met teachers who are brilliant, I've also met ones whose IQs were marginal. Many have very low self-esteem, and that's the reason they teach. They think it's the only thing that they can do, and that is sad.

I have a friend who says there are three big reasons to teach: June, July, and August. Still, I don't really understand what all the moaning and groaning is about. After a few years you can make $30,000 in about nine months a year. That's not bad.

Teachers also complain about overbearing principals who stifle you. But I found that teachers have more autonomy than most workers, and in my district, mothers are interested. They help out.

No problems?

No problems other than very pushy parents who can go for the jugular with an inexperienced teacher.

I get mothers to help, but I screen them very carefully. You do not want one of the mothers who stand over their kid all day long to make sure he behaves like a star.

What's wrong then? Why not continue to teach?

Teachers don't get enough respect, and that drives them to other occupations. With some parents and administrators I felt like the low man on the totem pole. It's interesting—the lower the grade you teach, the lower the respect. Kindergarten and first-grade teachers are considered overpaid baby-sitters.

Yet kindergarten is not easy to teach. You can't just write something on the board and have them do it. Being with the five-year-olds, it's great.

I wonder why so few male teachers seem to think so.

It's terrible. In the lower grades everybody wonders, *why* is he here? If you're a woman and not married, that's the kiss of death. You are not going to meet a male teacher. Male teachers are considered either wimps, gay, or even child molesters.

It's terrible, it's absolutely sexist and awful. But you know what's worse? [Laughs] It's true. Every guy I have personally met who is a lower-grade teacher has had something wrong with him.

[Silver elaborates, but her examples seem to me to say more about her than about wimps and the other categories she's mentioned.]

What worries you most about our schools?

Their continuance. I think public schools are very important; they are the foundation of everything.

I very much resent it when parents in our affluent district take their kids out of public school, which is among the finest in California, and put them in Chadwick and other private schools.

Private schools foster a terrible elitism. Kids feel they are the best of the best. They think they are hotshots, and what they are is snotty little snobs.

Still, if I lived in the city, I'd send my kid to private school.

MARY SINCLAIR: SEVEN YEARS AS A TEACHER
(NEW YORK, NEW YORK)

In the seventies Mary Sinclair first taught and then became the director of New York's Acorn School, a private early-childhood and elementary school in lower Manhattan. Now that lower Manhattan has become yuppified, she said, Acorn is quite an affluent school. In her time, however, cost was moderate.

Sinclair stayed at the Acorn School for seven years and moved to California in 1978. She then chose to remain at home in order to raise her own children—itself a commitment to early-childhood development about which she feels very strongly.

I wanted to know what had led her to teaching:

I had just graduated from college, having majored in classics, and I wanted to remain in New York. If I taught, my parents would accept my remaining in the city.

I loved it. I taught at the Acorn School, and it was really the best of your open-classroom situations—mixed age groups, no walls, and clustered areas but with a structured curriculum and terrific teachers.

I taught in a team-teaching situation, and that was great. The team-teaching approach allows one to compensate for weaknesses and emphasize strengths. My own strengths were in teaching skills, not in crafts, and in the interpersonal area.

I'm good with parents, good with the children, good with other teachers. That's what I enjoyed most—the camaraderie I had with other teachers and also learning how people, both parents and children, behave. I seemed to be effective at that and was made director of the school after three years of teaching.

I was 24. Being director gave me a new perspective. I negotiated our rent, and at one point, we instituted five full-term scholarships for youngsters from a nearby housing project.

How did scholarships for low-income kids work out?

At Acorn it worked very well. We used a lot of manipulative materials, and language was taught at school. Three- and four-year-olds pick up the language if they are in small groups.

The kids did not have to play catch-up ball?

It depended on the kids. Sometimes we chose on the basis of the greatest need, and then we did have to play some catch-up ball. But when we tilted toward ability, this didn't happen.

The problem is that we had these tremendously talented kids who went on full scholarship. Later on, when they went on to second and third grade in other schools, they did not always get that full scholarship. The private schools in New York are so expensive, maybe $8,000, $9,000 a year. When they got a $6,000 scholarship, it was not enough.

We wanted to get them into the best possible school, either a magnet program or a top private school, but sometimes it did not happen.

What about public versus private schools?

Most of my experience is in private schools and as a trustee on an education committee at Sarah Lawrence College. I was a trustee for eight years, and our committee talked a lot about privilege and other explosive social issues. I don't think there are any answers, but the important thing is to be able to formulate and come up with significant questions.

I think that is what you do when you teach. In addition to skills, you're trying to get students to learn how to think, to know how to ask questions, and that means a liberal-arts education. The ability to think will do you more good in the long run that training yourself in a particular field.

My major in the classics was certainly not on the surface the most job-oriented major to have, but I feel that Greek and Latin have served me well.

Then again, I did come from a family of wealth. I did not have to pay for my own schooling, and I could not have lived in New York on my teacher's salary. I was living with a man who was making a good income, and he was subsidizing my teaching. My top salary as director of the Acorn School in 1978, my last year, was $13,000. You don't go into teaching for the money.

The salaries are reprehensible. Teachers are a very altruistic group of people in general. They are probably the last population group to ask for significant salary raises, and they constantly underrate themselves.

What is your response to people who criticize private schools as elitist?

Part of it is justified. There are some people who send their children to private schools because they want their children to go to school with children from that elitist group. But I believe that private schools enable teachers to teach from a curriculum that is not dictated by state standards, and that is probably all to the good.

Good public schools are free, and you get a mixed population without having to work for it—decided advantages. If there were a good public school for my kids, I'd send them to it. [Her two children go to a private school in L.A.] In most urban centers it's difficult to do that. If we were in Lake Forest, Illinois, where I grew up, then I'd send my kids to public school without question.

Also, because private schools are not subsidized by the state, they cannot pay teachers nearly as well as public schools. Therefore, some teachers in private schools come from a moneyed background and are not dependent on their salary. That is really a disadvantage because you are not getting that full pool of teaching experience.

Still, those who do stay on as teachers take it pretty seriously, and I don't think they'd choose to stay on if they were dependent on the salary unless they really liked it and felt they were good at it. In private school you do feel that commitment to the children.

The teaching field is really filled with people who have tremendous integrity. Those people for whom it is just a job are weeded out very quickly.

I stand up for teachers. I think most teachers take pride in what they do. Most teachers, if they are good teachers, will not hesitate to study other teachers and pick up what they can. A friend of mine from New York who is a teacher came out to visit me. I took her to our children's school, and she took notes constantly—everything from how the shelves were arranged to the activities. Even on vacation she was involved.

You do not think the best and the brightest get out?

I've gotten out, and I consider myself a very good teacher. I can't take enough financial pressure off my husband by staying in the teaching field. I'm working toward a doctorate in counseling psychology, which I don't think is a great leap from teaching. Most of my strengths are in my ability to read people.

I think that the teaching field has its work cut out trying to keep good teachers. It's a tremendous problem. They are going to lose good teachers. The teaching profession is looked upon with contempt by most people.

Was the low status a problem for you?

No [laughs], but I don't have a problem with what others think of me. Look at my haircut! [It is very short.]

The teaching profession will probably lose wonderful people because of the lack of respect with which it is treated by people in general. People get out because of the lack of respect and the very real inability to meet expenses.

What are the three biggest issues facing education today?

Issue number one: having some real way to evaluate who is a good teacher and trying to keep those teachers in the classroom. This has nothing to do with degrees or credentials. I have a master's degree from Columbia Teachers College, and the fact that I am a good teacher has nothing to do with the degree I got.

Good teachers aren't the result of education programs. Having working teachers as role models, not teaching professors, is important. You can only learn by being in that classroom. Just put new teachers in a classroom as quickly as possible and expose them to a master teacher.

Second issue: improving conditions in the classroom, reducing class size, and educating parents not to expect too much in terms of skills at the expense of teaching children how to think. I realize that sounds like very late-sixties-liberal thinking but it really is true. We need to teach people how to think.

Why should learning how to think and acquiring skills be at odds?

The fact that a two-year-old can recognize a van Gogh is not different from his being able to say "ducky." It's the colors and the textures and the feeling that you want to teach that child.

The basic skills have already been tremendously accelerated. "Sesame Street," public TV in general, is giving children that pre-kindergarten foundation. Now children come into kindergarten, and they are reading; that is not necessarily a good thing.

Culturally deprived children are a different issue. But your average middle-class child is getting a battering of stimuli: I mean, too many lessons, baby gym and kinder gym, and Mommy and Me, instead of being able to just run around.

I think also we have to teach middle-class parents not to be so greedy for material things at the expense of their children. I'm not talking here about two-income families that need the two incomes, but two-income families who need to upgrade their car to a BMW. Probably two-thirds of the children in my daughter's class are from two-income families who do not need two incomes. Those children are being raised for the most part by Spanish housekeepers who are terrific, but it gives the children a very misguided perspective on one, the Spanish population and two, their own language. The children are learning early language from a caregiver who does not use English as a primary language—because their parents are greedy.

Materialism at the expense of family life is your third issue?

Yes, I feel very strongly about the way teachers are expected to take up the slack for the lacks in family life. To effectively handle career and a family is near to impossible. I acknowledge the need for many women to bring in money, but for those who are doing it to fulfill their self-image and who have young children, I think they should question it. Again, they should be able to formulate questions and ask, "Why am I doing this?" Early childhood is so important.

And it seems to be still a largely female province. Were there many male teachers where you taught?

No, but the nursery school I sent our daughter to was staffed primarily by men. It was geared toward female single parents who thought having male teachers was important. But now, with all the adverse publicity about child molestation, it is a very tricky thing to pull off. People have become very squeamish about males being with nursery school children.

When the whole McMartin thing [a nursery school child-molestation case in L.A.] was going on, the insurance at my daughter's school went up five times—to cover potential lawsuits. There was a rule that there had to be two teachers taking the children to the bathroom. Frightening isn't it?

It is also frightening to assume that males are more likely to molest children than females. Is there any reason to think this is so?

No, the McMartin episode implicated as many females as it did males. But it relates to the contempt in which teaching is held. It's dumb enough for a woman to go into teaching, but, God, if you are a man, you must be a moron.

Any child you especially remember?

I remember one girl, Emmy Townsend, whom I taught for three years. Her mind was like a sponge. I got a card from her last year. She went to Bryn Mawr and now runs a shelter for battered women in Philadelphia. She was an exquisite delicate child, but she had that strength and tremendous inner resolve. She wasn't afraid to think or to say no–isn't that what teachers should nurture?

SARAH REYNOLDS: AFTER TEN YEARS, FROM PUBLIC TO PRIVATE SERVANT (WESTCHESTER COUNTY, NEW YORK)

Sarah Reynolds is an ex-elementary school teacher turned gourmet cook and caterer. She taught for ten years and then quit to open a gourmet shop, since expanded to two locations.

When I interviewed Sarah Reynolds, I was tempted to ask about her recipes, not her insights as an ex-teacher. But when she began to talk, I changed my mind. Her business is in the same town in which she taught– an affluent New York suburb whose school system is labeled one of the nation's best. Because of the system's acclaim and her continued contact with the town, I was especially interested in what she had to tell me.

Reynolds's own background also made a difference. As a young woman she worked many different dead-end jobs simply to survive, and she managed, finally, to sell herself to a small and well-heeled girl's college as a full-scholarship student. "Developmental psychology"–in this instance a fancy name for a teacher-education program–was the closest her college had to a psychology major, and she enrolled. She never intended to teach and envisioned a career in business.

When she student-taught, however, the school's administrators were impressed enough to offer her a job–unusual in a system that can afford to recruit more-experienced teachers. She worked at two elementary schools, the first under a wonderful principal and the second under someone whom she could not stand. She says that the first experience made her a teacher, and the second drove her out.

I think she must have been a great teacher. I know she loved it, and her career change–she joked about going from being a public servant to a private one–was foreshadowed in the classroom:

I always cooked with the kids. It's part of what I really loved about teaching–the way I shared creative parts of my life with the children and turned them into great learning experiences.

At one point we even started something called the "Company."

It was a cookie company and an exercise in just about any subject you can imagine—economics, cooking, English. We set up a little company store and actually sold shares of stock to get started. We were a big business, and it became a little embarrassing after our first dividend was declared.

It was a great experience for the kids and for me; and it was the complete freedom allowed in this school system that made it possible.

But I don't know if it would be possible to set up the Company today. There is much more uniformity today and more pressure to follow an elaborate, highly structured curriculum—maybe because the school budget is now so large that schools want to account for how every minute is spent.

In fact, the community wants so badly to have every educational facility and opportunity available for every child that there is hardly any time left in a day to teach. When I was teaching, I was always amazed by the limited contact time I actually had with my students. They had music and recess and lunch and art and special-ed. classes. They would be leaving my classroom for this special activity and that gifted program. None of those things are bad. They are all great, but it does limit the person who is put in the school to teach the kids.

Psychologist David Elkind and others say that this generation has overprogrammed its children.

I think the programming is too much. We all live at such a hectic pace. These kids have all these activities at school, and then they go home and they've got Girl Scouts and swimming and riding and volleyball. There isn't a day when these kids are not scheduled for something.

A lot of people who live here lead a very fast life, and that's how their kids are too. It's sad because many of these kids never had a chance to be kids or to do kid things. They are all nine going on nineteen. They are very aware of designer jeans, Gucci bags. Many have been skiing in the Alps, but they probably could not use a pay phone by themselves.

That raises an interesting question. What was the relationship between these highly privileged kids and their teachers?

It varied tremendously. The children's values reflected their families' values. Those parents who were supportive of the educational community and who respected educators themselves raised children to have that same respect.

I certainly had plenty of kids who said (I thought it was funny), "If you don't do this, my father is going to have your job." And in fact, there *were* parents who came in and said, "I'm going to have your job."

You're kidding.

No, no, I'm not kidding. In this community parents are very vocal, very involved, and they have very definite ideas about what they want for their kids. And that became a real burden for me.

The parents were too involved?

The school tried so hard to please every parent. One week the principal would call me in to tell me that six parents complained that I was not doing enough creative projects in the classroom. Two weeks later she'd again call me to tell me that half a dozen parents had called her up because I was doing too many creative projects.

In the end I felt compromised. If I wasn't a high-priced baby-sitter, I was a high-priced performer—what I was really doing was putting on bigger and better shows each day.

Parents want the wrong things?

Let's just say they don't see what the teachers see.

The people that I worked with were so dedicated, so involved, and everybody was trying so hard for these kids; and yet the community always seemed kind of against us. The parents did not really see the whole picture.

People would come in and demand *the* first-grade teacher. They never understood all the effort and thought that went into student placement. We really worked very hard to try and suit the class environment to each and every child. Hours were spent discussing each youngster and which situation would be the best for him.

I understand the parents' concern, especially now that I am on the outside. But it's a sad situation. Here is a community that goes out and hires the absolutely best educators that it can find. There is an unbelievable screening process. The district has a great reputation, and people apply here from all over. Teachers are paid a lot of money, and then the district doesn't let them do what they know how to do best.

Yet few teachers leave this district to do something else.

Many feel stuck. Teaching can be a very isolating experience, and there are few contacts with the adult world. People don't know how to get out, and they need the income.

I was lucky. I was divorced and had no children—free as a bird. A lot of teachers don't have that freedom of choice.

I loved teaching, and I really did not find it a hard job compared to many others I'd had. It's a humanistic setting, and everyone in elementary school is trained to never say a negative word. Every one is very complimentary—not at all like the business world.

But teaching was a very wearing job. It was an emotionally draining job. It is hard to return year after year and retain that spark, no matter how great the kids and the administration may be.

When you did leave, how did the community react to your new role?

That's a funny thing. When I taught, I felt that the community held us to mid-Victorian standards. Teachers must be morally superior to the rest of the population—an understandable attitude.

When I left, I was still held to a holier-than-thou standard, and it was a problem. If you are a teacher, then you should be a teacher —period. There's a feeling that teachers should be above making money. It was very nasty that I was making money, or at least trying to.

My biggest supporters were other teachers.

The first three years in business I worked eighteen hours a day, seven days a week—I had no life and had lost the financial cushion of having a job. In many ways, you know, teaching was a great job. Whatever goes wrong—medical, dental—they take care of it.

Thinking back on your years as a teacher, what educational issue strikes you as most important?

This is in many ways a wonderful school system. But there is one issue that I feel very strongly about: the school is losing the whole idea of quality, of the need to work for what you get.

In this school system no child is allowed to fail. No child ever does anything wrong. Whatever they do is always praised, and we were never allowed to make demands on them.

That's a problem I had. I do have very high standards, and I wanted my students to have those same high standards. I wanted to be able to make demands on them, and sometimes it meant that they were not going to be having fun.

It was a real conflict for me, and I found it very hard to accept that it was not up to me. It was not my school, and I had to do what they were paying me to do—keep the kids happy. If that meant we could not make demands on them or ask that they try to meet high standards, then that was the way it would have to be.

I'm confused. On the one hand this is a school system noted for high standards—

[Interrupts] High standards, but the most important thing, I always felt, was that these children *must be happy*. That's why I said I put on a bigger show every day until I sometimes felt I was a performer and not a teacher. It's really true. That was the primary objective—that these children were happy at school.

It is important for kids to come into school with a good attitude and to feel that school is going to be a positive experience. But there's a big difference between work and play: we call it "work" because it may not be fun 100 percent of the time.

I do think that we are losing the ability to help children see the difference: I saw it a lot and I see it now—young people who come to work for me and are shocked because it is not fun.

There is a value that we lost in the school system: this whole idea of doing something that is really hard and challenging, having it be a struggle and maybe not being fun, and shedding a few tears over it—agonizing over something and then having that great feeling of having succeeded. I don't think we are allowing kids to do that any more.

Is that an educational issue? A cultural one? I'm not sure we can separate them.

I don't think we can.

I think it's a crime to have youngsters graduating from high school who can't read or write, who can't spell, who can't do arithmetic, who can't look up something in the dictionary.

In this top-rated school district? Children who can't read?

There surely are; there are kids who are getting out and cannot read or write. They are moved along, and it's all explained by the new hot label "learning disabled."

They do seem to have discovered a lot more learning disabilities than were around when I was a kid.

[Mutual laughter] Don't get me started—that's another book!

JUNE LASKI: FIVE YEARS AS A TEACHER (NEW YORK, NEW YORK)

June Laski taught junior high school in a New York ghetto in the mid-seventies. She was fired, or what schools call "excessed," during New York's big fiscal crisis. By the time she was offered her job back, she had gone into business. She is now the president of a personnel company. Would she return to the classroom if the salary were far higher?

No. The environment and the way the school system was run were extremely frustrating. The system seemed to work against the education of the children. Education seemed to be a minor issue in the great scheme of things.

I taught at a community-run school, and it was a classic case of everything being done to benefit the higher levels of the administration. The administration had no interest in education, only in whether things were quiet.

We did what we wanted in the classroom with no input from administration. In one respect that was nice. We were independent. But there were many classrooms in which nothing was going on, and this was allowed. In fact, I walked into several classrooms where words were misspelled on the blackboard, and the children were just asked to copy what was on the blackboard. Many teachers weren't literate enough for the job and could not themselves speak proper English. Others were very talented and taught almost in spite of the system. But the kids were falling through the cracks.

None of the people with whom I taught are still there. All have gone into business and are successful, often using skills they learned as a teacher. My business—personnel—is a logical progression for teachers, and I have hired many ex-teachers.

What do you think of teachers?

The ones in my son's school are extremely motivated and are doing the job that I would have liked to do—if I'd been in a school conducive to learning. I respect teachers and feel they have a very hard job to do. I don't have that feeling that anyone can be a teacher. It requires a lot of talent.

VICTOR LASKI: EIGHT YEARS IN THE CLASSROOM
(NEW YORK, NEW YORK)

June Laski's husband Victor is the man who told me he woke up one morning and realized he was not Albert Schweitzer. His elementary school was in the South Bronx and was populated by black and Hispanic children. He started out in the late sixties and was there for eight years. During his time he saw community control "dismember" the central power of the New York City Board of Education:

Community control had taken over, and the administration was hostile–to white Jewish teachers. They wanted to do their own thing, have their own say and control. I empathized, but they did not want my empathy. They just didn't want me around.

There was a backlash. I could understand it, but I was its victim. I felt I was a victim to some conditions and circumstances that were really alien to me and my well-being. I was threatened on many levels–personally, physically, and professionally.

How so?

I remember one experience I had with a child. I attempted to stop her from leaving before dismissal time, and I was accused of beating her! The administration tried to have me expelled, and that was at a time when the administration itself was inflicting corporal punishment on children.

You saw that?

There were a number of incidents that I saw. Sometimes it was almost what had to be done to establish control in what was an intense, horrific environment for a lot of people and their children.

Is this the same area where the recent scandal over a corrupt school board erupted?

Yes. It was corrupt then. The people in charge were not interested in education. And the depth of the feelings some of the children had for white people–the hatred. These were a lot of very poor, very frightened people–ghetto people, disenfranchised, ignored.

Do you agree that ghetto schools cannot compete with the streets?

Wow! Is that what teachers say? Somehow I cannot accept that. That's anarchy.

The street was in the school, and that's what the problem was. If you are going to let a ghetto mind govern a ghetto area, then you are increasing the problem.

There's a tendency to blame the victim, and that bothers me.

But there is a statement being made about responsibility. It goes beyond the schools to the state of these people in our society. On that level there's a part of me that says we all—not just the schools—have an obligation.

When I taught, I had a boy one year who was sharp as a tack. But all his intelligence was going into being the class clown and being street smart. I wanted to help him and arranged to visit his home.

When I went home with him and saw the conditions in which he lived—the horrific conditions—I decided that I could not help him. The odds against him were almost insurmountable.

Did your being a male teacher in an elementary school present a problem?

The salary did. When I taught, I was in my late 20s. I saw what other people—and my friends—were making, and I knew I was not up to speed. If you measure success by income (and to some degree we all do), I knew I had to make a change.

You are now a success by the usual measure. Do you ever regret or miss the classroom?

I am more fulfilled today. I feel more challenged by things that are [he pauses when he realizes what he is saying] *easier* than teaching a class of angry children.

IN A REAL-ESTATE OFFICE

Real-estate offices are filled with ex-teachers. I asked four ex-teachers in one suburban New York realty office why they had become teachers and why they had left:

Jo Lang: I grew up being told I was going to be a teacher. It was my mother's decision. She said that my brother was going to be a doctor, and he is now a doctor.

My mother had her reasons: good pay, steady income, good benefits, if you got married and had a family, teaching was something you could always leave and come back to later on. Teachers are respected. The decision never had to do with what I wanted to be.

I taught second grade for two years. It was really a challenge because I was teaching in the South Bronx, working with under-privileged children. I enjoyed it. I enjoyed the breakthroughs—the really deprived ones who came in not knowing how to read and who left being able to. I remember I had three children the second year who could not read at all and who left reading on a third-grade level.

This was in the late sixties. Then I had my own children, and when I went back, I was a substitute teacher. And subbing is what really turned me off. Again I was in the South Bronx, this time at an inner-city intermediate school that was just wild.

What turned you off?

I just felt that it took too much out of me. I was dealing with children, not with adults. I didn't like the teaching environment. I found that teaching was a very stifling environment. It was a very closed society, and there were no opportunities to really grow.

So it wasn't money then?

At the time, no. Now it would be. Here I can make far more money.

[Marsha Kalko, whose husband is a teacher, has been standing in the background as I talk to Lang. Every so often she interjects a comment: "Nobody wants his kid to be a teacher anymore. Not one parent in my husband's classes wants his kid to be a teacher."]

Marsha Kalko: When I was a little girl, my parents said I had to decide what I wanted to be. I said that I wanted to be a stewardess and they said, "Jewish girls are not stewardesses." And I decided I was not smart enough to be a doctor, so I said, "Okay, I'll be a teacher." They thought that was wonderful. You know, they thought teaching was a great occupation for a girl: when I had children, I could stop, and I could always go back to it and still spend vacations with my children.

I taught for a year and a half and then stopped to have my child. Then we moved to New York, where I couldn't get a teaching job; so I substituted for a while. I was also going to school to get a master's in special education when my husband's school had the longest strike in New York State history. I decided I never wanted to go through that, and I stopped on the spot.

Mary Ann Romer: I became a teacher because I always knew I was going to be a teacher. We played school, and I was always the teacher. Getting out was an accident. I couldn't find a summer job one year, and people told me to go to one of the real-estate brokers. I did, and she hired me.

And you liked real estate so much that—

[Interrupts] I made so much money.

Money drove you out?

Yes, I think so.

Would you go back if it paid as well as real estate?

I don't know.

Ruth Frame (who taught from 1955–1958): My mother said teaching was a wonderful insurance policy. Once you had a teacher's license, you were good for life. Little did she know what the eighties would bring. And I liked it very much.

Then why did you stop?

I had a family. When I went back, I went back to substitute-teach because I did not want to work full-time. I found that substituting was not the satisfaction that teaching had been.

Since I was a substitute teacher, I was largely a baby-sitter. Most teachers did not want to leave me their lesson plans; so my main job was just to keep the kids from killing each other. Also, teaching had changed. The kids' attitude was different, the parents' attitude was different. There was no awe of the teacher, or even respect.

Isn't All Education Special?

Beth Johnson is an ex-teacher turned administrator. She heads the special education program in the same district that employed Sarah Lessing (and still employs Dr. Julius Applebaum and Eleanor Blaine). Though now a bureaucrat, Johnson herself called her department the "biggest paper shuffle I have ever seen."

She taught for many years and now trains teachers in workshops that she runs year-round. We spoke because I wanted the insights of someone responsible for special education (special ed.)—the world of emotionally, psychologically, and academically handicapped kids. (As previously discussed, the classification of handicapped now includes the gifted as well as the learning-disabled. Both are considered out of the mainstream, or handicapped, conditions.)

So many interviews had been peppered with phrases like "emotionally disturbed" and "learning-disabled" that I began to wonder about it. Are more kids learning-disabled today than when Dwight David Eisenhower was president? And do far more show emotional disturbances than at any earlier time in our history? It appears that way from these interviews with teachers, and yet one cannot be sure what to believe in an age of psycho-babble.

275

(My skepticism is shared by others. In Daniel Calhoun's The Intelligence of a People we learn that eighteenth-century teachers assumed that when a pupil did not learn, the fault lay with the method of instruction or the teacher. But, argues Calhoun, the nineteenth century changed all that. A child's inability to learn was now called a "learning problem"—a defensive strategy invented by educators to explain their own failures.)

The reality may not be quite so extreme. Some of the time, as Sarah Lessing had suggested, a teacher may find it a relief to label a kid "special ed." Then he is out of the classroom and out of her hair or, equally convenient, he is at least not measured (and his teacher is not measured) by difficult, standardized tests.

Beth Johnson, who has found that even administrators' hands are bound in red tape, agrees that special ed. is misused. But she sees the problem as more complex—yet another case of teachers being asked to deliver on 101 fronts and being overwhelmed by the magnitude of their job.

She is sympathetic—to a point. But her awareness of the teachers' difficult job and her high regard for what they do achieve is often at odds with her efforts to reorganize how special education works. As we talked, she bumped into the catch-22 life of our schools and could not, for long, get away from it. Even the origin of special education, which I first asked about, is mired in contradictions:

You don't remember special ed. as a child because there was no formal special-education system in place prior to 1975. In that year it became federal law that all school districts had to provide free appropriate public education to all children, including the handicapped. If services were not available within the school district, schools had to pay for and provide outside placement.

But it got out of hand. More and more kids were referred to special ed. because it was the only game in town—the one place to find speech therapists, psychologists, resource rooms, and so on. As students began to have difficulties and to struggle in school, they were sent to special ed. even though they were really part of the regular educational population.

In New York the special-ed. population shot up to about 15 percent, and that's when the state intervened. The state saw it had created a monster, and it tightened the criteria for admittance to special ed. The trend now is that programs should not exceed 10 percent of the school population.

But more than 10 percent of the kids need extra help?

There should be more services, but we do not have the money to provide them.

In the meantime our dual system—regular versus special ed.—creates problems. In order to help kids, we pull them out of the class, and that in itself stigmatizes them. And right now we also pull out kids from the regular population who are slow readers or need help in math, because it is the only way they can get help.

Eligibility for special ed. is not black and white. Data can be interpreted different ways, and some districts stretch things a little bit. Their intentions are good. They do it to support kids. But I think a lot more could be done in the regular classroom.

In fact, research suggests that it is better for the handicapped child to remain in the classroom, and a new state initiative, known as the Regular Education Initiative, seeks more of a marriage between regular and special ed. The idea will be to bring kids back into the classroom rather than pull them out.

Back to square one?

Not exactly. I think many regular-ed. teachers want to keep handicapped kids in the classroom, but they want to be shown how to do it. Is the teacher expected to work one-on-one with them, and if so, how does she manage the other students in her class?

Who was going to teach special ed. when it started in '75?

There were always special-ed. teachers, just not a formal system. In 1969 I was doing speech therapy, and the system was informal; a teacher would say, "I think Johnny has a lisp. Can you see him?" And I'd agree, and Johnny would come to me for a test. I didn't have to get parental consent or go through a whole formal procedure.

That sounds better than what it became.

I have to tell you that in districts where those services were in place —albeit informally—it was better. But how about districts that did not provide those services? There was no mandate to put those services in place, and you really had differences between the rich and poor districts.

There was less of a stigma attached when it was informal?

I think so, although on the elementary level, kids don't know. They just know they go down to that nice lady for help.

You don't think some teachers use special ed. to get rid of a child they find difficult?

I do; that is my concern. A lot of that takes place. When you have the dual system, there is a place to send kids out. If it wasn't there, then teachers would have to take responsibility for those kids. The more special-ed. programs you have, the more they'll be used.

Also, special ed. has become a way to soften our new, stiffer standards. It was felt that the new Regents Action plan [involving higher standards] put extra pressure on borderline kids; and therefore, special ed. became a way to exempt them from some tests or modify others.

So we raise standards and then use special education to lower them again?

It's complicated. I used to do a workshop with teachers on their role, and what I saw was people under a lot of pressure. The pressure comes not only from all the beefed-up requirements and new standards, but from all the social issues teachers now must face.

Veteran teachers feel they have much more to deal with than in the past. There are drugs—they're destroying many children's lives, and people don't want to face it. Most people aren't prepared to deal with this, but teachers—who see kids nodding out in class—haven't much choice. They see kids today who are really troubled, and there is no one at home to support them emotionally. The kids come to school and are needy.

I myself see far more language problems even though these kids' parents are college educated. Very young children in affluent communities like this one are being raised by people who speak little English, and the parents are not around much.

The kids come to school, and they're fragmented, disorganized, immature...they just don't seem very intact. There is simply a lot of emotional disturbance.

The number-one growing program is BOCES [an alternative program for children who need special help—whether because they're gifted, learning disabled, physically disabled, emotionally disturbed, or whatever]. This is a program for children who have a lot of emotional problems. They started out with three classes, then went to four, five, six, seven. It's unbelievable: it is the number-one growing class. I'm talking about looking at a seven-year-old kid and saying, "This kid has severe enough emotional problems that he cannot be educated in a regular classroom." I have a real problem with that.

I do too. It isn't just our psycho-babble age causing this situation?

No, these are kids who cannot control their behavior and are extremely disruptive–like little animals. I'm talking about the Westchester-Putnam community, which includes some affluent districts as well as some that are not. In some areas where poverty and drugs compound the problem, the numbers of disturbed kids are even greater.

Parents in the more-affluent communities are reluctant to mix their kids with the kids from the poorer districts, and BOCES does mix them. Parents here won't accept that BOCES class; yet we are dealing with significant problems, and teachers are tearing their hair out. They are seeing behaviors they have never seen before–no wonder the word *burnout* was first applied to teachers!

Why the burnout?

The multiplicity of roles teachers have had to take on: if the parents are not parenting at home, if kids had no breakfast, haven't done the homework, and did not get a hug, then teachers end up with a refrigerator in the classroom in order to feed them a little breakfast. Then they do a little social work with the boy who went to his father's house for the weekend and witnessed a fight Mommy and Daddy had. Lots of teachers are finding they have to deal with these things before they can think about teaching.

That's what you hear when you run teacher-training workshops?

All the time. Remember, too, that this profession is still reeling from a Nation At Risk. Now the issue of whether our kids are being taught in the best possible way is an open question–a wound. When teachers face parents, it's almost a confrontation. Teachers don't feel respected, and they feel they are not getting much parental cooperation. In fact, at a parent-teacher conference they feel a lot of anxiety. They feel they will be somehow attacked and that parents will be demanding and critical. Teachers also feel they no longer have any clout: if a parent disapproves of an assignment, he may encourage his child not to do it.

It's like having 27 critical bosses, isn't it?

Very much so. Then there's also the paperwork, more than there has ever been before, despite the computers we now have. Because of the demand for accountability within the organization on every step of the ladder, there is report after report.

Special ed. is the biggest paper shuffle I have every seen anywhere. As an administrator I feel terrible about it. Sometimes teachers tell me that they feel all they are doing is paperwork. What happened to the time they could spend with the kids?

Everyone covers his or her backside?

Yes. But if we kick and scream to the state education department–which has given us all this paperwork–they tell us it comes from the feds. There are reports that ask for minutiae and that take hours to extract from reams of other reports.

Are the reports necessary?

Some are. Supervision is stronger today, and that's good. Years ago administrators would walk into a class and write a report on the level of "good," bad," or "the blinds were out of line." Now the report has some substance, and specific recommendations are made to the teacher involved.

But teachers say administrators left the classroom because they hate to teach and are therefore no help at all.

That is sometimes true. But some very good teachers wanted to move up, and unfortunately you cannot do that within the classroom.

It's really a problem. If you go into teaching and you are an absolutely incredible master teacher, you are still lockstepped into your salary increases. Every year you get the same amount as Mrs. So-and-So down the hall, who is absolutely the worst. It's demoralizing for teachers.

And many administrators–I guess I am speaking for myself and people I know–were very excited about the profession and about what they wanted to see for kids. They wanted to have a greater impact. That was my motivation.

Power?

Yes, power. I had a vision of what should be available for kids and how programs should be operated. I felt very limited within the classroom to make any of the changes. In order to empower teachers, I felt that I had to have decision-making power—what gets taught, how it gets taught.

And now, do you have any power?

[Laughs] I feel I have less than before.

Teachers are what it's all about. While we administrators talk about what should be in and out of the curriculum, teachers are the ones making it a good and worthwhile experience for those kids. Their contribution is not sufficiently acknowledged, but it is teachers who are in the trenches, the front lines.

Military metaphors always make me wonder who the enemy is supposed to be.

You hear all the time it is "the system," "the community," the "board of education," "the parents." There is a great deal of finger pointing all around. Parents feel teachers pressure the kids and give them unrealistic, lengthy assignments; and teachers then say parental expectations are one of the reasons we must make demands on the kids. But where are the shared values?

That's a good question.

But I haven't an answer. I really think our society's values have gotten a little out of whack, and the schools reflect that. Forget skills—teachers say these kids don't even show up on time. They're floundering, unable or unwilling to take direction.

Why don't teachers just get out?

There is very little turnover around here. Some figure they are tenured and secure, and they'll hang out and count down. When teachers are good and when they are dedicated, you don't want to lose them. (I come from a teaching family. Both my parents retired after 35 years.) But there are others who—quite honestly—it's time.

Many teachers feel that this is all they know, and so career changes are hard for them. Those who have left have the biggest smiles on their faces, which really upsets me, because they have found that there's a whole life out there. Some do come back. They are true teachers and know that their calling is to be with kids and to teach.